MW00933707

THE FANTASY SPORTS BOSS 2015 FANTASY BASEBALL DRAFT GUIDE

BY THE FANTASY SPORTS BOSS STAFF

TABLE OF CONTENTS

EDITOR'S NOTE

To Our Readers:

Yes is that special time of the year again. Fantasy football leagues have been decided, the winter is starting to ebb, and baseball gloves and bats are beginning to come out of the closet. Most significant to all of us however is the quickly approaching fantasy baseball season, which unofficially begins with the all-important draft that many deem the highlight of the year. In reality, there really is nothing as exciting as the draft, whether done online or in-person. With some beverages and hot wings included amongst your trash-talking league mates, the whole exercise is a tremendous amount of fun. The old adage certainly rings true that you can't win your fantasy baseball league with a good draft but you could certainly put yourself in good position to lose it with a poorly executed one. It is this reason why we once again left no stone unturned when it came to putting together the most in-depth and analytical draft guide we have ever published in our eight-year history. Whether it is our position rankings, top sleepers and busts, rookie report, and more, we feel confident that the information contained in the following pages will put you on the path to success in your league. In addition, our draft guide is just one extension of our fantasy baseball reach. Once the season begins, be sure to follow us all year long through our award-winning website www.thefantasysportsboss.com, which continues to update injuries, post features, adjust rankings, and more on a daily basis. We love nothing more than hearing from our readers that our advice helped them to win their leagues and it is that goal in mind that keeps us going in our never-ending pursuit of top notch analysis. And of course none of our success would be possible without each and every one of you. Our sincere thanks as always and once again allow me to wish all of you good luck as our six-month journey begins together.

Sincerely,

Michael E. Keneski
The Fantasy Sports Boss
www.thefantasysportsboss.com

10 BURNING QUESTIONS FOR 2015 FANTASY BASEBALL

BY ERIC C. WRIGHT

Each and every fantasy baseball season is like one big storybook. There is a plot, twists and turns, and ultimately an ending. Every individual who signs up for fantasy baseball each season proceeds to write their own story, told in bold-face numbers by the players who inhabit their rosters. No two stories are alike of course, which is what makes formulating a fantasy baseball roster such an inexact science. There is no clear-cut "perfect way" to win your league but there are certainly some themes and subjects that can help better define a path to success. With that in mind, we tried to put together 10 "Burning Questions" and their subsequent answers in order to get a better read on how the 2015 fantasy baseball season is shaping up. While these 10 questions and their answers are by all means far from the only topics worth discussing, they do serve as a barometer to some key storylines that are being talked about as drafts begin to unfold. So without further delay, let's get right to it.

1. Q: The last two years we had back-and-forth debates over whether Mike Trout or Miguel Cabrera was the number 1 player in fantasy baseball. I gather there is no such debate this time around?
A: You got that right. There is no doubt that prior to both 2012 and 2013, there were grounds for a lengthy discussion regarding whether or not Trout or Cabrera should be the number 1 pick in standard mixed league drafts. A year later no such discussion is needed as Trout firmly established himself as the number 1 player in the game by posting a monstrous MVP season. Meanwhile 2014 proved to be Cabrera's worst season in years, accompanied by depressed power numbers due to a variety of physical setbacks. While no one doubts a healthy Cabrera will be ready to reclaim his MVP status for 2015, the fact of the matter is that there has been no letup at all from Trout in his numbers as he made up for a drop in stolen bases by increasing his home runs and RBI. And at a still young 24, Trout has more than a few prime years left, which is a scary thought indeed. If Trout is NOT the number 1 pick in your draft, the owner who made the selection should be kicked out of the league for gross incompetence.

2. Q: With the number 1 pick issue out of the way, who makes up the other 11 slots in a standard mixed league 12-team league?
A: In no clear order, the 11 names who should hear their names called during the initial round of your draft should be Andrew McCutchen, Jose Abreu, Paul Goldschmidt, Clayton Kershaw, Robinson Cano, Miguel Cabrera, Edwin

Encarnacion, Adam Jones, Giancarlo Stanton, Carlos Gomez, and Felix Hernandez. In actuality, it was quite difficult to come up with a 12th player who absolutely deserved to go in Round 1, which was not the case with the other 11. Feel free to remove King Felix and insert someone else of your choosing but the other 11 should be near locks to go among the initial 12 picks.

3. Q: Has Jose Abreu overtaken Paul Goldschmidt for the top spot among all first baseman?

A: Close but not quite yet. While there is no debating the monstrous instant impact that slugging Cuban import Abreu had in 2014 when he slammed 36 home runs and collected 107 RBI, Goldschmidt retains his title for another season as the number 1 fantasy baseball first baseman in our opinion. Sure Goldschmidt hit only 19 home runs but that was because he didn't have a chance to finish out the season due to suffering a freak fractured left hand from a HBP. There are two aspects that separate Abreu and Goldschmidt in the latter's favor, with the first being runs scored. Goldschmidt's last full healthy season in 2013 saw him cross home plate 103 times. And before he suffered the fractured hand, Goldschmidt was on pace for over 100 runs scored again. Meanwhile Abreu didn't pass the injured Goldschmidt in runs scored for 2014 until more than a month later which is telling. In addition, Goldschmidt has the ability to steal bases, which Abreu does not. Goldschmidt stole as many as 18 bags in 2013, while Abreu had a grand total of 1 a year ago. Throw in the threat of a sophomore jinx and it becomes clear that investing in Goldschmidt is a safer bet.

4. Q: Who has fallen out of Round 1 consideration from a year ago and who has graduated to such a lofty status?

A: Exit stage left Joey Votto, Bryce Harper, Prince Fielder, Carlos Gonzalez, Chris Davis, Troy Tulowitzki, and Jose Fernandez. Welcome to the club Giancarlo Stanton and Jose Abreu.

5. Q: After missing all of 2014 due to Tommy John surgery, where do we draft New York Mets ace Matt Harvey this season?

A: To put Harvey's talent into perspective, we had the fireballer ranked as the number 5 starter in all of fantasy baseball before he went under the knife midway through the 2013 season. The term power pitcher was meant for someone like Harvey, who can touch 98 with ease, while also showcasing terrific secondary stuff. Now a full year-and-a-half removed from the surgery once the 2015 season kicks off, Harvey should be fully ready to go to reclaim his status as one of the best pitchers in the game. As with all Tommy John patients in their first year back on the mound, control may be an issue from time-to-time but on talent alone few are better. The best part is that the Tommy John surgery makes Harvey a much more affordable pitcher than he would have been if he had not gone under the knife. That means you can start looking in Harvey's direction in Round 5 where he would make for one of the cheapest fantasy baseball ace starters in our fake game.

6. Q: Is Rusney Castillo set to become the next instant impact Cuban import for the Boston Red Sox?
A: It is staggering when you consider how many Cuban signings over the last five years have had tremendous debuts right out of the gate. That class includes Yasiel Puig, Yoenis Cespedes, Jose Fernandez, Aroldis Chapman, and Jose Abreu. In fact no other country is even remotely close to Cuba when it comes to the quality of players coming into the major leagues during that span. The latest sensation very well could be multi-tooled outfielder Rusney Castillo, who the Boston Red Sox netted with a $72 million deal. Comparing to Cespedes with regards to his arm and pop, Castillo differs from his countryman due to his better speed and contact skills. While we always want to be cautious with any prospect regardless of the country of origin, Castillo has the classic skill set to be an outfielder 2 right away.

7. Q: Is David Wright finished as a top fantasy baseball third base option?
A: To say that Wright had an awful season in 2014 would be one giant understatement. Long one of the most productive third baseman in the game, Wright was comically bad last season as he hit all of 8 home runs and drove in only 63 batters while hitting .269. While Wright will still be a young 32 in 2015, there are two major issues to worry about here. The first and most glaring is the fact that Wright has now suffered serious injuries in three of the last four seasons. Whether it was a concussion, back fracture, or shoulder injury, Wright's body is staring to betray him. In addition to the health concerns, Citi Field has been a house of horrors for Wright since its opening. Wright hit 29 home runs as recently as 2010 but since that time (and since Citi Field opened), Wright's power totals have read 14, 21, 18, and 8. Not good. While we have always loved the very rare power/speed ability that Wright has produced throughout his career at third base, the reality is that the current version of Wright is a striped-down model.

8. Q: Now that we are squarely in the era of pitching dominance, can anyone hit 40 home runs this season?
A: Amazing that 40 home runs is now the hallowed ground mark for power hitters, whereas it was 50 and 60 just a decade earlier during the steroid era. Clearly the elimination of steroids have had a dramatic effect on pushing

down power numbers drastically around baseball. With regards to who can possibly reach the 40 home run mark this season, we can count the candidates on one hand. The most obvious of course is Miami Marlins outfielder Giancarlo Stanton who has the most pure power of any hitter in the game. Other possible candidates are the Toronto Blue Jays' Jose Bautista and Edwin Encarnacion, the Chicago White Sox' Jose Abreu, and the Los Angeles Angels' Mike Trout. Chris Carter and Nelson Cruz also could get there but we think both fall just short. As a result, the draft prices of the five 40-home run candidates are all sky-high, as all but Bautista will be first round selections. With power numbers as low as they are in today's game, all are well worth the sticker price.

9. **Q: Which veteran "name" players have now started going off the statistical cliff and thus should be avoided in this season's draft?**
   A: Age is the one factor that no player in any sport can avoid no matter how big the name is. One of the most often-repeated mistakes in yearly fantasy baseball drafts is to select a proven veteran bat or pitcher who at one time might have been right there at the top of the league in numbers but who now are fully engulfed in decline due to age. Injuries often go along for the ride when a player begins to age, which also helps to accelerate the problem. Widely known names who began to go through this negative transformation last season included among the following: Alex Rios, Dustin Pedroia, Yadier Molina, Matt Holliday, Brandon Phillips, Chase Utley, Ben Zobrist, Aramis Ramirez, Carlos Beltran, and Coco Crisp for the hitters. Among pitchers, try to avoid Cliff Lee, Justin Verlander, Matt Cain, and C.C. Sabbathia.

10. **Q: A first baseman and outfielder for the first two rounds and everything else comes next?**
    A: Once again we stick fully to our tried-and-true draft method of grabbing a slugging first baseman and a five-tool outfielder as your first two picks. It is imperative you get your hands on a 25-40 home run first baseman in order to collect a solid portion of your roster's power. With home runs being so scarce in today's game, going that route takes on even more importance. In addition, picking up a five-tool outfielder who can do a little of everything is also key to formulating a potent roster. While the price for these players is always expensive, their ability to help in all five standard categories is invaluable. You can flip flop these selections if you want in terms of which spot to take in Round's 1 and 2. For example, you can take an Andrew McCutchen in Round 1 and than follow that up with an Adrian Gonzalez or Anthony Rizzo in Round 2. Or you can go a Jose Abreu or Paul

Goldschmidt in Round 1 and than follow that up with a Jacoby Ellsbury in Round 2.

Once those two positions are addressed, you can than start filling out the rest of your roster by concentrating on hitting at least until Round 5. It is in Round 5 where you could take your first starter if you can't resist the pull to go there. Ideally we would wait until Round 6 given how deep the position is. From there, the only rules we have left are not drafting a catcher until the middle rounds and to avoid taking a closer until the LATE middle rounds given the volatility and high injury rate of those two groups.

Surely there are dozens of additional questions left to be answered but these are the ten we think help shape your 2015 draft in a more clear and concise manner. As always continue to check out our website at www.thefantasysportsboss.com for daily features and articles that will keep you on top of the game.

2015 FANTASY BASEBALL DRAFT SLEEPERS

By Robert Calcaterra

Every fantasy baseball season we see the same trends happen over and over when it comes to the so-called "sleeper." The hitter or pitcher that all of us just have to have no matter the cost. So certain are we of their imminent stardom that we drool all over the place when their names get mentioned. We often make rash decisions when it comes to chasing sleepers, who it turns out more often than not, fail to meet our unrealistic expectations. Which than leaves us cursing under our breath (or out loud when the mood calls for it) as we vow never to be so foolish in wasting such precious draft picks on unproven talent ever again. Which sixth months later we forget as we repeat the process all over again.

Now while I completely agree with the notion of using extreme caution and discipline when it comes to drafting so-called "sleepers," the fact of the matter is that not every player who falls into that category costs an arm or a leg to get. And it is under this type of scenario where major profits can be made when it comes to getting the most out of your fantasy baseball roster. While our 2015 Sleeper list contains some names that will be fought over vigorously at your draft, we also made a strong effort to compile players who may not be totally on the radar yet. It is these draft picks that could help propel your roster upwards for a very cheap price which of course is one of the keys to winning your league. Feel free to debate some of these choices but ultimately we have a strong inclination at least a few of these players will make us look smart for recommending them to you in the first place.

Travis D'Arnaud: We are always on the lookout for young catchers who possess hitting potential and such is the case with developing New York Mets backstop Travis D'Arnaud. Universally considered one of the best catching prospects in the game, D'Arnaud struggled so terribly with the bat during the first half of the 2014 season, that the team was forced to send him back to Triple-A. It during his return to the farm where D'Arnaud seemed to clear his head and unleash his potent bat which quickly earned him a recall from the Mets. Upon his return, D'Arnaud looked like a new player at the plate as he hit .265 with 7 home runs and 22 RBI in only 196 at-bats. Keep in mind that D'Arnaud was a .300 hitter in the minors who has the potential to hit 20 home runs. With his draft price depressed due to his early struggles, the potential payoff could be significant.

Wilson Ramos: Yeah him again. We just can't move away from Wilson Ramos and the annual potential he brings to the table each season. On the rare occasions when he is healthy, Ramos has hit for above-average power and been a solid run producer for the Washington Nationals. If he can only somehow manage to squeeze out 400 at-bats, we could be looking at 20-plus home runs to go along with 70-plus RBI. Give him one more chance.

Kennys Vargas: Kennys Vargas is pretty much a DH-only at the start of 2015 fantasy baseball but his power is interesting in an era where home runs are scarce. Vargas cracked 9 home runs in only 215 at-bats last season and it is that part of his game that has us wanting to see more.

C.J. Cron: We love pushing natural hitters such as C.J. Cron and the Los Angeles Angels have to know that they have something here in the hulking first baseman. The pedigree is certainly there as Cron was the team's first round pick in 2011 and he has done nothing but hit at all levels including the majors where he batted .256 with 11 home runs in only 242 at-bats during his debut last season. Cron clearly knows what he is doing at the plate and 20 home runs seems certain with a full allotment of plate appearances.

Kolten Wong: Post-hype sleepers such as Kolten Wong have always been terrific buys every fantasy baseball season, as the payoff is potentially significant when you consider the depressed draft prices such players present. St. Louis Cardinals second baseman Kolten Wong is one such player as he too was demoted in the middle of last season after a stretch of terrible results at the dish. Like Travis D'Arnaud, Wong was a different player when he returned to the lineup, hitting .255 in the second half with 6 home runs and 8 stolen base in the heat of a pennant race. Second baseman who can hit for power and run like Wong can are almost always fantasy baseball gold.

Mookie Betts: We were on the fence with regards to including Mookie Betts on this list due to the fact he might have done enough in his small stints with the Boston Red Sox last season to elevate his draft price beyond sleeper status. However the talent is obvious here as Betts is already a .300 hitter who has developing power to go along with top-end speed. This kid has the classic look of a future star. A future that could arrive as soon as this season.

Joe Panik: Few had ever even heard of San Francisco Giants infielder Joe Panik prior to the 2014 postseason but the former St. John's product opened all of our eyes with incredible poise in handling the bat during the team's World Series-winning run. Panik is not the most naturally gifted player out there but he knows how to handle the bat and could hit near .300 right out of the 2015 gate. The power figures to come around eventually as well and if hitting near the top of the Giants lineup, a solid amount of runs and RBI will go along for the ride.

Wilmer Flores: The New York Mets are still undecided when it comes to whether or not infielder Wilmer Flores is the future at shortstop for the team. Flores was a big-time producer who hit for power in the Mets' minor league system in Las Vegas but their affiliate there is part of the offense-inducing PCL which could call into question the validity of his numbers. Flores will struggle to hit .280 due to a tendency to strike out but his power looked legitimate. Citi Field is a challenge for any home run hitter but Flores did enough in his cup of coffee run in 2014 to warrant another look.

Nolan Arenado: We included Arenado here only for the fact that the broken hand he suffered last season took him out of action for two months. Those lost two months of potential production somewhat put a lid on what Arenado's numbers could have looked like if he had not gotten hurt. The Colorado Rockies third baseman was terrific when on the field last season, showing 20-home run pop to go along with the potential to hit .300-plus. We are reaching a round or two early here for this developing kid and we feel confident in saying Arenado will be a top five fantasy baseball third baseman by the conclusion of the 2015 season.

A.J. Pollock: Another case of a guy whose battle with injuries helped keep the lid on his numbers in 2014. The Arizona Diamondbacks' 2009 first round pick, Pollock began to unleash his power/speed ability last season as he hit 7 home runs and stole 14 bases while batting .302 atop the lineup. The fact those totals came in only 265 at-bats speaks to how good Pollock was. With full health, Pollock could move close to a 15/25 mark with another average around .300. Be aggressive getting this developing talent.

Avasail Garcia: It was thought that young Chicago White Sox outfielder Avisail Garcia would miss the remainder of the 2014 season after tearing the labrum in his shoulder last April. However Garcia rehabbed dilligently and returned in August as he tried to make up for lost time. The former top prospect with the Detroit Tigers hit 7 home runs and stole 4 bases in only 172 at-bats which hints at some interesting ability under the surface. The tools are there for more gains in Garcia's power/speed numbers.

Junior Lake: The Chicago Cubs gave the Dominican Republic's Junior Lake a chance to show what he could do last season as the team continued with its rebuilding effort. The extremely athletic Lake has good pop and speed which helped him hit 9 home runs and steal 7 bases in only 308 at-bats. Unfortunately Lake has some big holes in his swing as he has posted some truly ridiculous K rates in the minors and with the Cubs, making batting even .240 a challenge. Still there are tools to check out here.

Chris Coghlan: Yet another Cub appears on this list and this time it is old friend Chris Coghlan. The former Rookie of the Year for the Miami Marlins almost vanished from the scene since that terrific debut but he successfully fought back to post a solid comeback season in 2014 by once again showing the ability to hit home runs and steal some bases. Coghlan is getting older as he is flat in his prime but the cost is dirt cheap on a guy who can help in multiple categories.

Christian Yelich: We loved Yelich prior to last season and continue to push his prospects as the 2015 season dawns. While Yelich didn't have the breakout we expected in 2014, he continued to show his tremendous potential as he hit 9 home runs and stole 21 bases while batting .284. Yelich has the classic look of a guy who can be a 15/30 gem and 2015 could be the start on a run of terrific numbers as he settles into his ability as a major league hitter.

Jeurys Familia: While Jenrry Mejia got the saves glory in the ninth inning, New York Mets setup gem Jeurys Familia put himself in the 2015 closer picture with a tremendous full season debut in 2014 as he pitched to a 2.21 ERA while striking out 73 in 77.1 innings. Mejia has had trouble staying healthy in his young career and Familia is absolutely capable of being a dominant ninth inning pitcher.

Tajuan Walker: Sometimes long-term injuries the previous season allows for a player to qualify as a sleeper for a second year in a row. That is the situation facing Seattle Mariners top pitching prospect Tajuan Walker who battled shoulder trouble for most of the 2014 season. The result was only 38 major league innings that resulted in a 2.61 ERA and 34 strikeouts. The big-time power arm remains when it comes to Walker and his ballpark is obviously one of the best in baseball. Walks are the only thing that could interrupt Walker's rise to stardom but the fact that his star has dimmed a bit this season can only help you at the draft table.

Matt Shoemaker: It certainly looks like the Los Angeles Angels have something with regards to Matt Shoemaker being more than a serviceable starting pitcher for 2015. Undrafted out of Eastern Michigan, Shoemaker quickly showed that his stuff was major league-ready as he struck out 124 batters in only 136 innings last season. Accompanied by a 3.04 ERA and 1.07 WHIP, Shoemaker's light innings tally has kept the lid somewhat on his potential value which makes him a solid upside play.

Mike Fiers: For the second time in three seasons, Mike Fiers makes the sleeper list based on a tremendous second-half performance down the stretch of the 2014 season. After pitching in the minor leagues for most of 2013 and the first half of last season, Fiers came up at the beginning of August (after a brief stint in the bullpen in June) and absolutely dominated to the tune of a 2.13 ERA and 0.88 WHIP while striking out 76 batters in only 71.2 innings. The fastball is not impressive but Fiers collects his strikeouts on deception which is obviously working well for him.

Marcus Stroman: The ceiling is about to burst when it comes to the ace-like ability of the Toronto Blue Jays' Marcus Stroman. The organization's top pitching prospect looked like a natural in his 2014 rookie season, showcasing top-notch control for his age on the way to a 3.65 ERA and 1.17 WHIP. Those numbers are even more impressive when you consider Stroman pitched in a home run ballpark and in the rough AL East. This is a future All-Star power pitcher at its best and it will likely be the last time Stroman can be had for a mid-round draft choice.

Jake Odorizzi: The "other guy" in the haul the Tampa Bay Rays received from the Kansas City Royals for ace starter James Shields, Jake Odorizzi surprised many by striking out 174 batters in 168 innings last season. Odorizzi's 4.13 ERA and 1.28 WHIP show he has some more work to do before he reaches his optimal value but any pitcher who can post such a lofty K rate deserves all of our attention.

Shane Greene: It appeared as though the New York Yankees were beyond desperate when they were forced to call up a guy who had an ERA over 4.00 in the minor leagues due to their starting rotation being decimated by injury. Shane Greene was that guy but he got the last laugh as he showed big time poise and an eye-opening K rate in the form of 81 strikeouts in his 78.2 innings. Greene's 1.40 WHIP shows you that it wasn't all smooth for him last season but he will be given every chance to hold a rotation spot for the Yankees in 2015. The K rate alone makes him worth a speculative pick.

While we don't expect everyone on the list above to break out, we do feel confident that the majority of the names on this list can supply some solid value for the 2015 fantasy baseball season. Drafting a sleeper is never an exact science however so try not to reach too high. Also be sure to access our 2015

Draft Sleepers list which is updated on the web site all through spring training at <u>www.thefantasysportsboss.com</u>.

2015 FANTASY BASEBALL DRAFT BUSTS

By Michael E. Keneski

We all have the stories. The scars are still there, maybe even years later. We shake our heads in a combination of anger and disgust, so unnerved were the experiences. I am of course talking about the dreaded fantasy baseball draft "bust." The pitcher or hitter who you were ecstatic to see staring back at you on your roster after the draft but who eventually supplied nothing but an upset stomach and a receding hairline once the games started to count. Yes draft busts are prevalent each and every season and no matter how hard we may try to minimize their threat, sometimes downright bad luck can be blamed for everything going wrong. Whether or not these players gone bad drag down your roster altogether is another matter but doing your best to identify and in turn avoid risky players during your draft is paramount for giving your team the best chance to win. In order to help you avoid trouble, we came up with a list of players who we feel present solid to sizable risk for the upcoming season and who, unless the price is incredibly cheap, should be avoided if you can do so. A large part of having a successful draft is putting together a roster with as little risk as possible and it is these players who we believe bring the most potential for undermining that goal this season.

Yadier Molina: It already has been well-established that catchers over the age of 30 see a sharp decline in their hitting numbers. St. Louis Cardinals backstop Yadier Molina held off that trend longer than most but finally Father Time is taking its effect based on his 2014 numbers. Spending time on the DL due to a broken thumb, Molina posted his lowest average since 2010 and only hit 7 home runs in 404 at-bats as his pop is vanishing quick. The name brand remains expensive though and that alone makes Molina a huge risk.

Russell Martin: Many will notice the 2014 surface numbers of Toronto Blue Jays catcher Russell Martin and conclude that he was one of the better hitting backstops in the game last season. Molina somehow managed to hit .290 with 11 home runs despite being 31. Those statistics reek of being an outlier campaign as Martin had failed to hit above .250 since 2008 prior to last season. In addition, Martin's speed looks shot as he stole only four bases. While Martin's defense and leadership still are top notch, his offensive numbers are likely to fall off the map again.

Joey Votto: It is sad what is going on with Cincinnati Reds 1B Joey Votto who very well could be suffering from a degenerative knee injury that has robbed him of power and turned him into an ordinary player the last two seasons. Votto was a first round pick as recently as 2013 but now he doesn't even look capable of 20 home runs or even being healthy enough to amass 400 at-bats. The name brand will ensure Votto still gets drafted high enough but his body is betraying him and taking his numbers with it.

Victor Martinez: The biggest outlier number from the 2014 season has to be the shocking 32 home runs that Victor Martinez cracked for the Detroit Tigers. While no one ever questions Martinez' standing as one of the best pure hitters in baseball, the power was off-the-charts by his career standards. Consider that prior to last season, the most home runs Martinez had hit was 25 and that came back in 2007. Since that season Martinez has reached the 20-home run mark only once which was 20 on the nose in 2010. The career numbers always hold true for 99 percent of players and that means the aging Martinez will see a major slide back in his power output at the very least.

Jon Singleton: We all are suckers for young prospects, especially those who possess above-average power. However home runs are only one part of the hitting equation, as contributions in other categories are a must for a given player to reach move value. Young Houston Astros first baseman Jonathan Singleton is such a player, as he possesses terrific power but who **pretty** much is a one-trick pony in that regards given what we saw out of him as a rookie in 2014. Singleton was a strikeout king as he whiffed in almost half his 300 at-bats. The result was a truly horrendous .168 batting average that completely negates any gains in power. We always advise avoiding players who can't hit .250 and in the case of Singleton, he may not even reach .230.

Michael Cuddyer: One of the early shockers of the offseason was the fact the New York Mets signed free agent outfielder Michael Cuddyer to a two-year deal worth $20 million. Cuddyer certainly made out with that salary after he spent huge chunks of the 2014 season on the DL with hamstring and shoulder injuries. The problem now is that Cuddyer goes from one of the best hitting ballparks in the majors in Coors Field to one of the worst in Citi Field which undoubtedly have a major negative impact on his numbers. You can forget Cuddyer ever going anywhere near the .330 and .331 average he put up the last two years with the Rockies and the home run rare will drop noticeably as well given the chance of hitting locales. Go back to Cuddyer's numbers when he was a 20-home run/.280 hitter and that is pretty much where he should be expected to come in this season. Of course we didn't even mention how

Cuddyer turns 36 this March and how his body is clearly betraying him. All the evidence points to Cuddyer dropping off the statistical cliff this season.

Steve Pearce: After seven years spent as a major league baseball journeyman, Steve Pearce finally broke through in a big way last season when given a chance to help an injury-riddled Baltimore Orioles lineup. Pearce proceeded to hit 21 home runs and batted .293 in only 338 at-bats. There was a reason Pearce was a career major league nomad however and he could just as easily turn back into a pumpkin when 2015 gets underway. Again a career should always speak louder than one single season.

Dustin Pedroia: Already 32 years old, Boston Red Sox second baseman and former MVP Dustin Pedroia is on the fast track to decline. Guys with the type of slight frame that Pedroia has don't age well in the middle infield given all the wear and tear of the position. Pedroia's recent numbers certainly back this up as he sank to a .278 batting average with only 7 home runs and 6 steals in 551 at-bats last season. The speed has declined for four straight seasons, as have the home runs. Another sizable name brand guy who is not worth anywhere near what he will likely cost again this season.

Jimmy Rollins: The nice comeback from the cliff season that Philadelphia Phillies shortstop Jimmy Rollins engineered last season sets him up to make the bust list once again for 2015. Rollins surprised many by hitting 17 home runs and stealing 28 bases a year ago, which are numbers that would get most drafted as high as the third round. However Rollins is 36 and will no way stay healthy for a second season in a row. In addition, Rollins will struggle to hit even .250, which leave a smaller margin for error with his other numbers.

Nelson Cruz: Nelson Cruz could be this season's Chris Davis. One year he is leading the league in home runs and the next he crashed and burned under a hail of strikeouts. Cruz no doubt was spectacular for the Baltimore Orioles in 2014 on his one-year "prove it" deal but prior to last season, there was the whole 50-game PED bust and years with the Texas Rangers that were constantly marred by injury. The slugging outfielder certainly wouldn't be the first player to go the other way statistically after getting paid

Matt Holliday: The numbers started to leak badly for St. Louis Cardinals outfielder Matt Holliday last season, as he saw his average and power slide noticeably. Long one of the best pure hitters in baseball, Holliday is entering into his mid-30's with age clearly taking a chunk out of his numbers. Again don't chase the name but instead chase the actual current state of numbers.

Adam Wainwright: Already with a Tommy John surgery under his belt, Adam Wainwright generated a huge red flag in the 2014 postseason when he began to experience elbow discomfort. While Wainwright ultimately pitched through the ailment, the fact he does have a history of elbow trouble is very concerning. Also the fact Wainwright just completed an intense 244 inning season makes him a huge risk regarding his health on that issue alone.

Mat Latos: After enduring an injury-marred 2014 season, Cincinnati Reds starting pitcher Mat Latos was forced to go under the knife this past November in an effort to regrow tissue and cartilage in his elbow. Not the kind of news you want to hear a full FOUR months before the season gets started.

Michael Wacha: While we fell in love with Wacha after his 2013 debut, his first full season in the majors last year ended up disappointing as persistent shoulder trouble sapped him of strength and ruined his stuff. Bum shoulders tend to reoccur at a high rate and we have seen some other young, hard-throwing starters quickly disintegrate with similar injuries such as Josh Johnson and Tommy Hanson.

There you have it. We would make it a point to stay far away from the guys listed above if you can, so high is the risk they present when it comes to placing a 2015 investment. When you break it down, there really is no reason to increase your chances of suffering a setback with your team. In the end, avoiding high-bust candidates is always your best course of action when preparing for your draft and is a great way to set roster up with as little volatility as possible.

2015 TOP 25 ROOKIES

By Roger Miller

Along the same lines as the fantasy baseball draft sleeper, rookies are just as fiercely fought over each and every season. The tantalizing upside they bring is incredibly tough to resist and often we grossly overpay for guys who may not even make their debuts until halfway through the season. Be that as it may, we would be remiss if we didn't bring you our 2015 Top 25 Rookies where we delve in on all the hot names that are close to breaking into the major leagues, with an Expected Time of Arrival (ETA) included.

1. **Kris Bryant (3B Chicago Cubs):** Hands down the best prospect in all of baseball, Kris Bryant is expected to burst onto the scene in 2015 with his extremely powerful swing for the Chicago Cubs. Bryant demolished minor league pitching last season, putting up a total of 43 home runs spanning both Double and Triple-A. Bryant also stole 15 bases while batting well over .300, so there is pretty much nothing the kid can't do. Could be a top five guy at third base as soon as he gets promoted.
    ETA: May 2015

2. **Javier Baez (2B/SS Chicago Cubs):** We got a small preview of yet another top Cubs prospect in 2014 in the form of slugging infielder Javier Baez. While Baez struck out a ton, he also cracked 7 home runs in only 132 at-bats. The power is top notch for an infielder and Baez could hit 20 home runs and steal 15 bases right away. Just be aware that Baez could also struggle to hit .260 given that crazy K rate.
    ETA: April 2015

3. **Byron Buxton (OF Minnesota Twins):** If not for a ridiculously unlucky run of injuries, Minnesota Twins top outfield prospect Byron Buxton might have already been a regular for the team. Buxton has crazy speed and will be an instant 40-steal threat as soon as he makes the big leagues, while also batting .300-plus. There is little power at this stage of the game but Buxton is expected to develop that talent as he matures. Comparisons to a Mike Trout with less power are already making their way around the game. This one is going to be special.
    ETA: June 2014

4. **Maikel Franco (3B Philadelphia Phillies):** The Philadelphia Phillies are ready to turn third base over to this power-packed slugger. Maikel Franco has a terrific thunderous swing that could net 20-plus home runs right away.

There will be average issues early on due to a propensity to strike out but Franco is ready to be unleashed.

ETA: April 2015

5. **Joc Pederson (OF Los Angeles Dodgers):** The Los Angeles Dodgers have a very crowded outfield that at this point is still packed out as we go to press. It is that reason only that Joc Pederson is not already a regular outfielder for the team. Pederson has nothing left to prove on the farm after showing off amazing power/speed ability throughout 2014 and the Dodgers would be remiss if they didn't find a way to get him into the lineup on a daily basis this season. .

ETA: April 2015

6. **Jorge Soler (OF Chicago Cubs):** Yet another in a recent wave of promising Cuban imports, Jorge Soler is the third Chicago Cub among the first six players on this list. The power potential is immense as Soler compares to countryman Yoenis Cespedes, right on down to the high K rate.

ETA: August 2015

7. **Joey Gallo (3B Texas Rangers):** Joey Gallo might have to move to first base, so rough is his defense. However Gallo will be paid based on what he does with the bat and so far that means a bunch of home runs and RBI. The contact skills need a lot of work though as Gallo hit only .237 last season in the minors.

ETA: September 2015

8. **Addison Russell (SS Chicago Cubs):** You really got to hand it to the Cubs and the insane amount of top prospects they have in their system. Despite having Javier Baez ready to burst through the major league gate, GM Theo Espstein swung the trade with the Oakland A's for their top shortstop prospect Addison Russell at last July's deadline. The sky is the limit for Russell, who combines developing power and solid speed. Possessing better contact rates than Baez, Russell should post better batting averages as well.

ETA: April 2015

9. **Noah Syndegaard (SP New York Mets):** Noah Syndegaard looks to join Matt Harvey, Jacob DeGrom, and Zack Wheeler to give the New York Mets four young, high-velocity power pitchers sometime in the 2015 season. Syndegaard endured a trying 2014 when he got injured and struggled with his command in the challenging PCL league. Still the universal consensus

is that Syndegaard is going to be a good one and he is in line to make his debut sometime in the 2015 season.
ETA: June 2015

10. **Carlos Correia (SS Houston Astros):** The Astros won't waste much time in 2014 promoting top shortstop prospect Carlos Correia despite the fact he is only turning 20. Correia hit .325 with 6 home runs and 20 stolen bases last season in A-ball which hints at the power/speed talent he possesses. The future looks very bright for the Astros when Correia gets paired with George Springer real soon.
ETA: September 2015

11. **Corey Seager (SS Los Angeles Dodgers):** Younger brother of Seattle Mariners third baseman Kyle, Corey Seager is on the cusp of pushing his way to the majors with the Los Angeles Dodgers. While Seager is light on speed, he has above-average power and better batting average skills than his brother.
ETA: September 2015

12. **Jonathan Gray (SP Colorado Rockies):** The Colorado Rockies are giddy about their fireballing prospect Jonathan Gray and with good reason. Consistently hitting 98 with his fastball (and occasionally 100), Gray is ready to blow major league batters away with the heat. Gray has to work on his control like most young power pitchers but the ceiling is as high as any pitching in the minor league pipeline.
ETA: September 2015

13. **Dylan Bundy (SP Baltimore Orioles):** Tommy John surgery interrupted the rise to stardom for Baltimore Orioles top pitching prospect Dylan Bundy. Now a full season-plus removed from the procedure, Bundy is finding his 95-mph fastball and knee-buckling curve again. The Orioles had talked as recently as last summer about using Bundy initially in relief but as long as he continues to work through some control problems, a spot in the rotation should be his calling.
ETA: June 2015

14. **Francisco Lindor (SS Cleveland Indians):** The future is bright at the major league level when it comes to shortstops as Lindor is already the fifth player on this list. With Asdrubal Cabrera now out of town, the starting shortstop spot is there for the taking for taking in Cleveland. Unlike his counterparts listed above, Lindor's bat needs some work due to the fact he strikes out a bunch and has little power at this point. However Lindor is a

stolen base asset whose top-end speed will make him an instant impact player in that regard.

ETA: April 2015

15. **Archie Bradley (SP Arizona Diamondbacks):** Archie Bradley is another high-heat power pitcher in every sense of the word but his path to the majors depends entirely on him working through some very shaky problems with his control. Bradley's fastball also comes in a bit straight which could lead to a tendency to give up home runs.

ETA: August 2015

16. **Miguel Sano (3B Minnesota Twins):** Yes position players can have Tommy John surgery as power-hitting Minnesota Twins third baseman Miguel Sano fell victim to prior to the 2014 season. Sano compares to Pedro Alvarez, what with his 30-plus home run power and very shaky batting average, due to his tendency to strike out.

ETA: June 2015

17. **Julio Urias (P Los Angeles Dodgers):** Julio Urias has a magical arm that churns out 98-mph fastballs with ease. There are question marks about whether or not Urias will be a major league starter or a reliever due to a slight frame but the strikeout ability is off-the-charts.

ETA: April 2016

18. **Henry Owens (P Boston Red Sox):** There is nice ability here for a guy who the Boston Red Sox think could be a future bullpen weapon. Owens doesn't have the durability or vast repertoire to be a starter but his good fastball and solid offspeed stuff could get him into the bullpen at some point during the 2015 season.

ETA: August 2015

19. **Blake Swihart (C Boston Red Sox):** Reminding many of Carlos Santana, top Boston Red Sox catching prospect Blake Swihart can really handle the bat. Having a solid base of power to go with good hitting skills, Swihart's offense is his clear strength. Shoddy football and game-calling skills leave his future as a catcher in question however.

ETA: August 2015

20. **Aaron Sanchez (P Toronto Blue Jays):** Already having made his MLB debut out of the bullpen for the Toronto Blue Jays, Aaron Sanchez is already averaging a strikeout per inning. Sanchez was so good in the bullpen that the Blue Jays may decide to leave him there for the time being.

Blessed with an explosive fastball and decent enough secondary stuff, Sanchez has a bright future no matter where he pitches.
ETA: Arrived

21. **Andrew Heaney (SP Miami Marlins):** LHP Andrew Heaney is right on the doorstep to a major league rotation spot for the Miami Marlins as the three-pitch prime prospect is poised beyond his young years. Unlike most young pitchers, Heaney has terrific control and some sneaky good strikeout stuff.
ETA: May 2015

22. **Carlos Rodon (P Chicago White Sox):** The 4th pick in the 2014 draft, the burly hard-throwing Carlos Rodon is already knocking on the major league door. With a fastball that touches 95 and a good complementary slider, Rodon just needs to develop a third pitch to burst through.
ETA: May 2016

23. **Eddie Butler (P Colorado Rockies):** Again like other young power arms, Eddie Butler has some major control problems to remedy before his power arsenal can work at its most optimum. Rough control in Colorado is a bad recipe but Butler's potential is decent enough for him to remain a person of interest for another season.
ETA: September 2015

24. **Tyler Glasnow (P Pittsburgh Pirates):** Another Pittsburgh Pirates pitching prospect who can strike out batters at a high rate, Glasnow will likely need most or all of the 2015 season to get his control in order.
ETA: September 2015

25. **Lucas Giolito (SP Washington Nationals):** A UCL injury to his pitching elbow interrupted what would have been a rapid ascent for Washington Nationals top pitching prospect Lucas Giolito. Giolito goes along with the franchise mode of drafting high-K pitchers and without further injury, an appearance in the majors this September is not out of the question.
ETA: April 2016

During the course of the 2015 fantasy baseball season, we will continually update all the latest prospect news as it takes place. In addition, we will be posting "Welcome To The Show" features where we delve in on the expected statistical makeup of players who get promoted by their respective teams. All of this and more can be found on our website at www.thefantasysportsboss.com**.**

2015 FANTASY BASEBALL POSITION RANKINGS

CATCHERS

DRAFT STRATEGY: One of the more tried and true sacraments of fantasy baseball drafting that we firmly subscribe to each and every season is to ALWAYS wait on drafting a catcher until the middle rounds at the earliest. Year after year many make the foolish mistake of using a high round draft pick on a catcher which 9 times out of 10 ends up being the wrong decision. A few factors are at play here as to why drafting a backstop early in single-catcher formats is a big no-no. The first is the fact that outside of pitchers, catchers are the most injury-prone fraternity in all of fantasy baseball. No one has to be told that a catcher constantly is at risk for injury, what with getting hit with foul balls, back swings, and up until a year ago, collisions at the plate being part of the daily hazards of manning the position. In addition, the grueling nature of catching 140 games a season almost always takes a toll on offensive performance during the summer and into September. This is especially a big problem in September when you need your high draft picks to be operating at full efficiency in order to nail down your league title. A catcher is just not physically able to be that kind of player that late in the year for all the reasons already mentioned. Finally as we already noted, a catcher only starts about 140 games a season which has to be factored into the decision of using a high draft pick here. While the rest of your league is selecting hitters early in the draft who will play (health permitting) 155 games or so a season, you will be going with a catcher who will fall about 15 games short of that total bare minimum. Multiply those 15 games by 4 at-bats per and you get a total amount of 60 fewer plate appearances than the guys your opponents are taking in those early rounds. Thus the best course of action is to wait for value plays at catcher in the middle to late rounds. Our criteria for this remains the same as always. The first type of catcher to look for would be a prospect getting close to sticking with a big league club or who could get promoted sometime at or before June 1. In this space we recommended none other than Buster Posey and Carlos Santana a few years ago under this heading, which of course turned out well on both fronts.

The second type of catcher to look out for is a bounce back candidate who is coming off a rough season the year prior. Last season that guy was Miguel Montero who had a miserable 2013 season but than came back and produced a very solid 2014 campaign that restablished him as useful backstop. Such candidates this season under such a scenario could be Travis D'Arnaud from the New York Mets or Wilin Rosario from the Colorado Rockies. Some prime values can be had here if you look in the right places.

1. **Buster Posey:** It was another very solid season for three-time consensus number 1 fantasy baseball catcher Buster Posey in 2014 as he hit 21 home runs and drove in 87 while batting .310. By now it has become clear that the .336 Posey hit in 2012 was an outlier number but otherwise his stats have remained very consistent despite playing the always grueling catcher position. Turning 28 for the 2015 season, Posey is now flat in his prime so what you see now is what you get numbers-wise. In fact other than the injury risk that comes with any catcher, the only issue concerning Posey is whether or not you want to spend a third or fourth round pick on a guy whose offensive numbers may not measure up to the other guys picked in the same round.
   PROJECTION: .305 22 HR 89 RBI 72 R 1 SB

2. **Carlos Santana:** Santana retains catcher eligibility for another season despite playing most of his games at his new third base position. It was a volatile season for Santana in 2014 as he was arguably the worst everyday hitter in baseball in April and May when he hit .157 and .169 respectively. From that point on however, Santana caught fire as he slammed 21 home runs the last four months of the season, giving him a position-leading 27 to go along with 85 RBI. The holes in Santana's swing are stark and haven't gotten any better as he has reached his prime which means the average will continue to be a liability. However at catcher you can live with a shoddy average as long as the power there which is clearly the case with Santana who has smacked 27, 18, 20, and 27 home runs the last four seasons. In addition, many overlook the bonus value Santana brings in that he is the rare catcher who plays every day due to his move to third base. That boosts Santana's counting stats and eliminates the annoying issue of losing a game or two a week due to rest.
   PROJECTION: .255 26 HR 83 RBI 70 R 4 SB

3. **Devin Mesoraco:** We have heard for a few years about the potential of Devin Mesoraco but he never really got much of a chance leading up to 2014 due to the Cincinnati Reds being under the veteran-loving stewardship of Dusty Baker. With Baker out of town, Mesoraco finally got the chance to be an everyday catcher and literally hit the opportunity out of the park as he smashed 25 home runs and collected 80 RBI in only 384 at-bats. Many forget that Mesoraco was a 2007 first round pick (15th overall) by the team so the pedigree and expectations were always there. At 27, Mesoraco will likely repeat and not exceed his 2014 production but those are sweet

numbers either way. The value obviously won't be there this time around since the statistical cat is out of the bag but Mesoraco is worth the investment as a real-deal slugger at a thin spot.

PROJECTION: .271 23 HR 77 RBI 56 R 0 SB

4. **Evan Gattis:** When it comes to pure power, few are better irregardless of position than Atlanta Braves late bloomer Evan Gattis. In only 369 at-bats last season, Gattis crushed 23 home runs while also picking up eligibility in the outfield. Injuries continue to undermine Gattis, which is an issue that has derailed him more than once in the past. If Gattis could ever scratch out 450 at-bats, he could easily hit 30 home runs. Comparisons to Mike Napoli when he was catcher eligible (right on down to the high K rate and shaky average) are spot on and Gattis has some untapped potential still to his name.

PROJECTION: .259 26 HR 75 RBI 61 R 0 SB

5. **Jonathan Lucroy:** Lucroy is the only "do-everything" catcher in fantasy baseball, having the ability to contribute across all five standard categories including stolen bases which carries terrific value. In addition, Lucroy is the rare catcher who will help in batting average as his .285 career mark proves (plus having hit .300 in two of the last three seasons). Lucroy does come up a bit short in the power department, having never topped the 18 home runs he hit in 2013 but that is the only negative one can attach to the Milwaukee Brewers' veteran.

PROJECTION: .288 14 HR 73 RBI 66 R 5 SB

6. **Yan Gomes:** Moving Carlos Santana to third base virtually full-time was done with the idea of getting the powerful and intriguing bat of Yan Gomes into the everyday lineup. Gomes proved to be a smashing success as he hit for the power expected with 21 home runs but surprised a bit with the .278 average. Having fully earned the trust of Terry Francona and the front office, Gomes will be given even more responsibility as a prime run-producer in the Cleveland lineup for 2015 which could slightly boost his numbers even more. Not having the name brand that the guys listed above him have yet, Gomes arguably is one of the best values overall among all catchers.

PROJECTION: .280 .22 HR 77 RBI 64 R 1 SB

7. **Brian McCann:** It certainly didn't feel like it but overall Brian McCann put forth a solid set of numbers in his first season with the New York Yankees in hitting 23 home runs and collecting 75 RBI. Truth be told however, McCann's owners felt let down a bit amid all the spring training

hype that the veteran backstop would finally reach the 30-home run plateau as a lefty hitter taking aim at the short rightfield porch in Yankee Stadium. We can finally put the thought of McCann hitting 30 home runs out of our minds as it is never going to happen. In addition we also have to accept the fact McCann is now a clear batting average liability as he has hit .232, .256, and .232 the last three seasons as opposing teams continue to employ the shift against him. If you can accept the current version of McCann for what he is, the increasing discount he is supplies will make for a solid investment. **PROJECTION: .248 24 HR 76 RBI 59 R 1 SB**

8. **Wilin Rosario:** Rosario was a mild bust in 2014 as the young Colorado Rockies backstop lost 8 home runs and 24 RBI from the season prior due to both injuries and a continued issue with strikeouts. Despite the mild disappointment, Rosario stands a very good chance to have a bounce back season due to the fact he is still only turning 26 and is just two seasons removed from cracking 28 home runs. In addition, Rosario's K rate and advanced stats held steady which means health likely played more of a role than his actual hitting did in the depressed numbers. The ballpark remains a huge drawing card and Rosario presents as the type of catcher we always target as a value play coming off a somewhat down year. Give him another chance. **PROJECTION: .268 21 HR 75 RBI 66 R 1 SB**

9. **Yadier Molina:** The erosion is setting in. It has been more than a fun ride owning Molina in fantasy baseball the last 5-7 years but the gravy train comes to a halt eventually for everyone. At a very advanced age of 33 for a catcher, Molina noticeably slipped in 2014 as his average dipped below .300 for the first time since 2010 and the home runs dropped as well. Perhaps most alarming is that Molina dealt with injuries on more than one occasion last season, culminating in August thumb surgery that impacted his hitting when he returned in September. Keep in mind that you always want to abandon a player a year early rather than a year late. In the case of Molina, his name brand is now outpacing his actual production. **PROJECTION: .288 12 HR 71 RBI 62 R 2 SB**

10. **Wilson Ramos:** Ramos annually finds his name on our Sleeper Lists and rightfully so as the Washington Nationals' backstop has above-average power and the ability to hit .280 which is very enticing when it comes to catchers. Unfortunately Ramos is also one of the most injury-prone players in all of fantasy baseball which makes him one big source of frustration to own. Still despite all the annoyances, we recommend Ramos again due to the fact his draft value remains very low and the upside very high which

makes him a solid value play. 20 home runs and 80 RBI await if Ramos can finally stay on the field long enough.
PROJECTION: .273 16 HR 62 RBI 52 R 1 SB

11. **Salvador Perez:** Widely considered the glue that held together the World Series-bound Kansas City Royals, veteran catcher Salvador Perez is no slouch from a fantasy baseball angle as he proved once again in hitting .260 with 17 home runs and 70 RBI last season. What was really interesting about Perez is that despite those very solid numbers, his average was down more than a bit from the .301 and .292 he batted the two years prior. There is still a chance Perez could reach the 20 home run plateau this season, while at the same time bumping the average back to .280 or higher. That makes Perez' draft stock very attractive once again for a guy who always comes cheaper than he should.
PROJECTION: .282 18 HR 73 RBI 54 R 1 SB

12. **Matt Wieters:** Wieters was in the midst of his best start ever last April as he batted .308 with 5 home runs in his first 29 games before it was reveled he suffered a torn ligament in his right elbow which required Tommy John surgery. While Wieters is expected to be back at or soon after the start of the 2015 season, there is no telling how the procedure or the long layoff could impact him. Remember though that before the surgery Wieters was the rare catcher who could hit 25 home runs and drive in 80. In addition, the fact Wieters is coming off surgery should plummet his draft price which puts him squarely into the value bin.
PROJECTION: .265 19 HR 70 RBI 65 R 0 SB

13. **Travis D'Arnaud:** Like with most young catchers who come to the majors with a bunch of hype, the hitting aspect of the games gets stunted a bit due to the defensive responsibilities that come with the gig. That is exactly what took place with the New York Mets' Travis D'Arnaud during his first full big league season in 2014. Things got so bad for D'Arnaud that the Mets were forced to send him back down to Triple-A after he hit a listless .180 the first two-plus months. D'Arnaud didn't stay down for long however as he went on a ridiculous tear in the minors that included a near-.500 batting average. Once back with the big club, D'Arnaud proceeded to hit a respectible .265 with 7 home runs the second half of the year. This was a guy who was traded not once but TWICE for a Cy Young Award pitcher and D'Arnaud's stellar minor league work and second half of 2014 point to possibly top ten numbers being on tap.
PROJECTION: .267 16 HR 66 RBI 55 R

14. **Yasmani Grandal:** A PED suspension stained Grandal more than a bit in 2014 but he came back after his 50-game suspension determined to reclaim the polish that made him a much-talked about prospect in the San Diego Padres system. Showing off improved pop, Grandal swatted 15 home runs in only 377 at-bats. As surprising as the power was, it was also equally shocking to see Grandal hit only .225 which was in stark contrast to the string of .280-plus marks he put up coming through the Padres system. While we really don't have a handle yet on what Grandal is, he remains somewhat intriguing due to the fact he has produced whenever he has gotten a chance at the major league level.
PROJECTION: .256 17 HR 57 RBI 48 R 1 SB

15. **Dioneer Navarro:** The well-traveled Dioneer Navarro took almost a decade to find his footing in the big leagues but find his footing he did while hitting a decent 13 and 12 home runs the last two seasons. Never known for his average as he took his tour around the leagues, Navarro made gains there as well in batting .274 or better the last three seasons. If you are happy with solid but unspectacular numbers from your catcher, than Navarro is the guy for you. If you want upside, keep looking around.
PROJECTION: .276 11 HR 54 RBI 46 R 2 SB

16. **Jason Castro:** Prior to last season, we pegged Houston Astros catcher Jason Castro as a bust candidate despite coming off a breakout 2013 campaign when he hit 18 home runs and batted .276 at the age of 28. However we correctly pointed out that Castro's penchant for strikeouts would allow opposing pitchers the luxury of not throwing him anything to hit, thus knocking down the home runs and plummeting the average in the process. That is exactly what happened here as Castro turned out to be a colossal bust in hitting only 14 home runs and batting a ghastly .222. Having a long history of knee trouble that flared up again last season, there is very little to recommend here.
PROJECTION: .239 15 HR 51 RBI 48 R 0 SB

17. **Russell Martin:** How about that comeback season? The ageless veteran Martin had hit .250 or worse for five straight seasons before he somehow was able to post a .290 average in 2014. In addition, Martin was quite adequate in the power department with 11 home runs and 67 RBI. While we love the story and fully respect the career, there is absolutely no chance Martin comes anywhere near those numbers again at the age of 32. Best served as the second catcher in two-backstop formats despite the move to a more offensive ballpark in Toronto.

PROJECTION: .248 10 HR 61 RBI 48 R 2 SB

18. **Wellington Castillo:** We are squarely into the realm of catcher 2's in formats that play two backstops, which is a grouping that includes the Chicago Cubs' Wellington Castillo. Over the last two seasons Castillo has hit a total of 21 home runs and batted .274 and .237 which works well enough in that capacity.
PROJECTION: .267 9 HR 52 RBI 44 R 0 SB

19. **Miguel Montero:** It was a semi-comeback season for the veteran Montero in 2014, at least for the first half of the season when he hit .262 with 11 home runs. However the bottom completely fell out in the second half as Montero hit a horrid .218 with only two more knocks. Montero is aging at 32 and injuries have taken a firm bite out of his production. Just another guy at this stage of his career.
PROJECTION: .256 14 HR 66 RBI 46 R 0 SB

20. **Mike Zunino:** Meet the new version of J.P. Arencibia. If you didn't know any better, you would have thought Arencibia changed his name and played for the Seattle Mariners as Zunino did a flawless impersonation of his counterpart when you consider last season's 22 home runs and .199 batting average. Zunino has struck out at a ridiculous 35 percent clip since coming into the majors so expecting more than .230 is foolhardy at that rate. While the 22 home runs are a very good total, the damage Zunino's awful average causes offsets the gains there.
PROJECTION: .228 23 HR 63 RBI 52 R 1 SB

21. **Jarrod Saltalamacchia:** Moving from the hitting paradise in Boston to the pitching haven in Miami did a number on veteran catcher Jarrod Saltalamacchia's numbers in 2014 as he hit only 11 home runs with a .220 average. The 25 homers Salty hit in 2012 are a clear outlier and his .242 career average is a huge deterrent as well. With zero ceiling left to his name, Salty is a guy best left for the waiver wire.
PROJECTION: .221 14 HR 57 RBI 47 R 0 SB

22. **Derek Norris:** Norris did a nice job in a timeshare setup behind the dish for the Oakland A's last season as he hit .270 with 10 home runs and 55 RBI in 385 at-bats. With John Jaso getting almost half the work behind the plate, a repeat of last season's numbers is the best case scenario.
PROJECTION: .268 11 HR 56 RBI 50 R 3 SB

23. **Robinson Chirinos:** The definition of a late bloomer, Robinson Chirinos was a virtual unknown until he came up midway through the 2014 season and proceeded to slam 13 home runs and drive in 40 in only 306 at-bats. Texas GM Jon Daniels has already stated publicly he has no issues with Chirinos being the team's everyday catcher next season as he keeps the seat warm for top prospect Jorge Alfaro. A sneaky 15-18 home runs could be had here which makes Chirinos the perfect speculative catcher 2 in double-backstop formats.
    PROJECTION: .249 17 HR 59 RBI 46 R 0 SB

24. **John Jaso:** The flip-side of the Oakland A's catching platoon, Jaso pretty much replicated his counterpart's numbers in hitting .264 with 9 home runs. Jaso has good on-base skills which got him into the leadoff spot of all places during his stint with the Tampa Bay Rays but his lack of pop and lack of a full slate of at-bats makes him nothing more than a catcher 2/backup guy.
    PROJECTION: .267 7 HR 45 RBI 41 R 1 SB

25. **Kurt Suzuki:** Making the All-Star Game as Kurt Suzuki did last season for the Washington Nationals, doesn't automatically mean that player is worthy of fantasy baseball consideration. Such is the case of Suzuki who hit all of 3 home runs despite a tidy .288 batting average. While Suzuki at one time had some low-end upside value, those days are long since finished. Ignore.
    PROJECTION: .271 4 HR 51 RBI 43 R 1 SB

THE REST

26. **Alex Avila:** At one time an interesting power bat, Avila has not been anything more than waiver fodder in single-catcher leagues since 2011.

27. **Carlos Ruiz:** A PED stain and drastically reduced numbers the last two seasons have made Ruiz an almost non-factor.

28. **Rene Rivera:** Grabbed hold of the San Diego Padres' everyday catching job down the stretch last season as Yasmani Grandal was shifted to first base. Rivera proved to be no liability as he hit .252 with 11 home runs in only 294 at-bats. While Rivera is far from a sure thing and could quickly fade back to oblivion, he is worth watching in two-catcher formats.

29. **Josmil Pinto:** Pinto has been championed as the Minnesota Twins' catcher of the future and was part of the reason Joe Mauer was moved to first base. 2014 was a washout due to injuries which has put Pinto well off the fantasy

baseball radar but the promising bat remains. Could break through with good health.

30. **Ryan Doumit:** Was once a popular late round pick due to the fact Doumit played primarily as an everyday outfielder while making enough starts behind the dish to keep catcher eligibility. That was only as long as Doumit was hitting which he didn't due one bit last season. Aging and always prone to injury, this is one stock you can safely move away from altogether.

31. **Carlos Corporan:** Hit some home runs in limited time for the Astros last season but is not worth a look unless more injuries strike Jason Castro.

32. **Francisco Cervelli:** We include Cervelli here since there is a good chance he will be with a new team by the time you read this. Cervelli has hit whenever he has gotten the chance and so getting moved to a team who will give him everyday at-bats could turn him into an instant sleeper.

33. **Tyler Flowers:** Smacked 15 home runs in 407 at-bats but that is as far as positives go.

34. **Chris Iannetta:** After being moved out of Colorado, Iannetta pretty much lost all of his already limited appeal.

FIRST BASEMAN

Draft Strategy: This is where its at if you are on a mission for home runs and RBI. First base has historically been the top spot to find your power numbers and that remains true for the 2015 season. In fact, four of the first five picks in your draft may very well be first baseman (Miguel Cabrera, Edwin Encarnacion, Paul Goldschmidt, Jose Abreu) and it is recommended strongly from this peanut stand to double-dip here in order to fill out your UTIL or CI spots as well. You want to make sure you get a stud power-hitting first baseman with either your first or second round pick or else you will be chasing the rest of your league when it comes to power bats.

1. **Miguel Cabrera:** Despite moving to first base prior to the start of the 2014 season due to the trade of Prince Fielder, Cabrera retains both first and third base eligibility in leagues where 5 starts is the threshold (8 starts made at the hot corner). Whether at first or third base, Cabrera is the slam dunk number two overall player in fantasy baseball behind Mike Trout. Now as far as the

numbers are concerned, there is no denying the fact Cabrera had an "off" year by his incredible standards. After two straight seasons of slamming 44 home runs and RBI totals of 137 and 139, Cabrera saw massive declines in both categories. Cabrera wound up hitting 25 home runs and driving in 109 batters, which are still terrific numbers but they fell way short of his lofty standards. We always talk about outlier seasons in fantasy baseball and how inflated numbers from a guy's career norms usually can be thrown out. The same goes for an uncharacteristically off year like Cabrera had last season. Turning a still young 32 in April, Cabrera is much more likely to revisit his 2012-13 statistics which means 40 home runs and 120 RBI at worst. Don't let him slip past number 2 overall in your draft.
PROJECTION: .334 37 HR 129 RBI 107 R 1 SB

2. **Paul Goldschmidt:** A fractured hand right in August caused by an HBP was the only thing that stopped Paul Goldschmidt from having another stellar fantasy baseball MVP season in 2014. Once again Goldschmidt filled up all five hitting categories which is almost unheard of among first baseman. With full health, Goldschmidt is likely to come close to replicating or even exceeding his incredible 2013 campaign when he hit .302 with 36 home runs and 125 RBI and even stealing 15 bases. Tough call when deciding between Goldschmidt and Jose Abreu but the stolen base contributions decide things in the D-Backs first baseman's favor.
PROJECTION: .300 34 HR 119 RBI 104 R 14 SB

3. **Jose Abreu:** Talk about a smashing debut. Jose Abreu became the latest in an increasingly long line of Cuban imports who became instant stars in 2014 as he hit 36 home runs and drove in 107 while batting .317. Abreu's 10 home run/31 RBI month of April was one of the greatest run-producing stretches we have seen in years and his average got better as the season went on. What is truly amazing is that Abreu could even be better in 2015 as he continues to grow accustomed to major league pitching and he better withstands the rigors of a long season. Don't let him slip past the fifth overall pick. The guy is a monster.
PROJECTION: .310 38 HR 121 RBI 86 R 4 SB

4. **Edwin Encarnacion:** We took a lot of early heat a year ago after we gushed all over Edwin Encarnacion in last year's draft guide and strongly suggested he was a slam dunk first round pick. Only 2 home runs and a .260 average in April flooded our inbox with more than a few choice worded e-mails but we continued to preach patience. Ultimately those who had faith in Encarnacion won out as he slammed a ridiculous 16 home runs in April and finished with 34 to go along with 98 RBI. The average is a step

below the three guys listed above as Encarnacion has hit .280 or less in each of the last four seasons. In addition, Encarnacion has dealt with injuries throughout his career which has prevented a 600 at-bat campaign. Still Encarnacion can do a Paul Goldschmidt-like imitation right on down to the stolen bases this season which means middle first round territory once again.

PROJECTION: .271 37 HR 102 RBI 91 R 7 SB

5. **Todd Frazier:** Add Todd Frazier to the list of post-hype sleepers made good as the 2013 flameout found his footing at the major league level to say the least last season. Known for his pop coming up the minor league ladder that pointed to a future 25 home run bat, Frazier bettered that projection by sending 29 baseballs out of the park to go along with 80 RBI in 2014. In addition Frazier led all first base-eligible players in steals with 20 which is like 40 if he were an outfielder. A high K rate will not allow Frazier to hit anything better than .280 but his dual eligibility at first and third base to go with his five-tool production make him worthy of a mid-second round selection.

PROJECTION: .279 27 HR 89 RBI 86 R 17 SB

6. **Anthony Rizzo:** We told you all in last season's draft guide to stick with Rizzo for another season despite a 2013 campaign that left many abandoning him altogether after hitting only .233 with 23 home runs. Blessed with natural power and a massive frame, it was only a matter of time before Rizzo figured it out at the dish. Figure it out Rizzo did as he hit 32 home runs and knocked in 78 with a .286 average. Turning only 26, there is still time left for Rizzo to approach 40 home runs. The fact he plays for the woeful Chicago Cubs helps to keep his price down some as well. Go get him.

PROJECTION: .284 34 HR 89 RBI 92 R 3 SB

7. **Jose Bautista:** Reversing some troubling trends with a sliding home run rate and increasing injuries from 2012-13, Jose Bautista reclaimed his powerful name last season in hitting .286 with 35 home runs while clearing the 100 mark in both runs and RBI. In addition Bautista picked up first base eligibility for the first time in his career which added some bonus value to his aging (turning 35) name. We do have somewhat of a concern that Bautista could slide again with his numbers given the advancing age and the injury risk is getting more pronounced by the year. Still the fact of the matter is that Bautista provides top-end production in the one category (home runs) that is growing more and more rare by the day.

PROJECTION: .270 30 HR 92 RBI 88 R 5 SB

8. **Victor Martinez:** There was not a better value in all of 2014 fantasy baseball when it came to guys who swing a bat than veteran Detroit Tigers DH and sometime 1B Victor Martinez. Despite turning 35 the previous December, Martinez put forth an MVP-type season in hitting .335 with 32 home runs and 103 RBI. While the average and RBI total were no shock given the fact Martinez has always been one of the best pure hitters in baseball, the surge in home runs was beyond belief. Consider that the last time Martinez hit more than 20 home runs came way back in 2007 when he hit his previous high of 25. And in 605 at-bats in 2013, Martinez only managed 12. Thus we certainly have to look at the 32 home runs as an outlier and the smart approach would be scale back expectations there to the mid-20's. In addition, clearly hitting behind Miguel Cabrera gave Martinez plenty of fat fastballs to hit. Outside of that, Martinez remains a truly elite hitter who has another year or two of top production left. The real crazy aspect of all this is that once Martinez lost his catching eligibility prior to 2013, the consensus feeling was of him neing nothing more than a guy you plug in at UTIL if needed. Clearly we all wrote Martinez off too quickly as he showed in his remarkable performance a year ago. Sure there will be a bit of a regression but overall Martinez is a rock solid choice to anchor your 1B slot.
PROJECTION: .319 24 HR 101 RBI 86 R 1 SB

9. **Adrian Gonzalez:** Gonzalez has been a fascinating stock the last three seasons in that he continues to see depressed values in drafts due to the fact he longer is the 40-home run monster he was with the San Diego Padres or the MVP he was with the Boston Red Sox. An invasive shoulder procedure performed prior to 2012 no doubt robbed Gonzalez of some power as he is now firmly a 25 home run guy but his overall numbers remain excellent. Annually one of the best hitters in the game with men on base (an overlooked and very reliable stat when evaluating sluggers), Gonzalez led baseball in 2014 with 116 RBI to go with 27 home runs and a .276 average. Turning 33 in May, Gonzalez is holding steady as one of the more consistent and durable first baseman in fantasy baseball. Stop living in the past and take full advantage of the foolish discount he provides.
PROJECTION: .280 25 HR 105 RBI 81 R 1 SB

10. **Albert Pujols:** Along the same lines as Jose Bautista, Albert Pujols staved off decline at least in 2014 when it appeared he was on a steep downward slope with his numbers. The biggest key with Pujols last year was his health as he stayed mostly injury-free after dealing with ongoing foot

problems both in 2011 and 2012 which contributed to the sliding numbers. Be that as it may, Pujols is a somewhat stripped down version of his former number 1 overall self. For one, Pujols will never hit .320-plus again and .300 is likely well out of range as well. In addition Pujols' days of 40 home runs are a thing of the past as the 28 he hit last season are more in line with what we can expect for 2015. Pujols is now 35 and counting on him to stay completely healthy for two seasons running is asking a ton so cashing in your chips here may not be the worst idea in the world.
PROJECTION: .278 27 HR 103 RBI 90 R 4 SB

11. **David Ortiz:** Like a fine wine, David Ortiz seems to be getting better with age. While we can debate how Ortiz continues to manage being a 30-plus home run hitter as he approaches 40 given his past PED history, the fact of the matter is that he comes off one of his best season ever in 2014 when he hit 35 home runs and collected 104 RBI. The best part is that Ortiz still managed to make enough appearances at first base to carry eligibility there for those formats that use five games as the benchmark. We have been calling for Ortiz' demise for years now and been wrong every time, so we are out of that business once and for all. While the power remains as good as ever, Ortiz did in fact show some signs of slippage last season in regards to his .263 batting average, which snapped a string of three straight years of reaching the .300-plus mark. What is really interesting here is that everyone keeps thinking THIS is the year the big Ortiz drop-off comes which ensures his draft price is always somewhat affordable. And with the power numbers he annually provides, Ortiz actually qualifies as a value play.
PROJECTION: .268 29 HR 106 RBI 67 R 0 SB

12. **Freddie Freeman:** All in all, one had to be disappointed in the return on investment that Atlanta Braves first baseman Freddie Freeman provided in 2014 as he failed to make the jump to upper-tier status that had seemed to be his destiny. Freeman failed to crack the 20 home run mark (finishing with 18) and only collected 78 RBI which are not good numbers by any means for a fantasy baseball starting first baseman. The .288 average was tidy enough but Freeman still showed problems with K's as he whiffed 145 times. That tells you Freeman is not yet a finished product and that maybe we rushed to judgment a bit on him. Still before we get too down on the guy, Freeman will be turning only 26 this season which is right on the age cusp when players take a step forward in their power numbers. We don't think Freeman is the next Billy Butler but at the same time depending on him as your starting first baseman is not the safest investment that it looked like last season.

PROJECTION: .290 23 HR 94 RBI 95 R 1 SB

13. **Joey Votto:** It is all going incredibly wrong for Joey Votto in such a short time that it is stunning and somewhat sad to watch. A first round lock as recently as 2012, Votto's career looks like it is at a crossroads due to a knee issue that could be degenerative. Votto had two surgeries done on his left knee in 2012 and while he came back to play in all 162 games a year later, he managed to hit only 24 home runs amid whispers he wasn't driving the ball as hard as he used to. 2014 proved to be nothing short of a complete disaster as Votto played in only 62 games due to two separate DL stints (one for the same left knee and one for a quad injury) which resulted in a 6 home run season accompanied by a .255 batting average. At a still young 32, Votto's days of being a top tier fantasy baseball first baseman look finished and he is in jeopardy of being pushed out of starting status in 12-team standard leagues given the uncertainty surrounding his health. Again you always want to construct a team with as little injury risk as possible and on that front, Votto pretty much flies in the face of that plan as much as any other prominent player.
PROJECTION: .289 22 HR 82 RBI 88 R 2 SB

14. **Prince Fielder:** So much for being traded to the Texas Rangers serving as the impetus for Prince Fielder regaining his 40 home run status. Expectations went through the roof for Fielder after the deal sending him to the Rangers for Ian Kinsler was consummated due to the fact he almost literally was going from one extreme to the other when it came to moving from a pitching to a hitter's park. Ultimately Fielder was done before he ever really got started due to a neck issue that required season-ending surgery in May. After being drafted as high as the late first round in some leagues, Fielder netted a grand total of 3 home runs in 150 at-bats to go along with a .247 average. It was downright stunning how listless Fielder looked at the plate even before the neck issue was revealed and the year prior in Detroit was disappointing as well when he hit only 25 home runs with a .279 average. Many excuses have been made for Fielder the last few years such as distractions from a divorce, his giving up of meat, and his ballpark but maybe the guy is simply fading early like many other big-bodied sluggers have in the past. While Fielder is still only 31, there are way too many issues to concern yourself with to make him anything more than a UTIL or CI bat until we see a correction for the better.
PROJECTION: .275 26 HR 92 RBI 82 R 1 SB

15. **Lucas Duda:** Well it certainly looks like the New York Mets made the right choice in sticking with Lucas Duda and jettisoning Ike Davis in their

attempt to finally decide on a first baseman for the present and future. The hulking Duda always had the look of a classic home run slugger but a lack of confidence, struggles with strikeouts, and the pressures of trying to win the job over Davis resulted in numbers that weren't even attractive for bench duty. Once Davis was sent packing early last season, Duda seemingly turned into a monster slugger overnight as he would finish the season with 30 home runs and 92 RBI on a team in desperate need of power. Duda still has some ceiling left to him as he is still a young player at 28 but his awful .180 mark against lefties has to improve in order for him to reach his full potential. In addition, despite all the home runs, Duda hit only .253 due to his issues with the southpaws and strikeouts in general which speaks to his current status as a UTIL or CI bat for now.
PROJECTION: .259 32 HR 95 RBI 77 R 4 SB

16. **Buster Posey:*******SEE CATCHER RANKINGS!********

17. **Carlos Santana*******SEE CATCHER RANKINGS.********

18. **Mark Trumbo:** A stress fracture in his left foot caused the power-hitting Mark Trumbo to miss 71 games during his debut season with the Arizona Diamondbacks last season but his hitting rates remained as potent as they were during his stay with the Los Angeles Angels. Trumbo is what we call a "home run specialist" in that his best asset is the long ball which comes attached to some very shaky batting averages. Trumbo is only a .247 career hitter due to a massive K rate that totaled as high as 184 in 2013. Thus you have to weigh the damage Trumbo will cause to your team batting average with the positives he will yield in home runs and RBI. No longer third base eligible, Trumbo will qualify only at first and the outfield going forward.
PROJECTION: .252 32 HR 97 RBI 79 R 4 SB

19. **Chris Carter:** With Adam Dunn now retired, the Houston Astros' Chris Carter take the mantle as the top "all-or-nothing" slugger for fantasy baseball purposes. One of the strongest players in the game, Carter cleared the outfield fence 37 times in 2014 while also picking up 88 RBI on a bad Astros team. Still as glowing as those home run totals were, Carter managed only a .227 average due to striking out an insane 182 times in barely over 500 plate appearances. If you cover the rest of your roster with .300-plus hitters, Carter can surely be a help to you. If not than take a pass as those type of averages really do a number on your overall team mark in that category.
PROJECTION: .224 36 HR 90 RBI 67 R 2 SB

20. **Adam LaRoche:** It was another quietly solid season for Washington Nationals veteran first baseman Adam LaRoche in 2014 as he did his job in the home run department with 26 while also driving in 92 runs. The poster child for second half surges, LaRoche has flipped the script somewhat the last two seasons in the average department but his home runs have consistently went out at equal rates both pre-and-post All Star break. LaRoche is getting up therein age at 36 but this is as cheap a 20-25 home run haul for your UTIL or CI slot as you can possibly get.
PROJECTION: .255 25 HR 89 RBI 71 R 2 SB

21. **Matt Adams:** It was a weird first full season in the major leagues for intriguing St. Louis Cardinals first baseman Matt Adams who pretty much did the opposite of what was expected. For one, the hulking Adams hit only 15 home runs in 527 at-bats which was an astonishing number when you consider that he smacked 17 in only 296 plate appearances the season before. In addition Adams surprisingly hit .288 which didn't seem possible prior to the season when you look at the high K rates has always produced. Thus is it tough to figure what Adams truly is at this point as he turns 27 this August. The best course of action is to add some home runs while subtracting a bit in the batting average department for Adams in 2015.
PROJECTION: .275 24 HR 79 RBI 71 R 2 SB

22. **C.J. Cron:** Sleeper alert! Despite the presence of Albert Pujols at first base, the Los Angeles Angels will have to find a spot for the developing C.J. Cron for 2015. A former first round pick (17th overall) in the 2011 draft, Cron quickly showed an advanced hitting approach that points to a future .300/25 HR bat. Cron was no slouch in his 2014 campaign either as he hit 11 home runs in only 242 at-bats. At a hulking 6-4 and 235 pounds, Cron just needs a chance to realize his vast potential.
PROJECTION: .282 23 HR 79 RBI 70 R 0 SB

23. **Brian McCann:***********SEE CATCHER RANKINGS.*********

24. **Justin Morneau:** All in all the Colorado Rockies and the 2014 fantasy baseball owners of Justin Morneau did pretty well after buying very low on the former MVP. Clearly playing half of his games in Coors Field helped stunt the rapid drop in Morneau's numbers the last few seasons as he shockingly won the batting title by hitting .319. Unfortunately the home runs never came back around in his new locale as Morneau hit only 17 longballs and drove in 82. At 34 and with a long list of serious injuries in his recent past, Morneau at best can be expected to repeat last season's numbers minus a drop in average. That makes Morneau a solid enough UTIL or CI choice but far from a first base anchor.

PROJECTION: .300 16 HR 84 RBI 70 R 1 SB

25. **Brandon Moss:** We pushed hard for Brandon Moss prior to last season in seeing him as another very good value based on the strength of his power output. Moss fell into the underrated tier due to the West Coast Bias, his pitching-leaning ballpark, and his somewhat shaky average. However this is a guy whose per game home run output was near the top of the majors and he came off hitting 30 bombs in 2013. Moss would prove to be a first half monster last season as he hit 21 home runs with an extreme 66 RBI. Once the All-Star festivities were through though, Moss fell flat on his face as he put up one of the worst second halves of any hitter in the majors. The horror show included a .173 average and only four home runs. Sure Moss was dealing with some injuries but 153 strikeouts did him in when it came to his .234 average. Still Moss has hit 30 and 25 home runs the last two years which is a very impressive total in today's game. His second half fade in 2014 almost guarantees Moss will come cheap again in this season which is beneficial to you. We don't need to remind anyone how tough is it becoming with regards to finding home runs so Moss should remain squarely on your radar.
PROJECTION: .255 86 RBI 74 R 2 SB

26. **Mark Teixeira:** The declining fantasy baseball status of New York Yankees first baseman Mark Teixeira has been beyond stark over the last three seasons. A former first round pick as recently as 2010, Teixeira has seen his numbers and health spiral in the wrong directions since. It was more of the same for Teixeira in 2014 as he finished with an average 22 home runs while playing in only 123 games due to a variety of health woes. Specifically speaking, Teixeira struggled the first half of the year in coming back from offseason wrist surgery that robbed him of power and kept his status in the day-to-day mode for awhile. Making matters worse, Teixeira came down lower-body injuries after the All-Star Break that constantly had his owners checking on a daily basis to see if he was in the lineup. Now as far as the current hitting profile is concerned, Teixeira still has some solid pop that could net 25 home runs if he plays in enough games. However Teixeira's increased swing-for-the-fences mode has made him a batting average liability as he has failed to hit over .256 over the last five seasons. As a result Teixeira is now a clear shell of his former slugging self and at the age of 35, his decline won't be reversed. At this stage Teixeira is just a UTIL/CI bat.
PROJECTION: .253 24 HR 75 RBI 65 R 0 SB

27. **Chris Davis:** Called that one didn't we? Davis headlined our 2014 "Bust" list as his 2013 season was one big fluke, even before the PED bust. The .286 average that year was sustained by one of the most fortuitous BABIP's in baseball and Davis' always sky-high K rate meant that number was headed for a massive fall when his luck normalized. Well normalize it did in 2014 as Davis couldn't even muster a .200 average (.196) as he struck out a ridiculous 173 times in only 450 at-bats. Davis also was in clear outlier territory with the home runs in 2013 when he smacked 53 since that was 20 more than his previous high. Fast forward a season and Davis finished last season with only 26 and collecting a paltry 72 RBI. The only positive that can be said perhaps is that Davis picked up third base eligibility but right now he really just profiles as the next Adam Dunn at this stage of the game. The extreme damage Davis brings to your team batting average is not worth seeing if a rebound is in store.
PROJECTION: .230 28 HR 86 RBI 67 R 1 SB

28. **Michael Cuddyer:*****SEE OUTFIELDER RANKINGS.********

29. **Mike Napoli:** It has been a few years now since Mike Napoli was a top five fantasy baseball catcher and in that time he has lost power while continuing to be an average liability as he exclusively manages first base for the Boston Red Sox. While playing first theoretically should have kept Napoli more healthy, he has amassed only 352, 498, and 415 at-bats the last three seasons. Still Napoli is capable of hitting among the cheapest 20 home runs you can find so he still provides some solid value despite the hit to your team batting average.
PROJECTION: .253 21 HR 74 RBI 67 R 2 SB

30. **Brandon Belt:** There was one big dark cloud hanging over Brandon Belt's head last year to say the least. After coming out of the gates as hot as anyone in baseball by hitting six home runs in April, Belt suffered a broken hand via a HBP that cost him two months. Than only 11 games after his return, another HBP nailed him in the face which caused a concussion that kept him out for another period of games. The end result was another season of unmet potential as Belt hit 12 home runs and batted .243 in only 61 games played. Time is starting to run out on Belt's ceiling years as he turns 27 but he will be given every opportunity to finally show that the light bulb has gone on.
PROJECTION: .278 18 HR 71 RBI 77 R 4 SB

31. **Eric Hosmer:** For the second time in three seasons, Kansas City Royals 1B Eric Hosmer was a colossal disappointment after entering the year with a

ton of sleeper hype. After Hosmer hit nearly .330 the second half of 2013, many concluded that the talented former first round pick was on the cusp of stardom, with .300-plus/20-home run seasons in his future. Hosmer however failed to follow along with the script as he hit only 3 home runs the first two months of the season and 9 for the year. In addition, Hosmer drove in only 58 and batted a listless .270. While Hosmer is still a younger-than-you-think 26, we are getting very close to the what-you-see-is-what-you-get phase of his career. Which when you put it all together doesn't amount to a whole lot.

PROJECTION: .279 14 HR 68 RBI 75 R 10 SB

32. **Mike Morse:** Morse has been a guy we have always liked more than most due to the fact he annually provided some incredibly cheap power when home runs are becoming incredibly rare. Since Morse hit 31 home runs in 2011 however, he has been an injury-marred mess that has taken a huge chunk out of his counting stats. The San Francisco Giants took a low-risk chance on Morse for 2014 however and it looked early on like they had a huge bargain on their hands. In April and May Morse clubbed 11 home runs while collecting a tremendous 38 RBI. From that point on though, Morse went into the tank as his average and home run rate dropped off the map. In the end Morse hit only 7 home runs the last fourth months of the season and was benched down the stretch. At 34-years-old, Morse's injury risk will grow, while the offensive numbers could point south. Draft as nothing more than a bench bat to use when hot.

PROJECTION: .266 16 HR 62 RBI 61 R 1 SB

33. **Steve Pearce:** There are late bloomers and than there is the case of the Baltimore Orioles' Steve Pearce. After undertaking the journeyman's role in playing for five teams in 9 years without being able to stick as anything more than a bench bat, Pearce took full advantage of injuries afflicting the Orioles' infield last season to finally net some everyday at-bats. The results were shocking as Pearce hit 21 home runs in only 338 at-bats while batting a very solid .293. The Orioles have already said publicly that Pearce will be a big part of their 2015 plans so this story will have another chapter written. Having eligibility both in the outfield and at first base, Pearce could be in line to hit 25 home runs with a useful average. The best part is that most believe Pearce's performance was a fluke which means his draft price will remain very affordable. We smell another profit on the way.

PROJECTION: .266 24 HR 70 RBI 72 R 6 SB

34. **Adam Lind:** Lind has now hit .280 or better the last two seasons as the Toronto Blue Jays had figured out the best way to deploy his powerful bat.

That plan was to bench Lind whenever a lefty is on the mound and the results have worked given the gains in average we have seen the last two years. Lind has hit 23 or more home runs in four of the last six seasons so he has value on that aspect of his game alone. Will never come close again to the 35 home run/.305 monster he looked to be back in 2009 but Lind still has solid value in a home run-needy era. The problem now is that the Blue Jays dealt Lind to the Minnesota Twins which means he undoubtedly will lose home runs and RBI in moving from a hitting paradise to one of the worst power ballparks in the league in Target Field.

PROJECTION: .279 23 HR 78 RBI 65 R 0 SB

35. **Jon Singleton:** While Jonathan Singleton was touted as one of the better prospects in the minors, we were very tepid in our outlook on the Houston Astros' slugging first baseman. We correctly pointed out prior to his promotion in 2014 that Singleton could be more trouble than he is worth due to an extreme K rate and poor plate discipline overshadowing tremendous natural power. The result went right along with that forecast as Singleton hit only .168 with 13 home runs in 310 at-bats. Singleton almost struck out in half his plate appearances which is downright ridiculous and shows you how much of a liability he will be in the average department. Basically Singleton is a younger version of his teammate Chris Carter if that moves the interest needle for you.

PROJECTION: .225 25 HR 65 RBI 62 R 1 SB

36. **Billy Butler:** One of the biggest outlier numbers we have seen over the last five years was the 29 home runs Billy Butler hit back in 2012. While a power burst like he had that year was always being discussed as a possibility, Butler went back to his Sean Casey impersonation (solid average hitter with poor pop despite hulking size) by hitting only 15 and 9 baseballs over the outfield fence the last two seasons. Butler will turn 29 this year which means we are now fully past the ceiling portion of his career and even more disturbing is his usually solid average has been trending in the wrong direction the last two years. Signing a free agent deal with the Oakland A's does nothing for his value either as O.Co Coliseum is about as bad a power park as there is in baseball. Sorry but we can't get too motivated checking out a .280-hitting/10-15 home run hitter at a position where it is imperative to get at least 20-plus home runs and 80 RBI.

PROJECTION: .281 14 HR 81 RBI 65 R 2 SB

37. **Allen Craig:** What on earth happened here? One of the better pure hitters in all of baseball from 2012-2013, Allen Craig became washed up almost overnight in a truly awful season last year. After hitting .307 or better for

three straight years, Craig's bat was completely listless the first 97 games with the Cardinals as he hit .237 with only 7 home runs. The Cards threw in the towel on Craig as they shipped him off at the trade deadline to the Red Sox who were looking for some bats. Craig was even worse with the Red Sox as he batted a disgraceful .128 in 29 games with a single home run. So what in the heck went wrong here? Well for one Craig's long history of injuries could finally be taking a firm toll on his power and hitting in general. In addition Craig is an old 31 again due to all of the health woes he has suffered in his career. He will get a chance to have a comeback season with the Red Sox in 2015 but rest assured they won't be very patient if he continues to hit as poorly as he did in 2014.

PROJECTION: .278 11 HR 67 RBI 72 R 2 SB

38. **Brock Holt:** On eligibility alone, Brock Holt was the MVP of fantasy baseball as we can't remember when a hitter qualified at every infield position, to go along with the outfield. That aside, Holt was actually pretty good numbers-wise in taking advantage of a chance with the rebuilding Red Sox, showing a nice lone-drive swing that enabled him to bat a solid .281. The limitations were obvious though as Holt hit only 4 home runs in 449 at-bats. Holt will have to fight for a starting spot for the upcoming season but if he does stick, he is about as good as you can get with regards to eligibility and serving as the ultimate bench fill-in when needed.

PROJECTION: .275 6 HR 46 RBI 71 R 16 SB

39. **Joe Mauer:** It is tough to believe that Joe Mauer is already 32-years-old but one look at his declining hitting stats would be all you need to see to accept that fact. Striking out at a higher rate that ever before and walking less, Mauer hit only .277 last season despite moving full-time to first base in order to keep his body healthy. Mauer still spent time on the DL though despite the move and clearly has established himself as one of the more injury-prone players in the game. With very little in the way of power, Mauer's value depends heavily on his ability to bat .300, drive in, and score runs. He did none of the three well in 2014 and now that he no longer carries catcher eligibility, Mauer is pretty much nothing more than a bench bat if you can believe it.

PROJECTION: .288 8 HR 73 RBI 78 R 2 SB

40. **Casey McGehee:** Going overseas gave new life to the fledgling career of infielder Casey McGehee based on his surprisingly good 2014 numbers. Having once had a mini-run as a third base bat capable of hitting some home runs while with the Milwaukee Brewers, McGehee had to settle for a minor league deal by the Miami Marlins in order to get his foot back into big leagues. McGehee made good on the deal as he was right near the top

of basebal in RBI for a good chunk of April and May. In the end McGehee still showed that his past power was gone completely as he hit only 4 home runs in 616 at-bats. In addition, McGehee's RBI pace slowed tremendously as the year went on, finishing with a modest 76. Still McGehee hit .287 and has eligibility at first and third base. A bench bat who can help you in a pinch.
PROJECTION: .273 6 HR 70 RBI 59 R 5 SB

41. **James Loney:** Loney is the classic case of a guy who is better in real-life than in fantasy baseball. A .285 career hitter, Loney can spray line drives with the best of them. Unfortunately there is very little in the way of pop when it comes to Loney's bat and thus getting an empty average from a first base-eligible hitter is not very attractive. Loney can fill-in for short stretches when injuries strike your starting first baseman but that is the extend of his value.
PROJECTION: .288 10 HR 74 RBI 57 R 2 SB

42. **Kenny Vargas:** The Minnesota Twins have one of the better farm systems in baseball and they started showing off some of that bounty the second half of last season when they promoted their monstrous (6-5/273 pound) DH/1B Kenny Vargas. Vargas immediately went to work showing the team he could be a possible prime power source for the team as he hit 9 home runs and drove in 38 batters in only 215 at-bats. While we won't go so far as to say Vargas is a future 30-home run bat, he has the type of forceful swing that should net him 20-plus as soon as 2015. Upside play.
PROJECTION: .262 17 HR 65 RBI 55 R 0 SB

43. **Pedro Alvarez:******SEE THIRD BASEMAN RANKINGS.*******

44. **Juan Francisco: SEE THIRD BASEMAN RANKINGS!*******

45. **Ryan Howard:** It was prior to the 2011 season when we first started mentioning the fact that perennial home run monster Ryan Howard was looking more and more bust-worthy due to his increasing age, increasing K rate, and for his big body type which historically doesn't age well when it comes to sluggers. Well Howard did his 33 home runs that season but since than his career has bottomed out under a hail of strikeouts, injuries, and depressed power production. 2014 was no different as Howard hit only 23 home runs, batted a pathetic .223, and struck out 190 times. Things got so bad that the Philadelphia Phillies entertained the idea of cutting him loose and eating the remainder of his massive salary. At 36-years-old, Howard is

nothing but an average-destroying 20 home run bat who will miss games with injuries. Salute the career and move on for good.
PROJECTION: .232 19 HR 78 RBI 62 R 1 SB

46. **Yasmani Grandal******SEE CATCHER RANKINGS.****

47. **Lonnie Chisenhall:*****SEE THIRD BASEMAN RANKINGS.****

48. **Chase Headley:*****SEE THIRD BASEMAN RANKINGS.*****

49. **Ike Davis:** A change of scenery did Ike Davis little good last season as the New York Mets finally threw in the towel waiting for his bat to come around, shipping him to the Pittsburgh Pirates for a minor league pitcher. It can be argued that Davis was in the running as the worst hitting regular in the game the last two years, as he swatted a total of only 20 home runs with a batting average that threatened .200. Right now the 32 home runs Davis hit in 2012 are looking like a tremendous outlier and his inability to stem the strikeouts or to hit lefties has pushed Davis to waiver wire territory.
PROJECTION: .239 17 HR 57 RBI 52 R 1 SB

50. **Logan Morrison:** The most impact Morrison has had the last two seasons has been on Twitter which is obviously not saying much with regards to his fledgling fantasy baseball value. Injuries are a constant source of frustration, as Morrison has not reached 400 at-bats in each of the last three seasons. There are tools to work with here though as Morrison hit 11 home runs and stole 6 bases in only 336 at-bats in 2014 which hints at some decent potential. In addition, Morrison is only 28 so, health permitting, he could provide a sneaky 20 home runs and 10 steals with a mediocre average if all breaks right. Worth a very late round selection.
PROJECTION: .251 16 HR 63 RBI 61 R 8 SB

51. **Daniel Murphy:*******SEE SECOND BASEMAN RANKINGS.******

52. **Chris Johnson:*****SEE THIRD BASEMAN RANKINGS.*****

53. **Nick Swisher:** It was a frustrating season filled with injuries for the always excitable Nick Swisher in 2014 as he amassed only 360 at-bats that resulted in 8 home runs and a woeful .208 average. Swisher is much better than that hitting line and with good health he is a near-lock for 20 home runs. Decent bounce back appeal but Swisher is about as boring an investment as one can make.

PROJECTION: .255 21 HR 75 RBI 73 R 1 SB

THE REST

54. **Stephen Vogt:** Vogt was just the latest Oakland A's minor league hitter to come up and immediately start hitting ropes as he smacked 9 home runs and batted .270 in only 269 at-bats. Qualifying also in the outfield, Vogt could have a prime chance to grab hold of a starting spot for the A's this season which makes him somewhat interesting. Save a late round pick for him if you can.

55. **Kendrys Morales:** Has become a journeyman first baseman and not a good one at that the last two seasons as Morales has seemingly lost the ability to hit home runs and bat for average. One wonders what might have been if Morales didn't break his leg in that unfortunate home plate fiasco.

56. **Garrett Jones:** Jones pretty much duplicated his 2013 production last season which meant 15 home runs and a shaky batting average under .250. No longer outfielder eligible, Jones operates in a bad hitting park, turns 34, and no longer is a 20-home run threat. In other words take a pass.

57. **Scott Van Slyke:** Hit a home run on Opening Day which made everyone check him out but otherwise Van Slyke was just making his way through the season pretty much unnoticed. In part-time duty Van Slyke hit an impressive .297 with 11 home runs in only 212 at-bats but he has no shot at a staring spot for 2015 unless the Dodgers make a deal to open up space on the field.

58. **Justin Smoak:** Amazing that this was the "prized prospect" the Seattle Mariners got for Cliff Lee. Smoak has pretty much been a massive disappointment, what with his .220 average and only 20-home run power. Not for fantasy baseball purposes.

59. **Mark Reynolds:** Reynolds' home run swing is still in fine working order but he can't even hit .200 at this point in his aging career.

60. **Mike Olt:** Olt can hit home runs but that is pretty much the extent of the positives. His past as a top Texas Rangers prospect are long since finished.

61. **Tommy Medica:** There are some tools here as Medica has 20 home run power and 15 steal speed. A very high K rate though makes it tough to

expect Medica to hit anything better than .260 however. Could get a long look for an offensively-needed San Diego club. Monitor.

62. **Chris Parmelee:** A former first round pick, Parmelee is only a .249 hitter after three straight seasons of failing to stick with the Minnesota Twins. Stop chasing the potential.

63. **Yonder Alonso:** Alonso resembles James Loney in his ability to hit for average but not home runs. Injuries also have taken huge bites out of his last two seasons.

64. **Conor Gillaspie:** Gilleaspie qualifies at both first and third base which is about the only positive to speak of given his limited power and lack of impact in any one category. Leave on the wire.

65. **Corey Hart:*****SEE OUTFIELD RANKINGS!****

66. **Chris Colabello:** It certainly looked like the Minnesota Twins had a diamond in the rough at the start of 2014 when the undrafted Chris Colabello hit .286 with 3 home runs and a crazy 27 RBI in April. However once the book got out on Colabello, he completely hit the skids as he earned a trip back to the minors in July after a .125 May and a .217 June. Should be a non-factor.

67. **Darin Ruf:** Injuries almost completely ruined Ruf's 2014 season after he showed some power potential with the Philadelphia Phillies the year prior. Watch to see if Ruf can nab a starting spot but otherwise ignore.

68. **Daniel Nava:** Nava has been mildly interesting the last two seasons given his home ballpark and ability to hit the odd home run and steal the odd base. Has yet to break through though to be anything more than a backup bat.

69. **Kyle Blanks:** Blanks was always interesting due to his power potential but he has failed to stick after numerous opportunities the last four seasons. Don't bother with him unless a starting spot opens up at some point.

70. **Justin Turner:** Turner has found a role in the majors as a super utility guy who qualifies all over the diamond. He also hit pretty well last season in batting .340 with 7 home runs in limited appearances but overall Turner doesn't play enough to help you this season.

SECOND BASEMAN

Draft Strategy: When it comes to formulating a balanced roster, we historically like to group our second baseman and shortstops together in a quest for runs and stolen bases. While your first and third baseman should be supplying a large chunk of your power numbers, your middle infielders need to possess some speed and stolen base prowess in order to keep your team at optimum efficiency. As far as second baseman specifically are concerned, this is a very top-heavy group that saw some big names go bust in 2014. Of course I am primarily indicting Dustin Pedroia and Jason Kipnis who both came in well below what was expected from them stat-wise, while trusting in the always fragile Ian Kinsler is never a comforting thought. Robinson Cano meanwhile remains a late first round pick, as he has been since becoming a regular for the New York Yankees. Even after moving to the Seattle Mariners prior to last season, Cano offset a predicted drop in power by upping his batting average to its highest mark in his career.

We will remain consistent however in advising you to stay away from drafting Cano in Round 1, despite the instant advantage he gives you over the rest of your league at that shallow position. You ideally want to use your first two picks to get a slugging first baseman and a stud outfielder and that shouldn't change. Sort of along the lines of your catcher, you want to go value at second base in the middle rounds of your draft. A year ago that player was Jose Altuve who became somewhat of a forgotten man prior to 2014 and as a result dropped in drafts despite very good speed and a solid bat. Fast forward a year later and Altuve comes off a monster season when he was in contention for the batting and swiped a career-high total of 56 bases. We will go with that strategy again for 2015 as there are some names of interest who can exceed their expected draft position as Altuve did a year ago.

1. **Robinson Cano:** We all knew Robinson Cano moving from Yankee Stadium to Safeco Field would adversely impact his power numbers and that is exactly what happened as the perennial number 1 fantasy baseball second baseman went for only 14 home runs and 82 RBI. Still despite the drop in those two statistics, Cano continued to show that he remained one of the best pure hitters in the game as he challenged for the AL batting title for a chunk of the season with his .314 average. The ballpark and lack of lineup protection may keep Cano from 20-plus home runs and 90 RBI again but he remains flat in his prime with guaranteed solid to very good production across four different categories. Still we think Cano should fall

out of Round 1 for the first time since graduating into a regular as his overall numbers don't warrant him being one of the top 12 guys off the board.

PROJECTION: .315 19 HR 88 RBI 82 R 8 SB

2. **Anthony Rendon:** It took Washington Nationals second baseman Anthony Rendon all of a season-and-a-half to cement his status as the best at his position outside of Robinson Cano. Quite frankly there are a lot of similarities between the two as both came up the minor league ladder with MLB-ready bats that sprayed line drills all over the field and with burgeoning power. Rendon already had the .300 average swing down pat as he made his way to the Nationals but it was expected he would need a couple of seasons before he tapped into his power after he hit only 7 home in his 351 at-bat debut in 2013. Well Rendon would have none of it as he smacked 21 homers and drove in 83, while also scoring a massive 111 runs last season in a major breakout campaign. The .287 average was typical and even a bit below where Rendon should be going forward. The most pleasant surprise might have been the 17 steals Rendon collected and it was his performance there when combined with the home run advancement that put the new Nationals star into top tier status. At only 25, there is still some more growth seasons left or Rendon which is telling considering how good he already is. The sky is the limit.

PROJECTION: .302 23 HR 88 RBI 107 R 16 SB

3. **Jose Altuve:** Already a locked-in top ten fantasy baseball second baseman going into 2014, the Houston Astros' Jose Altuve had a truly magical year last season in taking his game to another level. Despite standing only 5-5 and 173 pounds, Altuve was impossible to get out for opposing pitchers both at the plate and on the basepaths as he took home the batting title with his .341 average and stole 56 bases. Incredible numbers for sure but let's examine them a bit further. As far as the average is concerned, Altuve had never hit over .290 in his previous three seasons prior to the batting title so there is a major outlier threat there. The 56 steals were also 21 more than his previous career-high as well. Speed is much less volatile than batting average however so even though a repeat there is not likely, 40 is certainly doable. The 7 home runs Altuve hit are about as good as you are going to get there and not scoring 90 runs last season with all those hits shows you how he gets hurt a bit with the lineup behind him. As long as you factor in the likelihood of the average slipping back more than a little, Altuve should remain a big-time impact player for you once again.

PROJECTION: .311 5 HR 89 R 57 RBI 48 SB

4. **Dee Gordon:** Los Angeles Dodgers manager Don Mattingly came out at the start of spring training and proclaimed unequivically that Dee Gordon would be the team's everyday second baseman for the 2014 season. Knowing all too well the fact Gordon had failed to secure a firm MLB job after three previous tries in each of the last three seasons, Mattingly was unbowed in believing he was the best option for the team's leadoff slot. Most fantasy baseball owners gave Gordon little attention last March when drafts were taking place due to the fact he had hit a miserable .234 and .228 the two years prior. This despite the fact that Gordon was already arguably the fastest player in the majors and that if he learned any sort of plate discipline, could easily lead the league in steals. Well lead the majors in steals Gordon did last season as he swiped 64 bags in 83 tries. Even better was the fact Gordon finally did break through with his hitting approach as he shocked everyone by batting .289. The key with Gordon and his fantasy baseball value always depended on the batting average, as no manager would stand for any .230 hitter with no power to go along with the fact no player has figured out how to steal first base. The jury is still out on whether Gordon can replicate that .289 average again this season but the speed and runs potential remain as good as anyone. This is strictly a 2.5 category guy (pluses in steals and runs, solid in average) as Gordon has zero power and RBI ability. Still as we have always advised, you want to receive a large allotment of your team steals from your middle infielders and on that front no one is better than Gordon.
PROJECTION: .272 1 HR 32 RBI 95 R 61 SB

5. **Ian Kinsler:** Us and many others pegged the aging Ian Kinsler as a prime bust candidate for 2014 for more than a few reasons, with the most significant being his move from perhaps one of the best hitting parks in the game to one of the worst when he was dealt from the Texas Rangers to the Detroit Tigers in the Prince Fielder deal. Kinsler got the last laugh however as he stayed healthy all year and proceeded to contribute across all five standard categories. While clearly no longer the two-time 30/30 monster he was in his younger days, Kinsler still hit 17 home runs and stole 15 bags while crossing home plate 100 times. In addition, he batted a good for him .275 and even drove in 92 runs out of the leadoff spot which is quite a feat. As a result, Kinsler should be back as a safe early round investment right? Well based on the numbers surely but there are still a lot of potential issues swirling here. For one, Kinsler is aging as he turns 33. We have seen age takes it toll on his speed as Kinsler has seen his steals totals go from 30 to 21 to 15 and than 15 again each of the last four seasons. In addition, expecting Kinsler to stay completely healthy for a second season in a row is asking a ton for one of the more historically injury-prone players in the

game. If all breaks right Kinsler could have one more season like he had in 2014 but if not we still think he will be very solid regardless health permitting. Just be aware of the age and injury issues before cutting the check.
PROJECTION: .270 15 HR 79 RBI 95 R 14 SB

6. **Josh Harrison:** Not even the most ardent fantasy baseball die-hard could have foreseen the incredible all-around breakthrough seen out of Pittsburgh Pirates super utility player Josh Harrison in 2014. That is true of the Pirates themselves who could have not been impressed with anything Harrison did his three previous seasons when he failed to hit and struggled mightily to stick with the big league club. It all somehow came together for Harrison last season however as he recovered from a rough April (1 HR/.227) to catch fire in May and June when he batted .317 in each month and began to show off his power/speed ability. When all was said and done, Harrison was a became five category stud in hitting .315 with 13 home runs to go along with 18 stolen bases. Qualifying at second base, third base, and the outfield, Harrison is a very hot fantasy baseball stock right now. There is some danger about the out-of-the-blue career year but Harrison played at such a high level for five straight months last season that the risk is somewhat decreased in our book. Sliding back the average just a bit would be smart but the rest of the package looks for real.
PROJECTION: .289 15 HR 57 RBI 80 R 20 SB

7. **Brian Dozier:** Dozier is the classic case about how many in the fantasy baseball community reflexively discriminate against a player who posts mediocre batting average ability despite possessing excellent numbers in the other four hitting categories. With batting average being such a black and white statistic that leads one to conclude whether a certain hitter was "good" or "bad" in a simplistic manner, guys like Minnesota Twins second baseman Brian Dozier find their stocks falling more than it should when it comes to the draft. Such was the case prior to the 2014 season when Dozier was coming off an 18 HR/14 SB semi-breakthrough with the Twins the year prior. Any young hitter like Dozier who is capable of being a power/speed force (especially in the middle infield) should be among the more sought after commodities during drafting season. However that was not the case for Dozier last March which meant that those who took advantage of the discount were tickled pink as he proceeded to up the power/speed numbers to another level by hitting 23 home runs and stealing 21 bases. In addition, Dozier became a top-notch run producer as he crossed home plate 112 times and collected a very solid 71 RBI. The average remained a clear liability as Dozier posted an ugly .242 mark as a result of 129 strikeouts. Still this is a

28-year-old second baseman who can help in four categories at a still very solid price. Ignore the average and buy in fully.
PROJECTION: .250 24 HR 68 RBI 108 R 22 SB

8. **Neil Walker:** Neil Walker was always that guy we selected really late when we somehow forget to address the second base position in the early and middle rounds of the draft. Or he was the first guy you picked up off waivers when Chase Utley or Dustin Pedroia got injured for you. Such was the life for Walker as a solid but unspectacular second baseman for the Pittsburgh Pirates since he made his debut back in 2009. Throughout his career, Walker would always be good for around 15 home runs, 7 steals, and a .275 average. Again numbers that wouldn't hurt you but left you always wanting more. Perhaps Walker was growing tired of that line of thinking as he proceeded to put up his best season in 2014 in passing the 20 home run barrier for the first time with 23, while also driving in 76 with a .271 average. The power boost was what clearly stood out but the total package of numbers were not exceptional once again. For one, Walker stole only 2 bases and his .271 average was nothing to write home about. In addition, he netted only 76 RBI with those 23 home runs. And with regards to the homers, Walker's previous career-high was 16 which meant last year's 23 could be an outlier number. At 30-years-old, there is no ceiling left to Walker's game and he is much more likely to slide back to his regular norms than hold onto the power gain.
PROJECTION: .275 19 HR 77 RBI 74 R 5 SB

9. **Daniel Murphy:** There was some stat-correction done on New York Mets second baseman Daniel Murphy in 2014 as he lost 10 stolen bases, 4 home runs, and 21 RBI from his career-year 2013 haul. Still despite the drop, Murphy proved himself a rock solid top ten fantasy baseball second baseman once again last season with a quietly very good season. Murphy is the classic player who will help you in all five standard categories but not excel in any one of them. We will gladly take that at second base and Murphy even picked up first and third base eligibility as well during the year as an added bonus. What you can count on is Murphy being a batting average asset to go along with 10-plus home runs and steals. The counting stats are also very good as Murphy has proven quite durable the last few seasons as well. Not everyone's cup of tea for sure as Murphy lacks flash but the bottom line is that he will do more than enough to justify a mid-round investment.
PROJECTION: .290 11 HR 74 RBI 80 R 14 SB

10. **Javier Baez:** The future has become the present for the Chicago Cubs as the team called up perhaps MLB's top shortstop prospect in Javier Baez last August and threw him right into the deep end against major league pitching. The results were part disturbing and part exhilarating as Baez hit 9 home runs and stole 5 bases in only 213 at-bats but he also batted a pathetic .160 due to striking out a ridiculous 95 times. At only 22 at the time of the recall, Baez clearly has some growing pains to fight through but the talent is obvious. Before his promotion, Baez hit 23 home runs in 434 Triple-A at-bats and stole 16 bases which highlights the power/speed game he possesses. Unfortunately there are some big holes in Baez' swing and lack of plate discipline as he even posted a 30 percent K rate last year at Triple-A. Baez is likely going to be a batting average liability for a few seasons before he hopefully works out the kinks and that has to be factored into his soaring draft price. In addition, Baez is eligible only at second base as Starlin Castro held down the shortstop spot last season so that is a minor negative as well. Baez no doubt has immense natural power for a middle infielder and comparisons to Brian Dozier seem spot on. Unfortunately there is also a risk that Baez struggles so much with the strikeouts early on that he gets sent back to the minors to clear his head, of which he would be the latest in a long line of prospect players to do have done sorecently. Ultimately we feel the hype surrounding Baez has inflated his draft price beyond where it should be and the bust factor under that scenario is sizable. Tremendous talent no doubt and a future star eventually but for the time being Baez is far from a sure thing.
PROJECTION: .253 23 HR 65 RBI 74 R 15 SB

11. **Danny Santana:** We are always on the lookout for emerging middle infield talent, even if it comes out of the blue like in the case of the Minnesota Twins' Danny Santana last season. Not on anyone's top prospect list, Santana immediately started hitting when called up in May and never stopped as he finished with a .319 average to go with 70 runs scored in only 405 at-bats. Known for his speed when coming up the farm system, Santana didn't disappoint there either as he stole 20 bases in 24 tries. What was really surprising were the 7 home runs Santana hit as his minor league high was only 8 which came in a 547 at-bat/A-ball campaign. Eligible at second base, shortstop, and the outfield, Santana looks here to stay as a daily impact player.
PROJECTION: .293 8 HR 54 RBI 86 R 27 SB

12. **Jason Kipnis:** Well that was a disaster. After being drafted as high as the second round prior to the 2014 season, Jason Kipnis fell flat on his face in hitting only .240 with 6 home runs and 22 stolen bases. The dropoff from

the year prior was incredibly stark as Kipnis lost 11 home runs, 8 stolen bases, and 44 points of batting average. And it came when most thought Kipnis was on the verge of becoming a 5-category monster as he reached his prime. The fact of the matter is that Kipnis has some work to do on his plate discipline and swing as he struck out in 20 percent of his at-bats last season and even in 2013 whiffed 143 times. So unless Kipnis gets some BABIP help, he will be a batting average liability. In addition, opposing pitchers stopped throwing Kipnis fastballs last season, instead choosing to let the Cleveland Indians second baseman chase to get himself out, which he often obliged. Kipnis is still only 28 however and remains talented enough to be a 15 HR/30 SB force. His depressed sticker price actually makes him a decent investment in an attempt to capture a comeback season.
PROJECTION: .261 16 HR 80 RBI 84 R 25 SB

13. **Kolten Wong:** A 2011 first round pick of the St. Louis Cardinals, it was only a matter of time before the talent bubbled to the surface for second baseman Kolten Wong. With the Cardinals having quite possibly the best track record in the game when it comes to developing prospects, Wong's power/speed ability was almost assumed to be there from the start when he got a cup of coffee with the team in 2013. Wong was not ready however as he hit only .153 in 32 games. Given a fresh start the following year, it seemed to be more of the same for Wong who struggled mightily once again in hitting .221 in April. While Wong rebounded to hit .333 in May, a .103 drought in June got him sent back down to the minors to clear his head. That seemed to do the trick as Wong came back up at the end of the month and proceeded to hit .255 with 6 home runs and 8 stolen bases the rest of the way. What is really interesting about Wong is the fact that despite some pronounced cold spells and the demotion, he still hit 12 home runs and stole 20 bases which is a terrific sum for a fantasy baseball second baseman. Wong has to do a better job drawing walks (only 21 in 402 at-bats) in order to boost up his .249 average but that really is the only area that is holding him back from top ten status. This is a player who is clearly on the upswing with his development and production so get on board now before the dam bursts on Wong's numbers.
PROJECTION: .267 14 HR 55 RBI 75 R 22 SB

14. **Dustin Pedroia:** Each season certain players' name values exceed their actual on-field production. Joe Mauer and Bryce Harper quickly come to mind and those two should be joined by Boston Red Sox second baseman Dustin Pedroia based on what we saw in 2014. The former MVP was just an ordinary player last season as he hit only .278 with 7 home runs and 6 stolen bases. Injuries were an ongoing problem for Pedroia and that was not

a new phenomenon as he spent a few extended DL trips in the previous four seasons. Second base is a tough position on smaller players like Pedroia and the wear and tear from playing there has been known to cause players' offensive numbers to drop off at a quicker rate than at other spots on the diamond. Think Carlos Baerga and Juan Samuel as prime examples. At 32-years-old, Pedroia is moving past his prime and by the looks of it, is following that same bath as Samuel and Baerga. Since 2011 Pedroia's home run totals have read 21, 15, 9, and 7. His steals have followed suit as they have come in at 26, 20, 17, and 6. The numbers and trends speak for themselves. Pedroia is just an ordinary player now and by the looks of it, is no longer a top ten fantasy baseball second baseman.

PROJECTION: .289 10 HR 62 RBI 89 R 8 SB

15. **Ben Zobrist:** Ben Zobrist is now entering his 10th season in the majors, all spent with the Tampa Bay Rays where he has been known for near 20/20 ability and for his eligibility all over the diamond. Zobrist is aging however at 34 and his home run totals the last three seasons have gone in the wrong direction from 20 to 12 to last year's 10. In addition, Zobrist's speed is also fading as his stolen base totals have dropped for five straight seasons. Still Zobrist remains eligible at second base, shortstop, and the outfield and another 10/10 season is likely. Boring as heck but still effective.

PROJECTION: .275 12 HR 57 RBI 81 R 9 SB

16. **Martin Prado:** Faced with a glaring hole in their infield, the New York Yankees completed a deal with the Arizona Diamondbacks for infielder Martin Prado at last year's trade deadline. A .291 career hitter, Prado's best asset has always come in the average department. In his nine year career, Prado's career-high in home runs is a modest 15 back in 2010 and his high in steals came in 2012 when he picked up an outlier 17 (his next highest total is only 5). Despite the solid but unspectacular numbers, Prado was terrific with the Yankees the last two months of the season as he hit .316 with 7 home runs. The second base spot has been reserved for Prado for 2014 and playing half his games in Yankee Stadium could have him in the neighborhood of 15-18 home runs, 90 runs scored, and 80 RBI to go with his customary .300 batting average. If you choose to wait on drafting your second baseman, this is one of the better value plays to target.

PROJECTION: .300 17 HR 78 RBI 91 R 5 SB

17. **Mookie Betts:** Top Boston Red Sox infield prospect Mookie Betts left us excited for his future after he hit .291 with 5 home runs and 7 steals in only 189 2014 at-bats. Betts has terrific bat control and a short, compact swing that will help him post good to very good batting averages. In addition, Betts has developing pop to go with top end speed which means 20/20 could

be in his future as well. Overall Betts didn't play enough last season in his two MLB stints to get the sleeper hype out of control which could work to your advantage at the draft. Go get him.

PROJECTION: .290 10 HR 54 RBI 72 R 19 SB

18. **Chase Utley:** One of the all-time great hitting second baseman, Father Time is really taking a toll on the Philadelphia Phillies' Chase Utley. And it is not only physical as Utley hit only .270 with 10 home runs and 10 stolen bases last season in 589 at-bats. Turning a very old for a second baseman 37, Utley's power fell off the map last year and he has now hit below .280 in four of the last five seasons. The tools are fading and Utley is always one of the more injury-prone players in the game as it is, a fact that will be more pronounced at his age. It is clearly time to move on for good here.

PROJECTION: .272 12 HR 75 RBI 72 R 8 SB

19. **Brandon Phillips:** Along the same lines as Chase Utley (although he was a step below his counterpart career-wise), the Cincinnati Reds' Brandon Phillips is succumbing to age and injury as he reaches his late 30's. Once a 20/20 early round stud, Phillips has completely lost his speed (only 7 total steals the last two seasons combined) and has failed to hit over .266 during that span as well. In addition, Phillips hit only 8 home runs in 2014 as he missed extensive time with injuries, which is a growing concern due to the fact he is now 34-years-old. There is not much to like anymore when it comes to Phillips so let him be someone else's problem.

PROJECTION: .262 12 HR 77 RBI 81 R 2 SB

20. **Howie Kendrick:** We all at one time heard the ridiculous talk that Los Angeles Angels infielder Howie Kendrick was destined to someday win a batting title but that was a foolish prediction from the start due to his utter lack of plate discipline since becoming a regular back in the 2006 season. Kendrick has been allergic to walks in his career, showing a hacking style that would make Vladimir Guerrero proud. After a few of his early seasons were ruined by injuries, Kendrick has settled into a solid player since 2011 in averaging 12 home runs, 13 steals, and a .290 average since that point. Another guy you may want to corral if you wait to draft a second baseman.

PROJECTION: .291 8 HR 68 RBI 77 R 14 SB

21. **Brett Lawrie:** Some guys just can't ever stay healthy no matter what and this ugly fraternity includes Toronto Blue Jays infielder Brett Lawrie, who only two short seasons ago was one of the most sought after sleepers in the game. By now it has become crystal clear that Lawrie's video-game numbers at Double-A in the Pacific Coast League were grossly inflated in

that hitter's paradise, as he has looked nothing but ordinary at the major league level since. Through four seasons Lawrie is a mediocre .265 hitter and he has never recorded 500 at-bats which is a testament to how injury-prone he has been. While Lawrie's 12 home runs a year ago in only 259 at-bats was a very solid rate, he failed to record a stolen base and batted a career-low .247. The amount of angst in owning Lawrie is as high as any player in fantasy baseball and the payoff numbers if he does somehow stay healthy are not looking like they will be impressive.

PROJECTION: .258 15 HR 61 RBI 73 R 6 SB

22. **Dustin Ackley:** We are now four seasons into the career of Seattle Mariners second baseman Dustin Ackley, who was the number 2 overall pick by the team in the 2009 draft, and thus far the results are nothing but disappointing. Showing none of the batting-title ability he portrayed in the minors, Ackley has a career major league mark of only .245. There were some tiny signs of development last season however as Ackley hit a career-high 14 home runs and he also chipped in with 8 steals. Again nothing earth-shattering and certainly not deserving of his lofty draft status but at least it is something positive. The bottom line however is that Ackley has not done nearly enough to be anything but a late round grab and only as a backup second baseman until we see a breakthrough that is not guaranteed to occur.

PROJECTION: .257 15 HR 67 RBI 65 R 9 SB

23. **Aaron Hill:** We got burned by Hill last season after pushing for all you to draft him as an affordable second base option with hitting upside. After all, Hill hit 26 home runs during his first full season in Arizona in 2012 and the 11 he clubbed in 2013 were only in 327 at-bats due to injury. In staying true to his career-long tendency to do the opposite of what was expected, Hill was simply awful last season in hitting only .244 with 10 home runs and 4 stolen bases in 501 at-bats. Hill's numbers have literally been all over the map in his career, with home run highs of 36 and a stolen base high of 16. The flip side to this were complete bust seasons in 2010 and 2014 which make Hill one big source of frustration. We don't blame you for moving avoiding Hill altogether as he is now 33 and has no track record of dependability.

PROJECTION: .270 14 HR 62 RBI 65 R 6 SB

24. **Jurickson Profar:** If you started playing fantasy baseball in 2014, you may have no clue who Texas Rangers top infield prospect Jurickson Profar is since he missed the entire year with a serious shoulder injury that never healed in time for him to get on the field. Making matters worse, Profar re-

injured the shoulder in September while rehabbing which cost him the opportunity to play in the Arizona Fall League and get some much-needed work. Turning only 22 in February, on talent and ceiling alone, Profar is as good a young hitter as any in baseball as he combines burgeoning power with terrific speed. Unfortunately Profar can't help us if he is on the DL and his outlook is very murky going into drafting season due to the re-injury of the shoulder. While the talent is not questioned, Profar has to be looked at as nothing more than a late-round lottery grab.
PROJECTION: .263 12 HR 55 RBI 67 R 7 SB

25. **Jordy Mercer:** A former third-round pick of the Pittsburgh Pirates in 2008, Jordy Mercer may have finally staked a claim to an everyday role with the team in 2014 as he hit .255 with 12 home runs and 55 RBI in 506 at-bats. There is nothing flashy here as Mercer will struggle to hit over .270 due to a lack of walks (35 last season) and his power ceiling is right around the 12 he hit a year ago. Although eligible at second base for another year, Neil Walker's presence there will have Mercer serving as the everyday shortstop.
PROJECTION: .261 14 HR 59 RBI 61 R 5 SB

26. **Omar Infante:** Despite not being blessed with natural skills, Omar Infante has made a nice career for himself as a good average hitter who makes some small contributions in the home run and stolen base categories. A .276 career hitter, Infante has only reached double-digits in home runs and steals twice in his 13-year career. At 34, Infante showed some signs of erosion in 2014 as he batted only .252 which was the second time in three years he posted an average less than .260. Classic backup infielder who can help when injuries hit.
PROJECTION: .259 7 HR 65 RBI 52 R 7 SB

27. **Brock Holt:************SEE FIRST BASE RANKINGS!*******

28. **Arismendy Alcantara:** While Javier Baez got all the pub, the 10 home run/8 stolen base/.210 hitting debut season by Arismendy Alcantara was not a whole lot different from his more heralded counterpart. Of course we are not suggesting Alcantara will hang with Baez into the future stat-wise but there is some interesting power/speed ability here and upside befitting someone who is only turning 24. Worth a late round grab to see where this goes.
PROJECTION: .248 17 HR 45 RBI 53 R 14 SB

29. **Joe Panik:** This is a name to store away for your late-round sleeper lists. The former 2011 first round pick for the San Francisco Giants came up in the heat of a pennant race last season and proceeded to hit .305 with 31 runs

scored in 269 at-bats. Panik than went out and hit rope after rope into the postseason which speaks to the already rapid development going on here. Panik is already a .300 hitter who will score runs due to the fact he likely will hit near the top of the 2015 lineup. He lacks in the home run and stolen base departments though which speaks to his fantasy baseball holes for the time being. Still Panik is the type of developing prospect who can break through with even better numbers as he gains more experience this season and his high upside is well worth the cost of a late round selection.
PROJECTION: .291 7 HR 46 RBI 62 R 5 SB

30. **Didi Gregorious:** Through two partial seasons in the big leagues, Didi Gregorious has flipped his minor league script. A string of .300-plus seasons on the farm didn't come over to the major league side as Gregorious has batted .252 and .226 the last two years. However Gregorious has hit 13 home runs over that span after doing next-to-nothing in the power department in the minors. Eventually Gregorious will find his average footing and if the power holds steady, he could be a sneaky late-round grab.
PROJECTION: .265 8 HR 42 RBI 55 R 7 SB

31. **Roughned Odor:** The massive injury epidemic that hit the Texas Rangers in 2014 opened the door wide open for the MLB debut of international free agent signing Roughned Odor at the ripe old age of 20. Considering how young Odor was, he did a tremendous job as he hit .259 with 9 home runs in only 386 at-bats. Even the Rangers had to be surprised at how poised Odor was right out of the gate and he earned himself every opportunity to be a starter somewhere on the team for 2015. Odor has hinted at 20-home run power and his average will get better with more experience and shows more patience (only 17 walks taken). The ballpark checks out as a huge plus and Odor has a good 3-4 years of ceiling left. Never a big prospect name prior to 2014, Odor will likely be a very affordable upside play.
PROJECTION: .267 12 HR 61 RBI 56 R 6 SB

32. **Yangervis Solarte:** It certainly was an eventful debut season for multi-eligibility infielder Yangervis Solarte in 2014. With injuries creating a dire need for infield help right out of the gate for the New York Yankees, the team brought hot-hitting spring training sensation Solarte up north to begin the year. The results were startling early on as Solarte cranked out 52 hits and 6 home runs in April-May while hitting .299. Solarte's output was even more shocking given the fact he was considered a Quad-A player who at 27 was already past prospect age. Eventually the league caught up with Solarte who endured a .164 June that got him shipped right back to the minors. Solarte got new life however as the San Diego Padres acquired him in the Chase Headley deal and he helped out his new team by hitting .267 with 4

home runs in 217 second-half at-bats. What we have here is a mediocre overall skill-set as Solarte has only 10-12 home run pop and zero speed. What he has going for him though is eligibility at third, short, and second base, That makes Solarte as decent bench help to fill-in on light schedule days.
PROJECTION: .268 9 HR 50 RBI 56 R 2 SB

33. **Scooter Gennett:** Years of awful hitting and poor health from Rickie Weeks forced the Milwaukee Brewers into moving the intriguing bat of Scooter Gennett into the starting second base spot right out of the 2014 gate. Showing Martin Prado-like ability as far as posting high averages with decent enough contributions across the board, Gennett made himself into a useful play in deeper mixed leagues and especially in NL-only setups. Gennett has now hit .324 and .289 in his first two seasons in the majors and the 9 home runs and 6 steals he supplied in 2014 keep him somewhat viable in those categories as well. The numbers fall short when it comes to using Gennett as a second base starter but he should be on rosters as a solid backup.
PROJECTION: .290 10 HR 57 RBI 61 R 8 SB

34. **Asdrubal Cabrera:** By now it is crystal clear that 25 HR/17 SB/.273 career year put up by Asdrubal Cabrera was nothing but an outlier anomoly. Since that time, Cabrera has struggled to hit .250 amid a slew of injuries. On the positive side, Cabrera has been very consistent the last two years with his power/speed numbers as he hit 14 home runs each of the last two seasons and stole 9 and 10 bases respectively. A free agent at press time, Cabrera is still young enough at 30 to hold onto his 2013-14 numbers for another year or so. You can do a whole lot worse.
PROJECTION: .253 14 HR 65 RBI 68 R 8 SB

THE REST

35. **Brad Miller:** Miller was a sleeper gone bust in 2014 as his big spring training failed to carry over into the season where he hit a woeful .221. 10 home runs in only 367 at-bats is decent but Miller is likely running out of chances.

36. **Alexi Amarista:** Another Padres infielder who qualifies all over the place (2B, 3B, SS, OF), Amarista's .234 average is an instant turn-off since he doesn't hit home runs and has moderate speed.

37. **Luis Valbuena:** The 16 home runs no doubt play very well at second base but Luis Valbuena's impact ends there as he is a career .229 hitter with zero speed.

38. **Jedd Gyorko:** Gyorko's power is not in question but instead his awful plate approach and K rates are severely stunting his growth. Batted only .210 in 2014 with an unfathomable 25 percent K rate. Petco Park further removes Gyorko from consideration.

39. **DJ LeMathieu:** Put up a 5/10 power/speed line which doesn't move the needle much, especially considering LeMathieu plays half his games in Coors Field. Not guaranteed a starting spot as well.

40. **Mike Aviles:** A former favorite of ours, Aviles has now settled into a utility role (eligible at 2B, 3B, SS, and OF) as he ages. 14 steals in 344 at-bats show Aviles can still be a help there but a .247 average and very poor pop make him interesting only if injuries open a starting spot for him.

41. **Jonathan Schoop:** Was a nice shot in the arm power-wise for the Orioles as Schoop came up and smacked 16 home runs in only 455 at-bats filling in at second and third base last season. Unfortunately Schoop was pretty much an all-or-nothing guy as he batted only .209 due to striking out in more than 30 percent of his at-bats.

42. **Chris Ownings:******SEE SHORTSTOP RANKINGS!*******

43. **Marwin Gonzalez:** Through three seasons with the Astros, Gonzalez has yet to amass 300 at-bats as the team views him more as a backup infielder or stopgap starter if injuries strike. That is not conducive to consistent fantasy baseball usage despite a solid .277 average and 6 home runs in 285 at-bats last season.

44. **Rickie Weeks:** Weeks lost his job to Scooter Gennett before spring training was even through last season as the Milwaukee Brewers clearly grew tired of his injuries, strikeouts, and pathetic batting averages. Pressed into a part-time role, Weeks' .274 average was his highest since 2006 but he got his walking papers soon after the season ended.

45. **Danny Espinosa:** Not since 2012 has Espinosa carried any sort of solid fantasy baseball value. Capable of a 15/15 season if all breaks right, Espinosa has struggled to stay healthy the last two years and is only a .228 career hitter.

46. **Derek Dietrich:** Made more news regarding his run-in with hitting coach Tino Martinez than anything done on the field. Was a 2010 second round pick who thus far has failed to impress. Will get a chance to claim the second base job in camp but until he makes that spot his own, there is no reason to bother here.

47. **Nick Franklin:** A former 2009 first round pick by the Seattle Mariners, the team threw in the towel on Nick Franklin's development last season by trading him to the Tampa Bay Rays in midseason. While Franklin possesses some intriguing power and some speed, his utter lack of strike zone awareness has left him a whiffing machine to the tune of 145 K's in 450 at-bats for his short MLB career. The Rays love reclamation projects such as this which means Franklin should remain on your watch lists for another spring but Quad-A status could be his calling.

SHORTSTOP

Draft Strategy: It was not that long ago when drafting a shortstop in the first round was a recommended strategy. Going back to Alex Rodriguez' arrival with the Seattle Mariners and subsequent years with the Texas Rangers, through both Hanley Ramirez and Troy Tulowitzki at times over the last seven years, the idea of taking a shortstop in Round 1 was not as absurd a notion as it is today. While Tulowitzki remains a truly dominant player and a firm first round pick on talent alone, his inability to ever stay healthy makes him too much of a risk for such an early pick. In addition, Ramirez has battled ongoing injuries himself, not to mention numbers which are beginning to slip. Thus just like with second base, you want to try and grab a speed-oriented option for your shortstop in the middle rounds. Some guys who produced under this scenario a year ago were Alicides Escobar, Danny Santana, Yangervis Solarte, and in a tremendous manner, Dee Gordon. Same plan of action once again is recommended for the 2015 season.

1. **Troy Tulowitzki:** Once again when on the field, Troy Tulowitzki is in the discussion as the number 1 player in all of fantasy baseball. Tulowitzki hit

21 home runs and drove in a tremendous 52 batters while posting a monstrous .354 average the first half of the season. In fact Tulo was the top-ranked first half hitter in all of baseball with those numbers. In following with his career-long trends however, the inevitable DL trip arrived and it was a bad one. Tulowitzki would play in only two games after the All-Star Break due to a severe hip injury that ultimately required surgery. We are now seven seasons and counting as far as Tulowitzki injuries/DL stints are concerned and that has to be factored into his draft price. Again on talent alone Tulowitzki is a first round lock but as one of the most injury-prone players in the game, drafting him anywhere before the third round is foolish. Turning 31-years-old, Tulowitzki is still relatively young but all the injuries have robbed him of his speed. Once a guy who logged a high of 20 stolen bases, Tulowitzki has only four the last three seasons so that statistic is now out the window. The power, average, and RBI are as good as it gets though and at the most shallow position in fantasy baseball, Tulowitzki on a per game basis is pretty much unrivaled. But wow those injuries. The most boom-or-bust player out there.

PROJECTION: .315 26 HR 91 RBI 88 R 2 SB

2. **Ian Desmond:** While everyone always talks about Troy Tulowitzki, Jose Reyes, and Hanley Ramirez, Washington's Ian Desmond it could be argued is the most consistent hitting shortstop in fantasy baseball. Flat in his prime as he turns 30 in September, Desmond has posted three straight 20/20-plus seasons in a row, which is quietly one of the best runs of production out there when you factor in the position scarcity. It was more of the same excellence for Desmond in 2014 as he responded to being moved down the order into a more run-producing spot by hitting 24 home runs and stealing 24 bases while driving in a career-high 91 runs. The .255 average was the only negative as Desmond struck out a very scary 183 times (38 more whiffs than the year prior). While Desmond has always been prone to striking out, last season's number was extreme even for him and could go in the outlier bin. As long as you are all right with a somewhat ugly average, Desmond's power/speed combo and RBI potential are terrific investments, especially at shortstop. Better yet, his extreme durability puts him on a plateau that the other top-ranked shortstops can't reach.

PROJECTION: .265 25 HR 88 RBI 78 R 23 SB

3. **Hanley Ramirez:** Having turned 32 last September, Hanley Ramirez is starting to get old right before our eyes. The current version of Ramirez is an injury-prone one that contains some slipping stats across the board. The .345 average from 2013 was an outlier and so the .283 mark he posted there in 2014 is much more in line with what Ramirez is capable of. Ramirez also

has now failed to log 450 at-bats the last two seasons as his body is beginning to betray him. However the guy can still hit and run a little as Ramirez smacked 13 home runs and stole 14 bases to go with the .283 average. There is no chance Ramirez will ever go back to his former first round days but he has incurred enough wrath the last few years with his injuries that his draft price is coming down to decent investment territory.
PROJECTION: .286 21 HR 79 RBI 82 R 16 SB

4. **Jose Reyes:** Having more than earned the title of being injury prone, Jose Reyes seemed to want to really hammer that point home by not even making it out of the 2014 season opener with yet another leg injury. At 31, one had to wonder if the end was going to come quick for Reyes due to the fact a great deal of his game was built on speed. However Reyes got the last laugh and proved that he is far from done as he wound up hitting .287 with 9 home run and 30 stolen bases. Reyes was caught only twice attempting to steal which speaks to how his speed has not slipped much and how that crucial aspect of his game is still very effective. Another year older at 32, Reyes remains a huge injury risk prone to a blowout at a moment's notice, which means investing here is quite scary. His five-tool ability remains very much in play however and Reyes hits in one of the best ballparks in the game conducive to his speed. You feel lucky?
PROJECTION: .293 10 HR 53 RBI 88 R 28 SB

5. **Starlin Castro:** Even though it seems like he has been around forever, Starlin Castro will only turn 25 for the 2015 season. Castro has already ran the gamut in his young career numbers-wise after coming up at 19 as an instant-impact hitter who seemed destined to be a perennial star. Like with all young hitters, the elevator didn't move straight up to stardom as Castro got benched more than once during the 2013 season as he hit a woeful .245 and heard his name bandied about in trade discussions. With top shortstop prospect Javier Baez getting ready to burst onto the scene, it seemed only a matter of time before Castro was run out of town. Well Castro didn't go along with the plan as he had a nice comeback season in 2014, rediscovering his batting average knack by hitting .292 with a career-high tying 14 home runs. There remains another year or so of upside with Castro given his youth and a run at 20 home runs remains possible. However in order to optimize his value, Castro has to stop the stolen base slide from the last two seasons. After recording 22 and 25 steals from 2011-12, Castro logged only 9 and 4 the last two years respectively. Baez is now manning second base for the Cubs so Castro remains the team's everyday shortstop for whatever that means for his psyche. The shine has come off here

without a doubt but Castro also proved last season he can still be a very solid top ten starter at shortstop.
PROJECTION: .290 15 HR 71 RBI 56 R 8 SB

6. **Alexei Ramirez:** Now a veteran at 34, Chicago White Sox shortstop Alexei Ramirez is not letting age negatively impact his numbers. In fact one could argue that Ramirez had one of his best seasons ever in 2014 when he batted .273 with 15 home runs and 21 stolen bases. Ramirez is a strange case in that he should have begun losing speed when he reached the age of 30 but instead posted his two highest stolen base totals since that time. In addition, Ramirez ended a two year streak from 2012-13 when he failed to hit double-digit home runs by smacking last season's 15. The wheels could start to come off stolen-base wise at a moment's notice given Ramirez' age and his career average is a somewhat mediocre .277, so be sure not to invest too heavily here. Solid and steady is the name of the game with this Cuban import.
PROJECTION: 271 14 HR 73 RBI 74 R 19 SB

7. **Elvis Andrus:** We will say it again in order to stay consistent: Elvis Andrus remains one of the most overrated players in all of fantasy baseball. Andrus is a guy who has habitually been drafted in the high middle rounds, despite the fact he is generally only a plus in two categories (runs and steals), mediocre in another (batting average), and giant negatives in two others (home runs and RBI). And that was before Andrus posted only 27 stolen bases last season, hitting a shaky .263, and scoring a career-low-tying 72 runs. Only a .272 career hitter, Andrus is not a good leadoff threat where he could do his most runs/stolen base damage due to the fact he doesn't take walks and annually has a horrendous OBP. Andrus is still in his prime as turns only 27 in August but his statistical output remains as overrated as ever. Look elsewhere for more value if you can.
PROJECTION: .265 3 HR 55 RBI 81 R 29 SB

8. **Jimmy Rollins:** Just when we were ready to write off Jimmy Rollins forever, the veteran Philadelphia Phillies mainstay went out and hit 17 home runs and stole 28 bases which erased completely the memories of his horrific 2013 campaign. Rollins proved a year ago that he still retains his speed and his 15-plus home run power, which is certainly a very valuable combination. Clearly Rollins' awful 2013 could be blamed on the numerous injuries he had suffered that season and good 2014 health surely played a major part in resurrecting his numbers. However the fact of the matter is that Rollins will be 36 this season and his batting average now struggles to reach .250. The steals have to start eroding sometime and this

season could certainly be when we start to see that happen. The best part about Rollins for 2015 is the fear of his bust potential and age have made his draft stock sink to the point that he is almost a value play. Ultimately however, Rollins can't be counted on to stay healthy for a second season in a row and investing in aging stars is always a recipe for trouble.
PROJECTION: .248 14 HR 57 RBI 75 R 22 SB

9. **Javier Baez:*****SEE SECOND BASE RANKINGS!*******

10. **Danny Santana:*****SEE SECOND BASE RANKINGS!*******

11. **Mookie Betts:*****SEE SECOND BASE RANKINGS!********

12. **Alicides Escobar:** While not many talk about the guy, Kansas City Royals shortstop Alicides Escobar has now put himself firmly into everyday usage territory off his underrated 2014 campaign. Serving as the speed catalyst atop the Royals lineup, Escobar batted .285 with 74 runs scored and 31 stolen bases. Now entering his seventh MLB season, Escobar's statistical plane is pretty well established. Escobar has now stolen 22 or more bases for four straight seasons and generally has scored between 65-75 runs, which are the two categories where he makes his largest impact. There is next to no power here as Escobar has never hit more than 5 home runs in a season and his .263 career average is nothing to write home about. Overall however, Escobar provides the precious speed that you want from your middle infielders and his always cheap draft price works well if you want to address this position later.
PROJECTION: .278 4 HR 51 RBI 72 R 29 SB

13. **Jhonny Peralta:** The stain of Jhonny Peralta's PED suspension for getting caught up in the Biogenesis probe failed to dissuade the St. Louis Cardinals from handing the veteran shortstop a rich free-agent contract prior to the 2014 season. Peralta rewarded their investment by hitting 21 home runs and collecting 75 RBI while batting .263, which were numbers that pretty much went with his career norms. Peralta is one of those guys you either admire or yawn at given the fact he supplies zero speed from a spot you want to get stolen bases from. However Peralta has hit 20-plus home runs 5 times in his career to go along with three 80-plus RBI campaigns, showing valuable pop at a power-starved spot. The price is always affordable and if you have speed covered elsewhere, Peralta has shown himself to be a helpful shortstop addition.
PROJECTION: .267 19 HR 72 RBI 59 R 2 SB

14. **Ben Zobrist:*****SEE SECOND BASE RANKINGS!*****

15. **J.J. Hardy:** Persistent shoulder pain turned the always reliable power bat of J.J. Hardy into something so much less in 2014 as he only hit 9 home runs in 529 at-bats. That ended a streak of three straight seasons of at least 22 home runs from Hardy and pretty much ruined any value he had overall. If Hardy is not hitting at least 20 home run, he is pretty much useless since he doesn't steal bases and his career batting average is only .261. The Baltimore Orioles showed no hesitancy re-signing Hardy during the 2014 postseason however, possibly indicating their confidence in a rebound. We love the power here when all is right but Hardy is aging and any kind of shoulder issue for a hitter are two major red flags.
PROJECTION: .265 20 HR 75 RBI 62 R 2 SB

16. **Joe Panik:*****SEE SECOND BASE RANKINGS!*****

17. **Danny Espinosa:*****SEE SECOND BASE RANKINGS!*****

18. **Didi Gregorious:****SEE SECOND BASE RANKINGS!******

19. **Jed Lowrie:** Now only carrying shortstop eligibility, Jed Lowrie is quickly moving into the irrelevancy territory with his spotty hitting and ongoing injuries. After hitting 31 home runs between 2012-13, Lowrie sank to only 6 last year while batting only .249. Lowrie will be 31-years-old for the 2015 season and he has now hit .252 or below in three of the last four years to go with a ton of games missed due to injury. You can do a whole lot better with less aggravation.
PROJECTION: .262 12 HR 56 RBI 54 R 2 SB

20. **Everth Cabrera:** While Nelson Cruz and Jhonny Peralta both flourished after getting pinched for 50 games in the Biogenesis scandal, Everth Cabrera went the other way as he was pretty much a horrid-hitting/injury-plagued mess last season. Cabrera batted only .232 and saw his stolen bases fall off the map from 37 in 2013 to last season's 18. The memory of Alex Sanchez and how he went from a 40-stolen base monster to a nobody overnight after his own steroid bust comes to mind here and Cabrera's complete minuses in home runs, RBI, and average are a huge price to pay for a not-even-given 30 stolen bases. Avoid like the plague. This could get ugly.
PROJECTION: .248 5 HR 29 RBI 56 R 28 SB

21. **Jean Segura:** When you look at Jean Segura's breakout 2013 season, what stood out was the stark differences between his first and second half numbers. After having a fantasy baseball MVP-like .325/11 HR/27 SB monster first three months, Segura was being hailed as the new Hanley Ramirez. As great as Segura was in the first half however, he was that bad in the second as he hit only .241 with 1 home run and 17 steals. Opposing pitchers had found some holes in Segura's swing and the young shortstop failed to adjust. Thus as the 2014 season approached, there was great discussion about which half was more indicative of Segura's ability. Most chose to believe his April-June numbers however as Segura was drafted as high as the early third round as a result. Unfortunately 2013's second half proved to be more of who Segura was as 2014 was almost a complete bomb to the tune of a .246 average with only 5 home runs and 20 stolen bases. So now what? Well the fact Segura has struggled for his last six playing months going back to the second half of 2013 is a huge issue that can't be chalked up to youth. Yes Segura is still only going to be 25 but we need to see some sort of progress from all his struggles to be confident drafting him again.
PROJECTION: .271 6 HR 53 RBI 71 R 24 SB

22. **Brad Miller:*****SEE SECOND BASE RANKINGS!*******

23. **Xander Bogaerts:** Prospects who come up in big-market cities like New York or Boston tend to get over-hyped more often than not and in the process increase their already high bust potential. Such was the case with Red Sox top shortstop prospect Xander Bogaerts, who fueled the hype machine with his poised performances during the team's 2013 World Series run. Prior to last season, we warned anyone who would listen how Bogaerts was incredibly overrated due to the fact he doesn't possess above average power or speed. And with a very high K rate as part of the package, Bogaerts was set to disappoint. Disappoint he did as Bogaerts wound up hitting only 12 home runs and collecting a miniscule 2 stolen bases while batting .240. Bogaerts struck out 138 times in his 538 at-bats and that type of K rate will continue to make him an average liability. At only 23-years-old, Bogaerts should add some more pop as he matures but the lack of speed will remain. That makes it crucial for Bogaerts to up the home run output to at least the high teens in order to be suitable for usage as an everyday shortstop (or at third base where he also is eligible). There is no guarantee he will break through there however, which means Bogaerts could go from mid-round sleeper to maybe not even drafted this season.
PROJECTION: .265 15 HR 54 R 67 RBI 4 SB

24. **Asdrubal Cabrera:** *****SEE SECOND BASE RANKINGS!*****

25. **Eric Aybar:** Long time Los Angeles Angels shortstop Eric Aybar is one of those guys who has always been on the doorstep of daily starting status but in the end his career norms of being a stopgap option when injuries strike your starter remains. Now past his ceiling window as he turns 31, Aybar is pretty set in his numbers which means between 7-10 home runs to go with between 15-25 stolen bases. When combined with a .275-ish average, Aybar likely looks better than you thought he was. If you choose to address shortstop among the last few rounds of your draft, this is the guy to target.
    PROJECTION: .276 8 HR 57 RBI 75 R 17 SB

26. **Jurickson Profar:** ****SEE SECOND BASE RANKINGS!*******

27. **Wilmer Flores:** The New York Mets continue to waffle on whether or not Wilmer Flores is the future at shortstop for the team. Flores showed some good power while in the minors, while also showing a .300 bat. However most of those numbers were accomplished in the PCL which calls into question the validity of Flores' statistics. Flores showed some signs that he at least deserves a long look this spring however after hitting 6 home runs and driving in 29 batters in only 259 at-bats last season. His .251 average shows that more works need to be done before we fully dive in. We are always on the lookout for fresh shortstop blood though and Flores certainly qualifies in that quest. Decent final round lottery pick.
    PROJECTION: .267 14 HR 56 RBI 52 R 4 SB

28. **Josh Rutledge:** We are still waiting for Josh Rutledge to firmly grab hold of a starting infielder's job with the Colorado Rockies, now three seasons into his so far disappointing career. Rutledge remains intriguing however due to his ballpark and the fact he has shown the ability in spurts to hit some home runs and steal some bases. If all breaks right, Rutledge could be a 15/25 guy but we are far from that level at this point, given a .259 career average that is being pushed down by a very high K rate. The wait goes on.
    PROJECTION: .275 11 HR 48 RBI 65 R 14 SB

THE REST

29. **Brandon Crawford:** If you are interested in a guy who can hit 10 home runs, bat .240, and steal 2 bases, than Brandon Crawford is your guy. If Brandon Crawford is your guy, you should be playing fantasy golf.

30. **Jordy Mercer:** *****SEE SECOND BASE RANKINGS!******

31. **Mike Aviles:** *****SEE SECOND BASE RANKINGS!****

32. Yangervis Solarte: *****SEE SECOND BASE RANKINGS!*****

33. Alexi Amarista: *****SEE SECOND BASE RANKINGS!****

34. Yunel Escobar: Truth be told, Yunel Escobar never turned into the star many expected him to be, which is why both the Atlanta Braves and the Toronto Blue Jays gave up on him. Escobar has found a home with the Tampa Bay Rays but his numbers from a fantasy baseball angle remain ugly. A top Escobar season centers around 10 home runs and a .260 average which means you let him rot on the wire.

35. Zack Cozart: Once a curiosity, Zack Cozart has proven himself to be nothing but an overly mediocre shortstop in pretty much any fantasy baseball format given his awful batting averages and only 4 home runs in 506 at-bats last season.

36. Chris Owings: ****SEE SECOND BASE RANKINGS!*****

37. Chris Taylor: Speed option for the Mariners who could factor into the starting shortstop job if the team continues to sour on Brad Miller.

38. Marwin Gonzalez: ****SEE SECOND BASE RANKINGS!*****

39. Nick Franklin: *****SEE SECOND BASE RANKINGS!

40. Jonathan Villar: Villar is the classic case of a guy who needs to figure out how to steal first base since he can't hit a lick. Having barely hit over .200 last season (.207) Villar is not looking like the next version of Dee Gordon. When your real-life value centers on being a pinch runner, there really is nothing else to say.

THIRD BASEMAN

Draft Strategy: We have seen a big time erosion of offensive numbers among all positions in baseball during this post-steroids/greenies era. Perhaps no other position has seen such a drastic dropoff in top shelf players than at third base. With Miguel Cabrera losing eligibility there in some leagues for 2015, right off the top a huge bat is removed from the player pool at the hot corner. Throw in awful seasons by Chris Davis, David Wright, Evan Longoria, Manny Machado, and Ryan Zimmerman, and there surely was a lot of angst to go around from this group. The silver lining in all of this is that there is the potential for big time values here as some of the players mentioned above could be in line for nice bounce back campaigns. Put Wright and Longoria squarely into that group as both are still in their primes and each has the ability to at least reclaim some of their numbers from last season. In addition, there was a nice infusion of youth here in 2014 as Todd Frazier, Anthony Rendon, Nolan Arenado, and Josh Harrison all had significant breakout years. The bottom line is that third base goes pretty deep, meaning you can wait until the fifth or sixth round to grab your starter. We wouldn't touch the injury-marred Zimmerman, the average-liability of Davis, or the aging Aramis Ramirez and the prices on Rendon and Frazier figure to skyrocket. However the fact Arenado missed a big chunk of 2014 with injury helped keep his potential numbers down and the late emergence of Harrison also kept the top from coming off on his name as well. Each one of these two look like terific buys in the seventh round or so. No need to move too early here as there are plenty of bats to go around later on in the draft.

1. **Miguel Cabrera:*******SEE FIRST BASEMAN RANKINGS!****

2. **Edwin Encarnacion:*******SEE FIRST BASEMAN RANKINGS!*****

3. **Todd Frazier:********SEE FIRST BASEMAN RANKINGS!******

4. **Josh Donaldson:** What an encore. There were plenty of questions regarding whether or not the 2013 breakout season of Oakland A's third baseman Josh Donaldson was a fluke or legit. Well Donaldson was in fact legit as he upped his numbers even more last season by hitting 29 homers, scoring 93 runs, and driving in 98. As an added bonus, he even chipped in 8 stolen bases. The fact Donaldson was able to add five home runs to his ledger shows that his power is for real and his spot in the middle of the shockingly productive A's lineup means 90 RBI is within the realm of possibility once again. Donaldson's .255 average was a bit ugly but when you strike out 130 times, your not going to challenge for a batting title. The Oakland West Coast bias may allow you to get him a round later than the numbers suggest but Donaldson is here to stay as a top hitter regardless. **PROJECTION: .261 27 HR 96 RBI 91 R 6 SB**

5. **Anthony Rendon:********SEE SECOND BASEMAN RANKINGS!*****

6. **Adrian Beltre:** When you look at the fact Adrian Beltre hit .324 last season, you would think that the perennial Texas Rangers third baseman had another monster season for his fantasy baseball owners. However the fact

of the matter is that Beltre leaked numbers everywhere as he lost 11 home runs, 15 RBI, and 9 runs from the season prior. In addition, Beltre spent time on the DL as well. As he turns 36, it is fair to wonder if Beltre is starting to descend from his career arc. Beltre is still capable of hitting 25 home runs but 30 is looking out of reach now. Also more injuries could be on the way as Beltre has never been known for his durability. The risk here is at its highest point since his forgettable Seattle days but Beltre likely can squeeze out one more above-average season.

PROJECTION: .310 26 HR 88 RBI 86 R 1 SB

7. **Evan Longoria:** After years of saying how Evan Longoria was overrated, he may now finally have settled into his true draft price and overall value as his ceiling years have now passed. Longoria was looked at as a first round pick as recently as 2012 and that was foolish given the fact the Tampa Bay Rays third baseman lost interest in stealing bases and his always high K rate made him an average liability. Longoria continued with his maddening ways in 2014 as he hit only 22 home runs and batted an ugly .253 in 624 at-bats. The 22 home runs were Longoria's fewest since 2010 and it adds another layer of disappointment to a guy who has been testing the patience of his owners the last few seasons. Now 31-years-old, Longoria has lost quite a bit of appeal and his recent work has not engendered much confidence either.

PROJECTION: .267 27 HR 93 RBI 84 R 2 SB

8. **Kyle Seager:** Oftentimes in fantasy baseball, some sweet values can be had from the West Coast teams that play in poor hitting ballparks. Along the same lines of Josh Donaldson in Oakland is the case of Kyle Seager in Seattle. The veteran third baseman was ignored by more than a few prior to 2014 despite showing some David Wright-lite ability as a home run/stolen base guy at the hot corner. Seager in fact did a better impression of Wright than the man himself last season as he put up a hitting hat trick of a .268 average, 25 home runs, and 96 RBI. Seager also stole 7 bases and has swiped 29 bags overall the last three seasons. This is a locked in top ten fantasy baseball third baseman who can help across the board. Gladly take the discount.

PROJECTION: .266 25 HR 88 RBI 81 R 8 SB

9. **David Wright:** Whether it was the expansive dimensions of Citi Field or a nagging shoulder injury that eventually got him shut down for good in September, David Wright endured his worst offensive season since becoming the New York Mets' everyday third baseman back in 2004. Overall Wright hit a pathetic 8 home runs and drove in a tiny 63 batters in

535 at-bats. In addition, Wright's .269 average was nothing to write home about either. There are a lot of discussion points here and many are not good. For one, Wright is no longer anywhere near a 30-home run hitter, which he accomplished twice way back from 2007-08. Once again Citi Field was one of the worst home run parks in the game last season and that alone caps Wright's power potential. In addition, the Mets lack impact bats around Wright which also has been an ongoing problem (and takes a chunk out of his runs and RBI totals). Also, Wright's speed could continue slipping as he is aging a bit at the age of 32. Finally, Wright has now dealt with serious injuries in three of the last four years and that issue will only continue to be exacerbated as he ages. There are some positives to note however. The Mets will pull in the outfield fences in right-center which is Wright's power alley for the 2015 season after much internal debate. In addition, Wright is still fully capable of a 20-plus HR/80-plus RBI/.280-plus/15 SB season if he can somehow figure out how to stay on the field. His draft price is dropping quick which is something to be taken advantage of as well given the track record. Overall though the risk is among the highest at the always volatile third base spot so treading carefully is warranted.

PROJECTION: .286 21 HR 82 RBI 83 R 14 SB

10. **Matt Carpenter:** We featured Matt Carpenter prominently both in last season's draft guide and on the website last March regarding the very high bust potential he carried going into 2014. The hype surrounding Carpenter going into last season went into overdrive after he challenged for the batting title the year prior when he hit .318 and scored an MLB-leading 126 runs. The average and runs were both huge numbers for Carpenter and it was those statistics that helped inflate his value way beyond where it should have been going into 2014 drafts. The big problem is that as good as his average and runs scored were, Carpenter was pretty much a huge negative in the other three scoring categories (home runs, RBI, steals). And when you consider that batting average is the least reliable statistic in fantasy baseball, Carpenter was set up to fail for his owners when he was going as high as the fourth round in drafts. What happened next was predictable as Carpenter's average sank to a mediocre .272 and he also wound up losing 27 runs from the year before. Carpenter also went on to hit only 8 home runs and steal 5 bases while driving in 59 batters which was nothing to write home about. Perhaps even more of a detriment to Carpenter's 2015 value is the fact he lost second base eligibility and can only be used at third where his lack of power and RBI's stand out in a more negative way. While Carpenter is fully capable of scoring 100 runs and batting .300, those

numbers need to be supported by another category if you want to use him at third base. Unfortunately Carpenter is not capable of doing so.
PROJECTION: .298 9 HR 63 RBI 105 R 4 SB

11. **Carlos Santana:******SEE CATCHER RANKINGS!********

12. **Nolan Arenado:** Lost in the tremendous breakout seasons from Corey Dickerson and Charlie Blackmon for the Colorado Rockies, was the terrific campaign put forth by third baseman Nolan Arenado in 2014. While his outfield counterparts got most of the pub, one could argue that Arenado was just as good as those two on a per game basis. Arenado only was able to log 111 games due to missing almost two months with a fractured finger but when on the field, few were better at third base. Altogether Arenado hit 18 home runs and batted .287 in only 432 at-bats in his first full MLB season at the ripe old age of 23. There is 30 home run potential here if Arenado can log close to 600 at-bats and a .300 average could go along for the ride as well. From a fantasy baseball perspective, Arenado missing all those games was actually a good thing for those trying to nab him in 2015 drafts, as it helped to keep his numbers down a bit which buttressed some of the hype. In fact so high are we on Arenado that we fully endorse the strategy of passing over the names above and coming back here in the middle rounds. If all breaks right, Arenado should be challenging top tier third baseman status.
PROJECTION: .293 25 HR 86 RBI 83 R 6 SB

13. **Manny Machado:** Sometimes you just have to throw a season out the window and forget what you saw so as not to distort a certain player's value going into the next season. That is the case for emerging Baltimore Orioles third baseman Manny Machado who endured a completely injury-marred 2014 campaign. The former 2010 third overall pick in the MLB draft, Machado didn't make his debut last season until early May due to slow recovery from the previous September's knee surgery. After struggling to find his groove in a .270 first half, Machado seemed to lock in on all cylinders and allowed his talent to take over during the second half. Machado scorched the baseball in July and August, batting a ridiculous .333 and .378 before more misfortune took hold in the form of another knee surgery that finished his season early and required yet another surgery. The fact Machado already has logged two serious knee surgeries before 24 is a major cause for concern and bring question marks about his durability. The talent is obvious as Machado has been compared to a young Miguel Cabrera who can someday crack 30 home run with a .300 average. While the injury

risk is real, we can't resist the potential that Machado possesses. If we are to roll the dice with any one player, this is the guy to do it with.
PROJECTION: .288 22 HR 78 RBI 92 R 4 SB

14. Josh Harrison: *******SEE SECOND BASEMAN RANKINGS!*****

15. Ryan Zimmerman: It is widely known that Ryan Zimmerman has been one of the more injury-prone players in all of baseball but he took that tendency to an even higher and more ridiculous level in 2014. Zimmerman was only able to log 214 at-bats last season as he spent two separate and lengthy stays on the DL, further perpetuating his injury-prone label. That now makes it 5 straight seasons where Zimmerman has landed on the DL at least once and during that time, much of his former All-Star shine has worn off. Despite all the injuries, Zimmerman has hit 25 or more home runs 4 of the last 7 seven seasons so he undoubtedly can be a very solid player when on the field. However given the fact you can already pencil in at least once DL stint, the aggravation sets in when you wonder how long that stint might be for. Way too high maintenance for our liking.
PROJECTION: .281 21 HR 81 RBI 86 R 4 SB

16. Pedro Alvarez: Now five seasons into his career, the statistical book is pretty much set when it comes to Pedro Alvarez. Power clearly is the name of the game here as Alvarez hit 30 or more home runs both in 2012 and 2013 and would have done so as well last season if he had not missed time with injury. Unfortunately home runs and RBI are the only positives Alvarez brings but in actuality some of the impact he supplies in those two categories gets offset by a horrible career batting average of only .235. Alvarez will strike out more than 180 times if he plays a full slate of games and so expecting any batting average north of .250 is a false hope. We always advise staying away from players like Alvarez who will set you back dramatically in the batting average category (not to mention poor tallies in steals and runs). Draft only as a backup.
PROJECTION: .243 28 HR 89 RBI 67 R 2 SB

17. Aramis Ramirez: When all plans go awry in your draft when it comes to picking a third baseman, Aramis Ramirez is always there to bail you out. Annually one of the best third base values in fantasy baseball, the veteran Ramirez did more solid yet undistinguished work in 2014 when he hit .285 with 15 home runs and 66 RBI. With 369 career home runs under his belt, Ramirez falls into that category of player where you say to yourself "he was better than I thought he was." Part of the issue with Ramirez, even in his younger days, were injuries that necessitated at least one DL trip a season

and that trend tends to alienate a sizable portion of the drafting community which continually made him an affordable stock. Still when all broke right, you got a 25 home run bat who could hit .300 for a nice price. While we always have stumped for and held great respect for Ramirez, we have to be realistic about his current state. Ramirez' injury habit has only gotten more pronounced the last two seasons as he has logged only 304 and 494 at-bats respectively. Also Ramirez will turn 37 in June which is a scary age for someone playing the rough hot corner spot. It may finally be time to salute the career and move on by.
PROJECTION: .286 17 HR 71 RBI 55 R 1 SB

18. **Daniel Murphy:*****SEE SECOND BASEMAN RANKINGS!*****

19. **Chase Headley:** It was another disappointing season for Chase Headley in 2014 as the veteran third baseman once again failed to hit much as he batted only .243 with 13 home runs in a year split between the San Diego Padres and the New York Yankees. We are well past the point of seeing Headley's monster 2012 season for the outlier that it was and his baseline numbers leave a lot to be desired no matter where he is hitting. The Yankees want Headley back as the free agent hits the open market but even if a return is worked out, he remains nothing more than a bench option at best.
PROJECTION: .251 14 HR 59 RBI 54 R 5 SB

20. **Pablo Sandoval:** If fantasy baseball were based on postseason performances, Pablo Sandoval would be a first round pick. Unfortunately for Kung Fu Panda, the regular season is what we are interested in and on that front, he has been pretty mediocre. 2014 saw a typical Sandoval season in that he hit some home runs (16) and had a decent enough average at .279. Sandoval has failed to come anywhere close to his 23 HR/.315 2011 campaign which goes down as a clear outlier. Considering Sandoval doesn't do any one thing great, he works best as a backup guy who can be good insurance for your starter.
PROJECTION: .275 14 HR 77 RBI 61 R 1 SB

21. **Martin Prado:******SEE SECOND BASEMAN RANKINGS!******

22. **Lonnie Chisenhall:** After three years of shoddy performances at the dish, a mini-breakthrough finally came forth for Cleveland Indians third baseman Lonnie Chisenhall in 2014 as he hit 13 home runs in 478 at-bats and batted a respectable .280. The fact that those numbers so far represent the best we have seen out of Chisenhall shows you how much of a struggle it has been but he still is a young player at 26. We won't call Chisenhall a post-hype

sleeper yet until he puts back-to-back productive seasons together but he could make a run at 20 home runs if he can avoid his annual slow starts. Draft only as a backup with a tiny bit of remaining upside.
PROJECTION: .270 19 HR 72 RBI 62 R 2 SB

23. **Alex Rodriguez:** He's baaaaccckkk! The human lightning rod, otherwise known as Alex Rodriguez, returns to major league baseball after serving an unprecedented full-season suspension due to the Biogenesis probe. Rodriguez makes his way back to the New York Yankees at the age of 40 and with two serious hip surgeries in his recent past further clouding his outlook. Once the top player in the game, Rodriguez is a mess both health-wise and with his sliding post-steroid numbers. Rodriguez has spent at least one stint on the DL in every season since 2009, so you are not getting anywhere near a full year out of the guy if you do take a late-round gamble. The Yankees have talked about giving Rodriguez some starts at first base in order to preserve his body which could add some versatility but expecting anything more than 20 home runs and 70 RBI at his age is silly. Ignore the name brand and look anywhere else but here if you can.
PROJECTION: .273 15 HR 65 RBI 67 R 2 SB

24. **Nick Castellanos:** We never bought into the sleeper hype that was attached by many to Nick Castellanos as he came up the Detroit Tigers minor league system. While Castellanos did some nice things on the farm that earned the hype, his tendency to strike out and the fact he had only average power made him a bad fit in terms of possible fantasy baseball impact. That is exactly the profile Castellanos showed during his first full season in 2014 as he batted only .259 while striking out 140 times. In addition, Castellanos hit a paltry 11 home runs which is below-average power at any corner or outfield position. Still an extremely young 23, Castellanos has at least three years of ceiling left, which means an uptick across the board is likely. Ultimately Castellanos profiles as at best a 20 home run guy down the road, which is production we don't think he will reach this season. Not the worst late round investment given his youth but only as bench help.
PROJECTION: .274 14 HR 68 RBI 57 R 2 SB

25. **David Freese:** When the St. Louis Cardinals give up on you, there is not much to say in a positive about the player This is the current state that David Freese resides in as we enter 2015 as it now appears like his 2012 late blooming breakout (20 HR/.293) was a flash in the pan performance. Since that time, Freese has continued a career-long trend of getting injured and he has hit only 19 total home runs total over the last two seasons, while also batting a mediocre .261 in that same span. Freese is already 32-years-old,

which means he is more likely to fall off the statistical map than make any gains. Even in AL-only leagues he is nothing but waiver fodder.
PROJECTION: .263 10 HR 56 RBI 51 R 1 SB

26. **Chris Coghlan:** What a nice comeback that was. The 2009 NL Rookie of the Year, Chris Coghlan almost literally fell off the map over the following four years as rampant injuries and shoddy batting numbers forced the Miami Marlins to throw in the towel on a guy they thought would be a mainstay for years. The Chicago Cubs never met a reclamation project they didn't like however as they inked Coghlan to a minor league contract prior to last season. Summoned in May, Coghlan proceeded to re-open eyes by hitting .283 with 9 home runs and 7 stolen bases in only 385 at-bats. Coghlan is still young at 30 and he will be given the chance to be the Cubs' starting third baseman or outfielder for 2015. There has always been some power/speed ability here, which alone makes Coghlan interesting again. The average will not likely go much above .280, if it even reaches that level but Coghlan at least deserves a late round pick to see if his return to usefulness is for real.
PROJECTION: .271 12 HR 48 RBI 5 R 10 SB

27. **Chris Johnson:** When you have THE single highest (and most fortunate) BABIP number in the league, there is nowhere else to go but down the following season. So was the case of Atlanta Braves third baseman Chris Johnson who was coming off a 2013 campaign where he hit .321, a number that was boosted tremendously by a nearly .400 BABIP. Making matters more volatile, batting average was the 5 x 5 statistic Johnson made his biggest impact in, which of course is a huge red flag due to the up and down nature of that category. As a result, Johnson appeared on many 2014 "bust" lists, including our own. Thus it was no shock that Johnson's numbers tumbled drastically last season to a .263 average with only 12 home runs. When you break it down, Johnson is just an ordinary player when his BABIP is in neutral or negative territory as we saw a year ago. He does carry first base eligibility as well but the fact last season's 12 home runs represent his career-high means he is an even worse fit there. Leave on the wire.
PROJECTION: .275 11 HR 61 RBI 4 R 5 SB

28. **Brett Lawrie:*****SEE SECOND BASEMAN RANKINGS!*******

29. **Xander Bogaerts:*****SEE SHORTSTOP RANKINGS!*******

30. **Aaron Hill:*****SEE SECOND BASEMAN RANKINGS!*******

31. **Brock Holt:** ******SEE FIRST BASEMAN RANKINGS!****

32. **Matt Dominguez:** If you are looking for some cheap pop out of your backup third baseman, Matt Dominguez is your guy. Over the last two seasons for the Houston Astros, Dominguez has hit 37 home runs and collected 134 RBI. Of course we recommend Dominguez as a backup play only due to the fact he batted an awful .241 and .215 the last two seasons.
PROJECTION: .245 14 HR 55 RBI 52 R 2 SB

33. **Will Middlebrooks:** When you lose the battle versus strikeouts, your fantasy baseball status and maybe even MLB career are on thin ice. That is the exact scenario facing Boston Red Sox third baseman Will Middlebrooks whose hyped power has not been able to launch due to terrible K rates that sank his average to a pathetic .191 last season. Yes injuries were a factor but Middlebrooks has now struck out in more than 25 percent of his at-bats through three seasons with the Red Sox, a totally unacceptable number. Blessed with natural power, Middlebrooks could fall into 25 home runs if he can curb his free-swinging ways even just a little bit. We are not holding our breath though. Time to move on already.
PROJECTION: .236 14 HR 56 RBI 45 R 2 SB

THE REST

34. **Casey McGehee:** *****SEE FIRST BASEMAN RANKINGS!****

35. **Juan Francisco:** It certainly looked like early on in the 2014 season that the terrific home run tendencies of the Toronto Blue Jays' home ballpark helped the team uncover another potential discarded gem in Juan Francisco. The former Milwaukee Brewer hit 14 home runs the first half of the season but that was the end of the story as Francisco's lack of any sort of batting approach exposed him tremendously in the second half. Francisco would hit only 2 more home runs the rest of the way and he also wound up striking out in almost HALF of his at-bats. Back to the shadows he goes.

36. **Yangervis Solarte:** *****SEE SECOND BASEMAN RANKINGS!****

37. **Trevor Plouffe:** Yet another waiver guy who hits some home runs while posting nausea-inducing batting averages. The 24 home runs Plouffe hit in 2012 are now a distant memory as he logged 14 each of the last two years while posting .254 and .258 averages. Strikeouts are a major issue and playing in Target Field is no picnic either. He will be there on waivers if you ever somehow have a need for Plouffe's weak overall body of work.

38. **Juan Uribe:** Juan Uribe has been around for a long time now as he enters into his 15th MLB season. In order to hang around for as long as Uribe has (and to be a starter as he remains with the Los Angeles Dodgers), you obviously have to have some skills. Uribe managed to hit .311 with 9 home runs at the age of 35 last season but that solid line represents the absolute best case scenario for him moving forward. This puts Uribe into backup status at best and more likely as a waiver guy.

39. **Wilmer Flores:*****SEE SHORTSTOP RANKINGS!********

40. **Mike Moustakas:** It has become crystal clear the fact that Kansas City Royals third baseman Mike Moustakas will never live up to the power he carried coming up the team's minor league system. 2014 was a microcosm of the issues Moustakas brings to the table, primarily of which is a sky-high K rate that resulted in a .212 batting average and only 15 home runs. Four years into his career, Moustakas' high in home runs is only 20 and any power he does bring is offset by the damage his average inflicts.

41. **Cody Asche:** Keeping the third base seat warm for top Philadelphia Phillies prospect Maikel Franco, fellow youngster Cody Asche did a decent enough job for the team in 2014. Asche hit 10 home runs and drove in 46 batters in only 397 at-bats but Franco will likely unseat him for the position in 2015. Asche struck out in 25 percent of his at-bats last season, which resulted in a rough .252 batting average. He also flashed none of the decent speed he showed in the minors as he failed to log even one stolen base. The Franco Era is set to begin.

42. **Gordon Beckham:** We really won't waste time here with this perennial disappointment. Beckham managed 9 home runs and 3 steals in his 446 at-bats but the overall the guy flat out can't hit.

43. **Mark Reynolds:*****SEE FIRST BASEMAN RANKINGS!*******

44. **Mike Olt:******SEE FIRST BASEMAN RANKINGS!*******

45. **Josh Rutledge:******SEE SECOND BASEMAN RANKINGS!*******

46. **Emilio Bonifacio:** Once looked at as a stolen base dynamo and prime fantasy baseball sleeper, Emilio Bonifacio is now nothing more than waiver fodder given the fact he can't hit. In order to collect steals you first need to get on base and Bonifacio has failed miserably at that endeavor as he has

now moved through five teams in the last three years. Steals can be found in much more promising and abundant places late in your draft, so don't bother here.

47. **Mike Aviles:** *****SEE SECOND BASEMAN RANKINGS!*****

48. **Jedd Gyorko:** *****SEE SECOND BASEMAN RANKINGS!*****

49. **Kelly Johnson:** It is looking like the twilight of Kelly Johnson's career as he couldn't hit in Yankee Stadium of all places and than was cut loose by the team. He was soon picked up by the Baltimore Orioles but a .215 cumulative batting average shows you how much Johnson is finished as any sort of impact player.

OUTFIELDERS

Draft Strategy: As we discussed earlier, your best course of action in a standard mixed league draft is to get yourself a stud first baseman and outfielder among your first two picks . The first baseman we already talked at length about but the importance of getting your initial outfielder right away is just as crucial for your team's success. Specifically speaking, you want to do your best to get your hands on a five-tool outfielder among Mike Trout, Andrew McCutchen, Adam Jones, Carlos Gomez, Giancarlo Stanton, Justin Upton, and Jacoby Ellsbury. Obviously with Trout you need the top pick and McCutchen, Jones, Stanton, and possibly Gomez will need a first rounder. If you get your first baseman in Round 1, Upton and Ellsbury will be good targets in Round 2. Sorry we are not buying fully into the Nelson Cruz contract push from last season. Draft him that early at your own risk.

As far as the importance of taking that outfielder early, the first is that all leagues require between 3 and 5 starters which is at least two more than any other position on the field. Thus you want that anchor outfielder which will allow you to wait a bit on getting your second one. In addition, outfield is where you will get your monster 5-tool guys who contribute across all five standard hitting categories. These are the players who are pure fantasy baseball gold and who are beyond invaluable given their all-around contributions. Trying to pick up numbers in all five hitting categories is a lot of work and that effort will be helped greatly by having one guy who helps everywhere. The price will be steep but they are worth every penny.

Meanwhile as far as the other two to four outfield slots you have to fill, try to use one on a power bat like a Yoenis Cespedes or even someone a bit cheaper like a Hunter Pence. The other spot you want to address more speed like with a Brett Gardner, Christian Yelich, or Jarrod Dyson. While your number 1 outfielder will cover all five categories, you want to spread out the numbers among the rest of your bats there.

1. **Mike Trout:** With Miguel Cabrera having somewhat of an off year by his lofty standards, the mantle of number 1 player in both real and fantasy baseball belongs to 5 x 5 monster Mike Trout. Ever since he broke into the league with the most dominant rookie season we may have ever seen (30 HR/49 SB/129 R/83 RBI/.326), Trout has redefined how one player can boost all five standard hitting categories. Trout enters the 2015 season still only 23-years-old, which is amazing when you consider how incredible a player he already is. Predictably, the Angels moved Trout out of the leadoff spot last season in order to capitalize on his power and RBI potential. The only noticeable negative was the serious drop in steals as Trout collected only 16 last season after going for 49 and 33 his first two years. That is nitpicking however as Trout clubbed a career-high 36 home runs and drove in another career-high 111, so the tradeoff was well worth it. There is a chance Trout could reach the hallowed 40-home run mark as soon as this season and even a boost back above the 20-steal mark is also entirely possible to go with his .300 average and 100-plus runs and RBI. There is simply no reason Trout should not be the number 1 pick in all mixed leagues this season.
PROJECTION: .297 38 HR 114 RBI 117 R 23 SB

2. **Giancarlo Stanton:** We had a tough time deciding whether Giancarlo Stanton or Andrew McCutchen deserved the right to be the top fantasy baseball outfielder AFTER Mike Trout. Ultimately Stanton won out due to the fact he supplies the most precious and increasingly rare commodity in today's game, which of course is the home run. Stanton has few peers in that aspect of the game as his Paul Bunyon frame would suggest. The Miami Marlins slugger was heading for a possible MVP award and his first 40-home run season in 2014 when some bad luck interfered with the narrative. A fastball thrown by the Milwaukee Brewers' Mike Fiers nailed Stanton square in the face in a truly horrific scene. Stanton suffered multiple facial fractures, lacerations, and dental damage as he missed the last three weeks of the season. Still the fact of the matter is that Stanton had his best year as a pro as he smacked 37 home runs and drove in 105 batters. In addition, Stanton decided to add some steals to his game as he swiped 13 bags. What is also really interesting about Stanton is that his sky-high

strikeout rate has not destroyed his batting average as one would think. A .271 career hitter through four seasons, Stanton has managed to bat .above .285 in two of the last three years despite strikeout totals that ranged from 140 to as high as 2014's 170. With full health, Stanton should burst through the 40-home run barrier this season and is as good a selection as any from picks 3-5 in Round 1.

PROJECTION: .275 41 HR 111 RBI 92 R 10 SB

3. **Andrew McCutchen:** Along the same lines as Mike Trout but to a bit of a lesser degree, Andrew McCutchen is a five category behemoth who is a slam dunk early first round selection. After clubbing 31 home runs and hitting .327 in his MVP campaign in 2012, McCutchen has settled more into a 25 HR/.315 performer who also will chip in between 20-25 stolen bases. That's fantasy baseball gold no matter how you slice it and with McCutchen still in his prime as he turns 29 in October, another MVP-type season should be in the cards.

PROJECTION: .315 22 HR 88 RBI 95 R 21 SB

4. **Adam Jones:** Another year and another monster season from Baltimore Orioles outfielder Adam Jones in 2014. While Nelson Cruz got most of the pub, Jones had the better overall year as he hit 29 home runs, collected 96 RBI, and batted .281. We were the biggest Jones boosters prior to 2014 and remain firmly on his bandwagon due to his top notch durability and consistency which are two often overlooked aspects of a player's value. Anyone who invested a first or second round pick on Carlos Gonzalez can understand what we mean. You can write in ink around 25-30 home runs, 90-plus RBI and runs, around 10-15 steals, and a .285 average for Jones, which we will gladly take as our outfield anchor.

PROJECTION: .286 30 HR 95 RBI 97 R 10 SB

5. **Carlos Gomez:** Gomez is yet another classic late bloomer as the former failed New York Mets and Minnesota Twins prospect put together his third top-end season in a row for the Milwaukee Brewers in 2014. While Gomez still struggles with strikeouts, his power/speed game has sustained after taking off in 2012 when he hit 19 home runs and swiped 37 bags. Over the last two seasons, Gomez has even improved on the power as he has come in at 24 and 23 home runs while maintaining his speed with 40 and 37 steals. His spot atop the Brewers' lineup won't allow Gomez to cross the 80 RBI mark but last season's 95 runs are very likely to be repeated. For all the times Gomez has struck out, he has used his speed to post fortunate BABIP numbers that have helped him hit .284 the last two years. Despite it seeming like Gomez has been around forever, he will only be 29 for the

2015 season. Has replaced Carlos Gonzalez as the number 4 multi-tooled outfielder
PROJECTION: .281 22 HR 74 RBI 92 R 35 SB

6. **Jacoby Ellsbury:** All in all it was a very successful first season for Jacoby Ellsbury after signing a massive free agent deal with the New York Yankees. The expected uptick in home runs as a lefty batter aiming at the short rightfield porch in Yankee Stadium materialized somewhat as Ellsbury hit 7 more bombs than the season prior, finishing with a total of 16. His speed game remained as dominant as ever as Ellsbury swiped 39 bases but being moved out of the leadoff spot took about 10 of those away. The 71 runs scored from last season represent the floor for Ellsbury and an uptick to 90 is in the realm of possibility. Perhaps the most satisfying part of Ellsbury's 2014 campaign was the fact he avoided serious injury in logging 149 games played. It was not until the last two weeks of the season when Ellsbury's injury luck ran out but overall he stayed on the field which is a big deal for a guy who had has some major health woes in the past. Ellsbury is getting a bit up there in age as he turns 32 in September which means the speed could start to slip a bit. Also it is asking a lot to expect Ellsbury to stay healthy for two seasons in a row so the risk remains. Cross your fingers again.
PROJECTION: .284 15 HR 67 RBI 89 R 38 SB

7. **Jose Bautista:** This is one guy we missed on when it came to projecting players in last year's guide. After three straight seasons of declining home runs rates and two straight campaigns that finished early due to serious injury, Bautisa had the classic look of a slipping and aging slugger. Well Bautista changed the narrative in 2014 as he had his best season since 2011 by hitting 35 home runs and collecting 103 RBI, while also scoring 101 runs. Avoiding injury was key as Bautista showed his home run swing was still in fine working order. Forget about last season's .286 average as Bautista had some BABIP luck there and he strikes out way to much to repeat that number. Even though Bautista is an aging player at 33, we feel strongly that another top power production season is on tap for 2015 as long as his health cooperates.
PROJECTION: .266 32 HR 101 RBI 97 R 4 SB

8. **Justin Upton:** Justin Upton has proven himself to be one of the more annoying players to own due to his wild swings of production during the course of a given season. Prone to extreme hot and cold spells, Upton seems to alternate good and bad months during the year. However by the end of the season, the numbers are always attractive as Upton has settled

into the prime years of his career. The former number 1 overall pick in the 2005 draft may not ever be the next Ken Griffey Jr. as some had predicted but 25-plus home runs and 100 RBI are perfectly acceptable enough as a lower-end outfielder 1. As we have said many times over, power is a very precious commodity in today's game and it is the home runs and RBI where Upton does his best work. The negatives are a very high K rate (career-high 171 strikeouts last season) that won't allow Upton to hit more than .270 and a stolen base rate that has dropped to the high single-digits since being dealt to the Atlanta Braves. No matter, Upton is well worth being the top outfielder on a given fantasy baseball roster once again.

PROJECTION: .265 28 HR 99 RBI 81 R 9 SB

9. **Nelson Cruz:** It was exactly one year ago when we highlighted our 2014 All-Bust team with Baltimore Orioles 1B Chris Davis, who was coming off a 53-home run season that had fluke written all over it. Davis' year was propped up by a very lucky BABIP that greatly boosted his average, to go along with some steroid rumors that eventually proved accurate in 2014 when he was suspended after testing positive for amphetamines. We bring up Davis here due to the very close similarities to his teammate Nelson Cruz. Cruz of course was suspended for 50 games in 2013 after getting caught up in the Biogenesis probe and took a one-year "prove it" deal with the Orioles right before the start of the 2014 season. Showing off power never seen to that level before, Cruz led baseball in home runs with 40 and drove in 108 batters in a visually stunning campaign. However caution is advised here. For one, Cruz had not so much as hit more than 30 home runs in a season since way back in 2009 with Texas which alone is a red flag. In addition, the 613 at-bats Cruz accumulated last season were the most he had ever collected in his career due to a long history of injuries. The term "outlier" quickly comes to mind with Cruz and his performance last season, as there is almost no chance he stays so healthy again in turning 35-years-old. In addition Cruz has almost completely lost his speed and his batting average is always an issue given his high strikeout tendency. Cruz has bust written all over him and while his numbers may not fall completely off the cliff like they did with Davis, the signs are all there for major trouble. Avoid overpaying.

PROJECTION: .268 28 HR 88 RBI 86 R 2 SB

10. **Yoenis Cespedes:** Along the same lines as Justin Upton, the massive hype that initially followed Yoenis Cespedes when he first arrived in the major legaues has pretty much died down now that he has settled into his true statistical profile. The Cuban masher is a high-strikeout power hitter who was dealt right at last season's trade deadline from the Oakland A's to the

Boston Red Sox in the Jon Lester deal. The move from O.Co Coliseum to Fenway Park is about as big a ballpark improvement as a hitter can make and the new locale could put Cespedes on the path to his first 30-home run season. Cespedes has not come anywhere hear the 16 steals he posted as a rookie, having taken only 7 bags each of the last two seasons and his career .263 average is shaky due to his strikeout habit. What we are looking at here is a two-category star (home runs/RBI) in a prime hitting environment who falls into the outfielder 2 realm.

PROJECTION: .266 29 HR 92 RBI 77 R 5 SB

11. **Michael Brantley:** One of the best values among all hitters in 2014 fantasy baseball was surely Cleveland Indians outfielder Michael Brantley. Up until last season, Brantley was a guy who did a little of this and a little of that without any signature statistic going into the above-average realm. However turning the magical age of 27 (which is historically when a hitter first reaches their prime years) elevated Brantley to a level no one expected as he hit 20 home runs, with 23 stolen bases, while hitting .323. All three numbers were by far his career highs (not to mention his 94 runs scored and 97 RBI) and at the very least should give prospective owners a bit of pause when cutting the check due to the possibility of an outlier campaign. Brantley had hinted at production such as this however as he went 10/17 the season prior while batting .284. There surely is a chance for Brantley to fall back across the board a bit in 2015 but at the same time he also is now firmly into his prime which means a repeat is also a solid possiblity as well. Tough call if the price gets a bit high but from Round 5 and on we're buying.

PROJECTION: .295 19 HR 88 RBI 95 R 22 SB

12. **Yasiel Puig:** True to his maddening form, Los Angeles Dodgers outfielder Yasiel Puig was a bit of a letdown in his first full MLB season in 2014. After Puig took the league by storm the year prior as a rookie when he hit .319 with 19 home runs and 11 steals in only 382 at-bats, talk began to surface that Puig was following in the Mike Trout footsteps as an instant five-category star. Well the encore was discouraging as the book on Puig's undisciplined hitting got around the pitching fraternity. Seeing fewer fastballs due to his tendency to chase and swing at everything, Puig hit only 16 home runs in 558 at-bats while coming in with the same 11 stolen bases and a .296 average. Along the way Puig incurred the wrath of manager Don Mattingly and the front office with tardiness and immature behavior. Perhaps most alarming was the fact Puig struck out 124 times and things got so bad there in the postseason that Mattingly considered benching him outright. Of course Puig is still very young as he turns 24 for the 2015

season and he has incredible talents that could explode at a moment's notice. We really like the depressed price tag this season but also are realistic that some more growing pains could be on the way in the short-term. As long as you draft Puig as an outfielder 2, you did just fine. **PROJECTION: .291 20 HR 75 RBI 97 R 14 SB**

13. **Bryce Harper:** The wait goes on. Now let's be fair here before we move on. Bryce Harper will be only 22-years-old for 2015 fantasy baseball despite the fact he has already logged three MLB seasons and that needs to be kept in mind when discussing his so far disappointing numbers. For a guy who was talked about as a future Hall Of Famer even before he made his debut at the ripe old age of 19, Harper has thus far struggled to break through due to injury and some sizable holes in his swing. 2014 was a microcosm of those issues as Harper hit only .273, with 13 home runs, and a tiny 32 RBI while appearing in only 100 games. Harper has now missed 106 games combined over the last two years, which shows you just how snakebitten he has been with the injury bug. A lot has been made about Harper's all-out style that borders on recklessness being the primary issue when it comes to him getting hurt but thus far the Nats outfielder vows not to change his ways. This is not what you want to hear when it comes to possibly investing in Harper for 2015 and one has to wonder if all the injuries have caused his stolen base numbers to plummet from 18 to 11 to last season's 2. In addition to the injuries, Harper is showing a compete lack of hitting discipline as he struck out in almost a third of his 2014 at-bats. Opposing pitchers have no reason to throw Harper anything down in the zone, choosing to let him get himself out instead. It is that issue that has helped keep both Harper's batting average and power output from taking the next leap. Despite all the negatives, Harper still has a good four years of ceiling left to his name and the natural power is still bubbling under the surface. The name value and potential remains very high here so if you think you are going to get a steep discount on Harper for 2015, you can forget it. Still it is only a matter of time before Harper swats those 30 home runs and drives in 100-plus. Is it this year? **PROJECTION: .275 24 HR 73 RBI 75 R 7 SB**

14. **Hunter Pence:** Hunter Pence is about as underrated as they come. For some strange reason, Pence is never talked about when discussions turn to the more productive 5-tool fantasy baseball outfielders. Pence has made a career out of quietly going about his business of contributing in all five standard hitting categories, which he accomplished again in 2014 when he smacked 20 home runs, stole 13 bases, and batted .277. He also scored a career-high 106 runs and drove in 74 for a San Francisco Giants lineup that

gave him little support. What you see is what you get here as Pence should be able to replicate his 2014 numbers once again this season and in the process continue his career-long tendency to be overshadowed by more sexier names. The most dependable outfielder 2 in all of fantasy baseball. **PROJECTION: .280 23 HR 84 RBI 99 R 14 SB**

15. **Billy Hamilton:** Perhaps the most talked about player going into 2014 drafts was a guy who had all of 19 at-bats to his name and who would struggle to hit 5 home runs. The hype surrounding Cincinnati Reds outfielder Billy Hamilton went beyond overdrive last spring training as we all wondered if he would be the first player since Vince Coleman to steal 100 bases in a season. After Hamilton broke the minor league stolen base mark in 2012 with an unfathomable 155 thefts, his extreme ability in that part of the game made him a name we all put at the top of our sleeper lists once he finally got on the doorstep to an everyday MLB job. It was truly remarkable seeing Hamilton drafted as high as the fourth round when there were major question marks about if he could even hit major league pitching. A few weeks into the season, that fear was being realized as Hamilton almost went hitless, recording only two hits in his first 22 at-bats. However Hamilton soon settled in and his speed took front and center as expected. While he didn't come close to the 100 mark, Hamilton still managed to steal a monstrous 56 bases despite only a .250 batting average. The six home runs were a nice bonus but Hamilton remains pretty much a one-trick pony, as he only went past home plate 72 times last season despite all the running. There are still valid concerns about how much Hamilton can hit but he should be able to go at least past the 70 steal mark this year now that he has a full season against major league pitching under his belt. Clearly you are buying Hamilton for his steals and nothing else as he will continue to struggle to post useful batting averages given his high K rate. A gimmick player all the way but a difference-maker when it comes to steals. **PROJECTION: .267 5 HR 51 RBI 82 R 73 SB**

16. **Lucas Duda:*****SEE FIRST BASEMAN RANKINGS!*****

17. **Ryan Braun:** So that is what Ryan Braun looks like without being on the juice. After finally copping to purchasing steroids in the Biogenesis mess and taking a season-ending 65 game suspension to close 2013, there were a ton of questions regarding what Braun would look like statistically the next season. If you read our 2014 draft guide, you would have know that we had Braun down as one of the biggest bust candidates in the game, firmly believing his numbers would sink without the benefits of steroids. Our opinion was spot on as Braun was a shell of his former MVP self as he

batted only .266 with 19 home runs and 81 RBI in 530 at-bats. Braun's home run rate sank and his speed seemed negatively impacted as well as he collected only 11 steals (way down from the 33 and 30 he has in 2011 and 2012). In addition, Braun battled chronic injuries that had him under the "day-to-day" label nearly all season, That culminated in Braun having invasive thumb surgery in the offseason in order to remedy what was an ongoing issue that stretched back years. What we have here is a guy who can't stay healthy and who is nothing more than an outfielder 3 based on his current numbers being off steroids. One big headache that is really not worth the trouble.

PROJECTION: .282 22 HR 86 RBI 88 R 10 SB

18. **Carlos Gonzalez:** We never knew that a finger could cause so much trouble. Such was the case for Colorado Rockies outfieler Carlos Gonzalez, who first developed trouble with finger injuries during the second half of the 2013 season. Gonzalez was on an MVP hitting pace prior to suffering the injury and he wound up seeing his numbers fall off the map from that point on. Given a fresh start to 2014, we were very bullish on Gonzalez' chances to once again showcase his tremendous power/speed ability with full health. However Gonzalez once again injured a finger that greatly impacted his hitting numbers in a negative way during the first half of the season. That was followed by a left patella injury in his knee that ultimately required season-ending surgery in August. The result was a shoddy .238 average with only 11 home runs and 3 stolen bases in 70 games. While Gonzalez is still flat in his prime at the age of 29, his body is proving to be one big mess which, makes him one of the biggest injury risks in all of fantasy baseball. The potential is alluring as Gonzalez has a ton of natural ability but we are not looking here again unless the price reflects the injury threat.

PROJECTION: .291 23 HR 84 RBI 86 R 19 SB

19. **Charlie Blackmon:** Before teammate and fellow outfielder Corey Dickerson stole much of the pub, Charlie Blackmon was the one who first opened eyes with an out-of-nowhere breakout season for the Colorado Rockies in 2014. The late bloomer had broken through somewhat the year prior when he hit 6 home runs and stole 7 bases while batting .309 in only 246 at-bats but the Rockies surely didn't know that this was a hint of more to come. Wasting no time showing that he was a major leaguer to stay, Blackmon was as hot as any hitter in baseball in the month of April, hitting .389 with 5 home runs and 7 stolen bases. Some adjustments were soon made by opposing pitchers but Blackmon still managed a 19 HR/82 R/72 RBI/28 SB/.288 season that had numbers-wise qualified him as an outfielder 2. As we said earlier, Blackmon was a bit late to the show as he turns 29 this July but his numbers mostly check out as legit. At Blackmon's

age we can't expect much improvement, if there is any at all, so as along as you are buying last season's haul, you will do just fine.
PROJECTION: .290 20 HR 70 RBI 89 R 27 SB

20. **Corey Dickerson:** Word of advice: if the Colorado Rockies call up a prospect, pick him up immediately even if you never heard of the guy before. After seeing Charlie Blackmon and Nolan Arenado come right out of the April gate hitting everything in sight, it should have been predictable that Corey Dickerson would follow the same path when he was put into a starting outfielder's role in mid-April. Not considered a top prospect when coming up the Rockies' system, Dickerson took full advantage of Coors Field to post eye-popping debut numbers. In only 436 at-bats, Dickerson hit 24 home runs and drove in 76 while batting .312. While he was only successful on 8 of 15 steal attempts, Dickerson put himself squarely into five-category territory as 2015 dawns. He hit 9 of his home runs on the road so Dickerson was not just a Coors Field product. The fact that Dickerson seemed to come out of nowhere should give one pause but the ballpark at the very least should keep any dropoff to a minimum. We are onboard.
PROJECTION: .305 26 HR 84 RBI 81 R 11 SB

21. **Matt Kemp:** It was only three short years ago when Los Angeles Dodgers outfielder Matt Kemp was in the running as the number 1 player in all of fantasy baseball as he came off a truly remarkable 2011 season when he hit 39 home runs and stole 40 bases while hitting .324. The multi-talented Kemp could run like the wind and hit the baseball a country mile. Turning only 28 for the 2012 season, Kemp was looking at an extended run of truly dominant numbers and unparalleled power/speed production. Unfortunately Kemp's body betrayed him in very ugly fashion as he battled a wide-range of injuries that seemed to include every part of his body. There were serious surgeries on his shoulder and ongoing leg issues as well that ruined his 2012 and 2013 campaigns and sank his draft stock to all-time lows. Thus when last season came around, Kemp was looked at as not much more than an outfielder 3 which was about as steep a fall as one could have in such a short time span. Despite a sluggish start, Kemp fought back to reclaim some of his lost shine as he hit 25 home runs and collected 89 RBI while batting .287. Perhaps the most positive aspect of Kemp's year is that he got better as the season went on and stayed relatively healthy in compiling a total of 541 at-bats. Still the current version of Kemp is a bit scaled down from his MVP past. Specifically speaking, Kemp has lost a great deal of speed as he stole only 8 bags last season and was caught 5 times. His inefficiency on the basepaths and lack of burst could be attributed to all the leg and hamstring issues Kemp has had the last three

years. Thus Kemp can no longer be considered a five-tool outfielder or even an outfielder 1 at this stage. Yes Kemp won't turn 31 until September but his injury-risk remains high and we will never see his 2011 numbers ever again. Be sure you cement in your mind the current abilities of Kemp before cutting the check and avoid living in his statistical past.
PROJECTION: .288 26 HR 90 RBI 79 R 9 SB

22. **Starling Marte:** A leadoff hitter Starling Marte is not. In last year's draft guide, we discussed how Marte was ill-suited to being a leadoff hitter due to his high strikeout and poor walk rates. This despite the fact Marte possesses some of the more impressive athletic tools in the game such as top-end speed and developing power. Still expectations were through the roof on Marte prior to 2014, as he came off a 41-stolen base explosion in his breakout 2013, which went nicely with his 12 home runs and .280 average. The red flags centered on the 138 K's Marte accumulated but the Pirates still went ahead and penciled him into the leadoff spot going into the 2014 season. Fast forward a month as Marte finished April with a .225 average and an obscene 37 K's in only 102 at-bats. The Pirates finally came to their senses with regards to pulling Marte from the leadoff spot and almost instantly the fortunes of their young outfielder changed for the better. Having a much clearer mind due to not having to worry about getting on base leading off, Marte once again showed off an intriguing blend of power and speed that had him hitting a red-hot .348 the second half of the season to go along with 8 home runs. In the end Marte ended up with 13 home runs and 30 steals as he actually improved his average to .291. With Marte now locked in as a middle-of-the-order hitter, a fair Carlos Gomez impersonation could be in the offing. Marte still strikes out way too much (131 K's in 495 at-bats last season) but his speed helps overcome any poor BABIP luck. Still a baby at 26, Marte has a bit more growth possible. Make him your prime outfielder 2.
PROJECTION: .282 15 HR 62 RBI 79 R 32 SB

23. **George Springer:** Fantasy baseball outfielders who can both hit for power and steals bases with nice precision make all who play our fake game weak in the knees. Players who excel in both of those disciplines are among the most precious and fought over commodities and one can see with the first round of drafts being peppered with the Mike Trout's, the Andrew McCutchen's, and the Carlos Gomez' of the world. While he is not in that realm yet, Houston Astros outfielder George Springer is already knocking on the door based on what he has shown both on the farm and in his 2014 big league debut. Taking a quick trip down memory lane, Springer added his name to every top prospect list in 2013 as he compiled a crazy total of

37 home runs and 45 stolen bases in the Astros minor league system. Houston wasted little time in bringing up Springer a year later as he made his debut on April 16th and immediately showed everyone what all the fuss was about. In just 295 at-bats, Springer cracked 20 home runs and drove in 51 batters. Springer was only able to net the 295 at-bats due to a serious left quadriceps injury that finished him for good July 19th. Despite the small sample size, Springer showed that he was in fact the real deal, showcasing natural power to someday possibly reach the 40 home run plateau. It was not all positive however as the high strikeout rate Springer showed through all those home runs and steals in the minor leagues followed him to the Astros as he whiffed in a crazy 33 percent of his at-bats, the main reason he batted an ugly .238. In addition, Springer seemed a bit hesitant on the basepaths as he swiped only 5 bases, no doubt trying to size up the ability of major league catchers to throw him out. We are not so much worried about the steals as Springer has top end speed that will make him a force there. The strikeouts though are a big problem that has to be worked on in order to avoid seeing a string of .250 batting averages. The comparisons to an early Chris Young with more power are spot on however. Springer will be on everyone's "must have" list this season, so he will cost a bundle even despite those batting average issues. While we ordinarily shy from players who hurt you in the average category, Springer is such a potential force in the other four statistics that we can overlook that negative.
PROJECTION: .252 34 HR 78 RBI 86 R 14 SB

24. **Brett Gardner:** Already a veteran outfielder 3 in fantasy baseball terms, the New York Yankees' Brett Gardner is beginning to evolve into a different player as he moves into his 30's. A two-time 40 stolen base weapon, Gardner has lost some speed as he has swiped only 24 and 21 bags each of the last two seasons. However what Gardner has lost in speed he has seemingly gained in power as he hit a career-high 17 home runs in 2014 while batting mostly out of the precious leadoff spot. Last year's homer output was 9 more than he had hit in his previous high, so we have to watch out for a possible outlier. Be that as it may, Gardner is fully capable of a 15 HR/25 stolen base campaign, with a .270 batting average thrown in. Rock solid all the way.
PROJECTION: .271 15 HR 56 RBI 89 R 23 SB

25. **Jay Bruce:** He is what he is. When it comes to Cincinnati Reds perennial tease Jay Bruce, that means a bunch of home runs and RBI with little else. The 12th overall pick of the 2005 draft, Bruce had sky-high expectations attached to his name when he first arrived on the scene as a 21-year-old back in 2008. Possessing some immense natural power, Bruce has now

logged three seasons of 30-plus home runs and 95-plus RBI. Unfortunately that is pretty much it when discussing Bruce's statistical output in fantasy baseball terms as he is a terrible base stealer, has never reached the 90-run mark, and his career average is a horrid .251. Bruce is a strikeout machine and was punched out 185 times as recently as 2013. Now a veteran at 28, Bruce is the classic poor average/power hitter. He makes the grade as your outfielder 2 but that average needs to be covered elsewhere which is always an annoying thing to worry about during your draft. You are better off getting the very similar Brandon Moss five rounds later.

PROJECTION: .254 28 HR 96 RBI 88 R 9 SB

26.**Jason Heyward:** Now a full five seasons into his still-young career, the jury remains out on how good much-hyped outfielder Jason Heyward can be. The tools are all there as Heyward has a nice blend of power and speed but his bat is still a work in progress. The Atlanta Braves lost patience with Heyward apparently as they decided to trade him to the St. Louis Cardinals for starting pitcher Shelby Miller. The big problem here is that Heyward continued to lose the battle against strikeouts as he has been punched out 90 or more times in four of his five seasons. The result has been a very shaky .271 career batting average, which leaves a lot to be desired. In addition, Heyward has been all over the map both in the home run and stolen base departments. After smacking 27 home runs in 2012, Heyward managed only 14 and 11 longballs the last two years. And the stolen base totals have read 11, 9, 21, 2, and 22 in his five MLB seasons. Thus nailing down what you could expect from Heyward for 2015 is an almost impossible task. The best course of action to take is to anticipate a replication of last season, while keeping hope alive for an improvement based on the fact Heyward gets a fresh start with the St. Louis Cardinals and still remains very young as he turns only 26 in August.

PROJECTION: .273 19 HR 75 RBI 83 R 21 SB

27.**Matt Holliday:** With 11 major league seasons in the rearview mirror, Father Time is starting to call for St. Louis Cardinals veteran outfielder Matt Holliday. Long one of the better pure hitters in the game, Holliday began to show some noticeable slippage last season when his career .308 batting average slipped all the way down to a mediocre .272. In addition, Holliday hit only 20 home runs, which was his fewest since 2005. Holliday turned 35 in January and more slippage is very likely. Already having lost his speed years ago, there is not much left to get excited about.

PROJECTION: .279 21 HR 88 RBI 77 R 3 SB

28.**Marcell Ozuna:** The Miami Marlins have always been willing to take chances on young players and often this has led to the team uncovering some very good major league talent. That could certainly be said of slugging outfielder Marcell Ozuna who stepped up and hit 23 home runs with 85 RBI in his first full MLB season in 2014. The free agent signing from the Dominican Republic is a hacker all the way, having struck out 164 times in last season's 565 at-bats but at only 24 years old, Ozuna has time on his side to work through some of those struggles. While Ozuna is not Giancarlo Stanton by any means, he could belt 25 home runs and collect 90 RBI in 2015 if all breaks right. This is a rising talent whose best is ahead of him.

PROJECTION: .271 26 HR 88 RBI 74 R 4 SB

29. **Alex Gordon:** Yet another example of a guy who helped across the board without blowing up any one category. Alex Gordon has never fully lived up to the hype that was attached to his name after he was made the number 2 pick overall in the 2005 draft but he certainly has developed into a very useful fantasy baseball piece. Consistency is the theme here as Gordon pretty much churned out the same exact numbers the last two seasons (2013: .265/20 HR/81 RBI/90 R/11 SB, 2014: .266/19 HR/74 RBI/87 R/12 SB). Thus Gordon is a fairly easy player to project and grade out. Lastly, Gordon is among the most durable players in baseball who has accumulated more than 600 at-bats in three of the last four seasons, which is always a major plus in an injury-filled game.

PROJECTION: .267 20 HR 86 RBI 92 R 11 SB

30. **Michael Cuddyer:** Proof positive of the benefits of hitting in Coors Field, we present to you the two-year case of veteran Michael Cuddyer. After 12 solid but unspectacular seasons with the Minnesota Twins, where his highest seasonal batting average was a modest .284, Cuddyer took the money and ran off to Colorado on a two-year free agent deal. The results were spectacular as Cuddyer won the NL batting title in 2013 with his .331 average and he would have been in line to defend his crown in 2014 with his .332 mark if he hadn't failed to qualify due to so many missed games because of injury. After moving on as a free agent to the New York Mets, Cuddyer has some major bust potential due to the fact he is likely to go back to being a .280 hitter/20 HR hitter now that he no longer calls Coors Field home. Cuddyer is also now 36-years-old, which means more battles with injuries are likely. Nice run for sure the last two seasons but Cuddyer has nowhere to go but down from here on out.

PROJECTION: .281 19 HR 72 RBI 75 R 7 SB

31. **Ryan Zimmerman:*****SEE THIRD BASEMAN RANKINGS!*****

32. **Christian Yelich:** Upward and onward we go with the Miami Marlins' 2010 first round pick as outfielder Christian Yelich gave a preview last

season of what is to come as he continues to develop. Hitting primarily out of the leadoff spot in his first full major league season, Yelich did a little of everything as he hit 9 home runs, stole 21 bases, scored 94 runs, and batted a solid .284. Yelich has some rough edges to work out such as the 137 strikeouts he put up in his 582 at-bats but the 70 walks show that he is also learning plate discipline as well. Keep in mind that Yelich will be only 23 and that he hints at a 20/20 season which could come as soon as 2015. We continue to be major stumpers of Yelich and strongly advise you to buy in before the top blows off on his numbers.

PROJECTION: .288 12 HR 62 RBI 95 R 24 SB

33. **Rusney Castillo:** The Boston Red Sox joined the 'Cuban Craze' last season when they inked free agent outfielder Rusney Castillo and wasted little time in promoting him for a short September stint. Despite only collecting 36 at-bats, Castillo left us amazed with his talent as he hit two home runs and ran like the wind in stealing 6 bases while batting .333. Castillo's speed is ahead of his power right now but many point to the centerfielder as a future 30 home run bat. The tools are incredible here and we don't have to remind you of the high success rate of Cuban imports over the last five seasons or so. We are very admant about drafting aggressively here, as Castillo will be an All-Star real soon. Just terrific upside.

PROJECTION: .307 19 HR 72 RBI 82 R 23 SB

34. **Shin-Soo Choo:** Yeah that was pretty gruesome. Already a very dependable power/speed outfielder 2, expectations grew for Shin-Shoo Choo heading into the 2014 season after he inked a free agent contract with the Texas Rangers. Coming off a 21/20 campaign the year prior, moving into the hitting paradise in Texas was supposed to add some more pop at the very least. Instead Choo somehow crashed and burned in horrific fashion as he hit only 13 home runs and stole all of 3 bases while hitting .242. Age can't be blamed as Choo was only 32-years-old, which means a look at the advanced stats is in order. A quick examination there helped supply some of the answers as Choo saw his K rate shoot way up to 24.8 percent, which was a great deal higher than the 18.7 percent he posted the year before. Choo also was less patient at the plate as his walk rate dropped. It is likely that Choo felt some pressure to justify his new contract and moving back to the American League could be blamed too. Choo has made a comeback from a terrible season before, which he accomplished back in 2012 off his DUI/injury-filled 2011 campaign, which gives hope for a bounce back. However Choo is older now and a loss of speed at his age happens. We still love the ballpark and the pedigree so we will buy at an outfielder 3 rate.

Last season was so ugly though that we also have no problems letting Choo pass on by.
PROJECTION: .278 16 HR 59 RBI 81 R 11 SB

35. **Wil Myers:** Stardom will have to wait at least another season for Tampa Bay Rays power-hitting outfielder Wil Myers. The prized return in the James Shields deal for the Rays, Myers was lauded for his above-average power while making his way up the minor league ladder. After opening eyes with 13 home runs and a .293 average in only 335 at-bats during his half-season rookie debut in 2013, Myers was primed to take that next step as 2014 dawned. We tried to temper those expectations a bit however in pointing out that Myers was far from a finished product due to a high strikeout rate that afflicts many young power hitters. Myers fell right in line with our warning, as he was simply awful the first two months of the season as he batted .227 with only 5 home runs in 198 at-bats. Strikeouts proved to be Myers' undoing as he whiffed 52 times and showed little to no patience. Young hitters who get themselves out by swinging at everything make a pitcher's job so much easier and in turn gives them little incentive to throw anything down the middle of the plate to drive. Myers is certainly capable of being a 30-home run masher down the line but first he has to get his swing in order to even reach 25. Myers in actuality is falling into that post-hype sleeper territory however so don't let him fall too far into the discount bin.
PROKECTION: .266 23 HR 71 RBI 70 R 10 SB

36. **Marlon Byrd:** Many snickered when the Philadelphia Phillies gave Marlon Byrd a two-year contract in free agency off his hard-to-believe 2013 campaign with the New York Mets when he hit 21 home runs, collected 71 RBI, and posted a .285 average. This just a year after Byrd took a 50-game PED suspension and had to settle for a minor-league deal by the Mets. Given seemingly one last chance to stay in the majors, Byrd was shockingly good. There was a tremendous amount of doubt regarding the believability of the numbers however given Byrd's past but the Phillies bought in. The result was that Byrd improved on his Mets numbers as he slugged 25 home runs and collected 85 RBI while hitting .264. Clearly hitting in the homer-haven that is Philly had its advantages and Byrd has one more year at least to take advantage despite the fact he turns an ancient 37 in August. This is cheap pop personified and worth the cost of an outfielder 3.
PROJECTION: .262 23 HR 84 RBI 68 R 1 SB

37. **Kole Calhoun:** The Los Angeles Angels went into the 2014 season with their stated goal being to take superstar outfielder Mike Trout out of the

leadoff spot and instead move him down slightly in the order so as to better take advantage of his exploding run producing abilities. Their best hope to make that happen was the developing Kole Calhoun who opened some eyes the year before when he hit 8 home runs and batted .282 in only 195 at-bats. Despite dealing with the injury bug as times, Calhoun proved to be completely up to the task as the Angels' everyday leadoff man as he cracked 17 home runs and scored 90 runs while hitting .272. Calhoun clearly is not your typical leadoff hitter in that he doesn't steal bases (only 5 in 8 attempts for all of 2014) and his OBP is not stellar. However Calhoun does a little of everything outside of the steals which certainly passes the mustard test for an everyday fantasy baseball outfielder. Calhoun is already 27 despite going into his third season so don't expect much improvement going forward.

PROJECTION: .278 19 HR 61 RBI 95 R 6 SB

38. **Jayson Werth:** Yes he is grossly overpaid but veteran Washington Nationals outfielder Jayson Werth continues to log very useful numbers for his fantasy baseball owners as he reaches his mid-30's. Outside of losing 9 home runs from the year before and a bit of his batting average, Werth pretty much matched his 2013 numbers. No stranger to injury, Werth remains a prime health risk, which grows even more pronounced as he enters his age-36 season. Getting back to the money issue, Werth has served as a strange case where his draft value has been hurt by the public disgust of his massive contract. Thinking that Werth is overrated based on how much he is being paid, he has continually been drafted lower than he should be when you see that he hit 25 home runs with a .318 batting average just two years ago. Take the discounted rate and get on board for one more season.

PROJECTION: .286 19 HR 83 RBI 86 R 8 SB

39. **Gregory Polanco:** Universally considered one of the best outfield prospects in the game entering 2014, Gregory Polanco forced the Pittsburgh Pirates to promote him in June after he hit .328 at Triple-A. Compared by some to teammate Andrew McCutchen with regards to his ability to run like the wind and hit for power, Polanco was not fully ready for the major leagues last season as he batted only .235. Polonco won't turn 24 until this September so he is still very young and his upside is immense. Buy low on the somewhat "disappointing" debut and reap possibly big rewards.

PROJECTION: .272 17 HR 62 RBI 79 RBI 27 SB

40. **Melky Cabrera:** Yes there was life after Biogenesis. Right along the lines (albeit at a lesser extent) of Nelson Cruz' monster season after getting popped the year prior in the scandal, Toronto Blue Jays outfielder Melky

Cabrera took his career back from the cliff with a tremendous 2014 campaign. Batting at or near the top of an explosive lineup, Cabrera batted .301 with 16 home runs, 81 runs scored, 73 RBI, and 6 steals. In other words, Cabrera did a bit of everyting in terms of standard fantasy baseball leagues. One has to figure that Cabrera and every other player who has been suspended for steroid use would come back the next season clean which means we can feel more confident in the numbers he supplied last year. Since the whole Biogenesis scandal, Cabrera has kept up mid-teens power but his steals diminished greatly, not to mention his batting average after he put up an outlier .346 mark in 2012. Solid is the word to use here and Cabrera's sketchy recent history makes him somewhat of a value play relative to his 2014 numbers as an outfielder 3.

PROJECTION: .298 14 HR 70 RBI 77 R 5 SB

41. **Lorenzo Cain:** Sometimes it really is as simple as staying healthy. In the case of Kansas City Royals outfielder Lorenzo Cain, his tremendous speed and solid bat made him a decent sleeper candidate prior to both the 2012 and 2013 seasons. Unfortunately Cain missed extensive time in both campaigns due to injury and the results when on the field were underwhelming. The Royals were determined to see it through with Cain however, so perfectly did his skills fit into the team's speed-first mentality when it came to their batting lineup. Their persistence paid off last year as Cain finally posted that season many expected as he batted .301 with 5 home runs and 28 stolen bases. Cain loves nothing more than to wreak havoc on the basepaths and 30 steals is not out of the question to go with an uptick in runs for 2015. The threat of more injuries is real and Cain has little pop so be sure not to go overboard when it comes to what you will pay on draft day. Slot him in as an outfielder 3 and pass if the competition gets too fierce for his services.

PROJECTION: .288 7 HR 56 RBI 65 R 29 SB

42. **A.J. Pollock:** What might have been. It certainly looked like A.J. Pollock was heading for a major and unexpected breakout season in 2014 before a fractured hand caused by an HBP led to surgery that cost him three months. However in the three months Pollock was on the field, he was simply outstanding as he hit 7 home runs and stole 14 bases while batting .302. Keep in mind the pedigree is there as Pollock was the team's 2009 first round pick and his power/speed game is very enticing going forward. Last season's injury could be a blessing in disguise as Pollock is another guy whose lack of plate appearances kept his numbers down to where it didn't draw as much attention as it could have. Buy in fully to the legitimacy of the numbers and reach a round or two early.

PROJECTION: .288 15 HR 65 RBI 80 R 25 SB

43. **Carlos Beltran:** The New York Yankees took a big gamble in giving a three-year free agent contract to Carlos Beltran prior to the 2014 season, believing that two straight years of relative health in St. Louis and the use of the DH in the American League could continue to keep his body spry enough to give them around 25 home runs and 90 RBI. Beltran fell way short of those marks however as his old injury-marred ways returned in very ugly fashion. A persistent elbow problem nagged Beltran pretty much all year and robbed him of 53 games and a ton of his power when in the lineup. The ugly result was 15 home runs and 49 RBI and a .233 average. Clearly Beltran is a better player than that but only if he can stay healthy which of course is a major question mark as his already fragile knees are turning 38. We love the ballpark of course but investing in Beltran as anything but a bench outfielder in leagues that play three is foolish given his age and injury nature. With his speed completely vanished, the power waning, and his average quickly moving south, Beltran is looking ready to fall off the fantasy baseball landscape completely.
PROJECTION: .265 19 HR 77 RBI 72 R 2 SB

44. **Alex Rios:** The end looks near for outfielder Alex Rios who took some heat off teammate Shin-Soo Choo with his similarly awful 2014 season. The longtime 5-tool force saw his power fall almost completely off the map last year as he hit only 4 longballs in 492 at-bats while calling one of the best power-inducing ballparks home. Rios hit 25 home runs as recently as 2012 but he began the leakage in 2013 by sliding to 18, which than led to last season's paltry 4. In addition, Rios seemed to lose his speed overnight as he went from his career-high 42 steals to only 17 the last two years. Rios is now 34-years-old which is not ancient but at the same time is entering into the statistical danger zone. There is a glimmer of hope that Rios can grab back some of his lost numbers in 2015 as he has made a career out of doing the opposite of what was expected. Last seasons was so disturbingly bad however that Rios is best left as a low-end outfielder 3 at best.
PROJECTION: .278 11 HR 65 RBI 67 R 16 SB

45. **Josh Hamilton:** It certainly has been a roller coaster ride of a career for Los Angeles Angels outfielder Josh Hamilton. After battling back from a drug addiction that had him suspended from baseball, the former number 1 overall pick in the 1999 draft finally unleashed his mammoth power at an MVP level in a short four-year window from 2010-2013. Unfortunately Hamilton's years of hard living are taking a premature toll on his body, aging him at a quicker rate that other players his age. The result is that the current version of Hamilton is that of an injury-plagued, fading power hitter

whose "good" season now is 20 home runs and 80 RBI. Spare yourself the aggravation.

PROJECTION: .267 20 HR 75 RBI 74 R 4 SB

46. **Desmond Jennings:** At this stage of the game, it is now fair to say that Desmond Jennings has not developed anywhere near what most had expected, including the Tampa Bay Rays themselves. Compared to the Rays version of Carl Crawford when he started coming up the team's minor league system, Jennings instead has suffered from horrible yearly batting averages and stolen base numbers that leave a lot to be desired for somebody whose main strength was supposed to come in the run game. Jennings' 2014 was pretty much a carbon copy of his 2013 numbers, which is not a good thing as he batted only .244 with 10 home runs and 15 steals. At 28-years-old, Jennings is at the stage of his career where his current numbers are who he truly is as a player and that barely means outfielder 3 status. Over the last three seasons Jennings has failed to hit better than .252, has struck out over 100 times in each, and has seen his stolen base numbers drop in every year in that span as well. In other words there really is not anything to recommend here at all.

PROJECTION: .257 14 HR 53 RBI 82 R 22 SB

47. **Ben Zobrist:*****SEE SECOND BASEMAN RANKINGS!******

48. **Curtis Granderson:** Sometimes projecting players is easy such as in the case of New York Mets outfielder Curtis Granderson when the 2014 season dawned. The Mets signed Granderson to a four-year deal worth $60 million dollars to add much-needed punch to their previously listless lineup and also to give David Wright some more protection. On the surface it seemed like a sound move as Granderson reached the 40-home run plateau both in 2011 and 2012 while with the cross-town Yankees. Granderson in the Bronx was a match made in hitting heaven due to his lefty bat being able to take aim at the short rightfield porch for 81 games a season and the results followed suit. However in moving from the Yankees to the Mets, Granderson went from one hitting extreme to the other when it came to the home run tendencies of the ballparks. With Citi Field serving as one of the best pitching parks in the game since its opening, it was predictable that Granderson would lose a good deal of his power. That is exactly what happened as Granderson hit only 22 home runs, drove in a very light 66 batters, and batted an awfu .227. Flat out Granderson was a bust both in his first season with the Mets and for his 2014 fantasy baseball owners. Granderson will turn 34 in March and his hitting profile is already looking like age is setting in. For one thing, Granderson continues to strike out at a

very high clip (141 in last season's 564 at-bats) and his speed looks like it is close to being shot as he stole all of 8 bags in 10 attempts. Perhaps most alarming was that Granderson hit lefties (.245) better than righties (.220) which is not the split you want. And when you consider that in his career Granderson has pounded righties and struggled against lefties, one has to wonder just how bad things are getting for him at the dish. One possible saving grace here is that the Mets hired Kevin Long as their hitting coach, who of course filled the same job for the Yankees when Granderson had his 40-home run seasons. It is possible Long will get Granderson back on track like he did prior to 2011 but the signs and situations are pretty much all bad.
PROJECTION: .245 23 HR 78 RBI 79 R 7 SB

49. **Torii Hunter:** We always have had a soft spot in our fantasy baseball hearts for ageless veteran outfielder Torii Hunter who quietly had a great career. Perennially one of the better five-tool players in the game who could swat long home runs as easily as he could steal second base, Hunter will return for one more go-around after the Detroit Tigers' ugly postseason exit. As far as his current stock is concerned, Hunter is no longer a factor in the steals department, as he picked up only 4 steals last season in 7 attempts and 2009 was also the last time he reached double-digits in that category. Despite the loss of steals, Hunter still managed to be a four-category guy in 2014 as he hit 17 home runs, collected 83 RBI, and batted a solid .286. Those totals were even more impressive when you consider Hunter was 39. Despite turning 40 in July, Hunter can do a close replication of his 2014 numbers and be a useful outfielder 3. One more chance to salute one of the better players of his generation.
PROJECTION: .278 15 HR 80 RBI 73 R 2 SB

50. **Ben Revere:** We would venture to guess you didn't know that Philadelphia Phillies outfielder Ben Revere stole 49 bases last season. The leadoff speed demon surely has the goods when it comes to supplying plentiful stolen bases at a very affordable price. Since becoming a regular with the Minnesota Twins in 2011, Revere's season stolen base totals have read 34, 40, 22 (in only 315 at-bats), and last year's 49. In addition, Revere is not strictly a one-trick pony as he is a career .291 hitter who can score you between 70 and 80 runs. However that is as far as Revere's value goes as the 2 home runs he hit last season were the first two in his five-year MLB career and his high for RBI is only 32. This is not the worst place in the world to get a bunch of your stolen bases and we like Revere because of the positive contributions he makes in two other categories. Scott Podsednick he is not.
PROJECTION: .300 1 HR 29 RBI 77 R 45 SB

51. **J.D. Martinez:** Yeah hitting behind Miguel Cabrera certainly has its benefits. Just ask Detroit Tigers outfielder J.D. Martinez who took advantage of all the fastballs he saw behind his teammate last season to crack 23 home runs (12 more than his previous MLB high), 76 RBI, and a .315 batting average. Prior to 2014, Martinez had washed out of the Houston Astros organization after three years of listless hitting that included back-to-back years where his batting average came in at .241 and .250. The Tigers bought low in a "what the heck" move and won big based on the numbers. Expecting Martinez to repeat such out of the blue results is asking a lot considering the lack of track record but again hitting behind Cabrera will give him plenty of chances to at least come close. This is a very cheap source of 20-plus home runs to help round out your starting outfield.
PROJECTION: .280 21 HR 73 RBI 61 R 5 SB

52. **Josh Harrison:*****SEE SECOND BASEMAN RANKINGS!********

53. **Leonys Martin:** Leonys Martin ended up on more than a few sleeper lists heading into the 2014 season after he stole 36 bases and hit 8 home runs in a quietly eye-opening 2013 rookie campaign. Speed clearly was the main selling point when it came to Martin but the fact he could pop a few home runs made him more attractive than your standard stolen base guy. Despite calling Texas home, Martin actually hit one fewer homer (7) in 2014 even though he received an additional 76 at-bats. Still Martin swiped 31 bags and scored 68 runs while batting .274. In other words good but far from great. Martin will come cheaper this season as he was not a universally accepted player prior to 2014 and many will also conclude he failed to live up to the mild hype he had. Group Martin in with your Ben Revere's and Rajai Davis' of the world and select who comes the cheapest.
PROJECTION: .273 8 HR 44 RBI 71 R 34 SB

54. **Khris Davis:** Who knew that this version of Khris (Chris) Davis would be the better performing hitter in 2014? That is exactly what happened as the Milwaukee Brewers' version actually would up being a sleeper who made good on his potential last season as he hit 22 home runs in a little over 500 at-bats. However it wasn't all great as Davis got exposed as an everyday regular in terms of the holes in his swing. Davis became somewhat of a hacker as he struck out 122 times which went a long way toward him finishing with a poor .244 average. There is affordable 25 home run pop here and Davis could boost his average to a more useful .260 now that he has more experience against major league pitching. Ultimately we prefer Davis as your top outfield reserve but he sneaks in as a low-end starter.
PROJECTION: .258 23 HR 72 RBI 74 R 5 SB

55. Brandon Moss:**SEE FIRST BASEMAN RANKINGS!******

56. Chris Carter:***SEE FIRST BASEMAN RANKINGS!******

57. Mookie Betts:***SEE SECOND BASEMAN RANKINGS!*****

58. Evan Gattis:***SEE CATCHER RANKINGS!******

59. Martin Prado:****SEE SECOND BASEMAN RANKINGS!*****

60. **Nick Markakis:** It has been nearly six years since Nick Markakis was seen as one of the best young hitters in all of baseball as he finished the 2009 season with an 18 HR/101 RBI campaign at the age of only 25. However Markakis mysteriously lost his power and run producing abilities from that point forward when he should have been settling into his prime seasons. After nearly dropping off the fantasy baseball landscape, Markakis successfully turned around his spiraling career by settling back into a low-teens home run hitter who scored over 80 runs while batting in the .270 region. Nothing outlandish of course but Markakis can serve as a good enough outfielder 3.
PROJECTION: .271 14 HR 55 RBI 86 R 5 SB

61. Steve Pearce:***SEE FIRST BASEMAN RANKINGS!*****

62. **Dexter Fowler:** Once a top sleeper candidate that many fought over in drafts when he first arrived on the scene with the Colorado Rockies, Dexter Fowler has fallen into "just another name" status. This is especially true after Fowler was dealt by the Rockies to the Houston Astros prior to the 2014 season. Fowler failed to impress his new club as he battled injuries and hit only 8 home runs with a .276 average. Now in fairness, those who play in five outfielder formats could use the 10 home runs and 15 steals Fowler brings but his sleeper status appeal vanished for good once he left Coors Field.
PROJECTION: .272 11 HR 41 RBI 74 R 14 SB

63. Nick Castellanos:***SEE THIRD BASEMAN RANKINGS!****

64. **Angel Pagan:** While San Francisco Giants outfielder Angel Pagan has generally carried outfielder 3 status since becoming a regular, his extreme battle against injuries the last two years have greatly depressed his value. Pagan has played in only 167 games combined the last two years as he has suffered through more than a few health issues and his numbers have slipped badly as a result. Age has not been kind to Pagan's body and the

fact he will turn 34 in July drives that point home. If Pagan can somehow amass 500 at-bats, 10 home runs and 30 stolen bases would be the sweet payoff but that is a big question mark. As a veteran guy who was never a household name to begin with, Pagan carries some bounce back appeal for the cost of a very late pick.
PROJECTION: .284 7 HR 48 RBI 67 R 19 SB

65. **Mike Morse:******SEE OUTFIELDER RANKINGS!********

66. **Dustin Ackley:*****SEE SECOND BASEMAN RANKINGS!*******

67. **Shane Victorino:** Now the Boston Red Sox see why we all ridiculed that shortsighted three-year contract they gave Shane Victorino prior to the 2013 season. While Victorino made the Red Sox look smart that first season under the deal in posting a semi-comeback campaign that reversed some growing declines, the fallout came in 2014 when his body completely betrayed him. Victorino was a giant health mess last season as he logged only 30 games and 123 at-bats that yielded all of 2 home runs and 2 stolen bases. We can't imagine Victorino having much left in the tank as he enters his age-33 season and with a body that is failing him. The Red Sox will not hesitate to move Victorino to the bench or into a platoon situation if he struggles early on and as always, investing in aging "name" players is always a bad idea.
PROJECTION: .272 11 HR 60 RBI 77 R 14 SB

68. **Domonic Brown:** The red flags blared all around Domonic Brown in 2013 from this peanut stand, despite the fact the Philadelphia Phillies outfielder posted a breakout season with 27 home runs and 83 RBI. It appeared as though Brown had finally figured out how to stick with the Phillies after more than a few failed attempts from 2010 through 2012. However we included Brown prominently in our "Bust" list in last season's draft guide, not buying into the numbers. One of the big issues we had was the fact Brown struck out 97 times in his 496 at-bats and it was only for some fortunate BABIP luck that he was able to hit .272. In addition, Brown walked only 39 times which was another problem that would hurt him going forward. We correctly concluded that opposing pitchers would take advantage of the impatience Brown habitually showed, while also working on the obvious holes in his swing. That is exactly what took place last season as Brown got virtually nothing to hit down the middle of the plate and instead began chasing everything out of the zone as per his impatient approach. The numbers slid off the map as Brown posted an unsightly .235 batting average, while only being able to hit 10 home runs in 473 at-bats.

Now it is up to Brown to respond to the approach pitchers are taking against him which is certainly not a given. We can't stand investing in high strikeout/average liability players such as this as they historically supply more headaches than positives.

PROJECTION: .251 17 HR 68 RBI 56 R 7 SB

69. **Adam Eaton:** For the second season in a row, injuries derailed a chance for the speedy Adam Eaton to reveal his ability as a possible fantasy baseball asset. After Eaton was traded from the Arizona Diamondbacks to the Chicago White Sox in the Mark Trumbo deal, his new team immediately penciled him into the team's leadoff spot. Unfortunately Eaton didn't show a whole lot of flash as he hit all of one home run in a power-inducing park and collected a modest 15 stolen bases. The .300 average was nice and no surprise as Eaton put up a string of those in the minor leagues but it was as empty as could be. Eaton is starting to run out of time to prove he deserves our attention.

PROJECTION: .297 5 HR 38 RBI 82 R 19 SB

70. **Alejandro De Aza:** Now a veteran player at the age of 31, Alejandro De Aza moves along as a low-end outfielder 3 in fantasy baseball terms. The former free agent signing from the Dominican Republic has 20-steal speed to go with the ability to pop 10-15 home runs, which is nothing to sneeze at. However the Chicago White Sox showed little hesitation in shipping him off to the Baltimore Orioles at last season's trade deadline and his status as a starting player is somewhat murky. There is never a whole lot of competition with regards to getting your hands on De Aza and there are many players who are comparable as well, which eliminates much of his limited draft appeal.

PROJECTION: .253 10 HR 61 RBI 78 R 16 SB

71. **Oswaldo Arcia:** Cheap pop alert! While any Minnesota Twins hitter instantly carries a red mark next to their names due to the power deficiencies of Target Field, Oswaldo Arcia showed in 2014 that few ballparks could hold back his natural power. Arcia managed to hit 20 home runs in only 372 at-bats and he was a prospect who showed good long-ball skills in the minor leagues. Unfortunately Arcia does fit squarely into the classic "high strikeout/power hitter" mode (127 K's in last year's 372 at-bats), so the batting average is not going to look pretty. Still Arcia is extremely young at 24 and has every right to improve both his average and power with some more experience against major league pitching. Another guy to stash in your queue for the last few rounds of your draft.

PROJECTION: .259 23 HR 62 RBI 54 R 2 SB

72. **Dayan Viciedo:** Before the recent explosion of overnight Cuban imports-turned-All-Stars, Dayan Viciedo began to blaze the trail for his countryman when he defected before the 2010 season. Signed by the Chicago White Sox, Viciedo since that time has been a guy who has above-average power and not much else given his .254 career average. Viciedo has hit 20 or more home runs twice in the last three years which is nice but there is little upside left as he turns 26.
PROJECTION: .251 20 HR 59 RBI 67 R 0 SB

73. **Avisail Garcia:** The Chicago White Sox and fantasy baseball owners of outfielder Avisail Garcia didn't get much of a look at the promising youngster in 2014 as he missed most of the season with injury. Despite all the missed time, Garcia showed tantalizing ability in hitting 7 home runs and stealing 4 bases in only 172 at-bats. The power/speed ability is real and while Garcia could struggle to hit for a solid average right away due to strikeouts, the upside value here is very interesting.
PROJECTION: .275 15 HR 55 RBI 59 R 8 SB

74. **Gerard Parra:** A little of this and a little of that. That would be the fantasy baseball analysis of Milwaukee Brewers outfielder Gerardo Parra. Over the last two seasons, Parra has hit 10 and 9 home runs, while also stealing 10 and 9 bases. Parra is a pure leadoff guy all the way who carries better value in five outfielder fomats as he is only a .274 career hitter and his high for runs scored is a modest 79. He figures to lead off for the Brewers again in 2014 and will more than likely replicate his 2013-14 numbers again.
PROJECTION: .272 10 HR 45 RBI 74 R 10 SB

75. **Brock Holt:******SEE FIRST BASEMAN RANKINGS!*******

76. **Allen Craig:*****SEE FIRST BASEMAN RANKINGS!*******

77. **Rajai Davis:** Heading into the 2014 season, the Detroit Tigers planned to use a platoon in leftfield split between speedster Rajai Davis and thumper Andy Dirks. That plan quickly fell apart however as Dirks got hurt in spring training and never played a game during the season. That meant Davis was once again an everyday player and the results were pretty good as he batted .282 atop the lineup with 36 steals. Few in baseball are more potent than Davis when it comes to collecting stolen bases as he has picked up 40 or more in four of the last six seasons. Davis is also not a pure stolen base specialist as he cracked 8 home runs last season and picked up 51 RBI.

Dirks will be fully healthy when the 2015 season begins however and the Tigers could once again revisit the platoon idea. Even if that plan does take place, Davis will play often enough to steal at least another 30 bases. **PROJECTION: .267 7 HR 46 RBI 63 R 32 SB**

78. **Denard Span:** The Washington Nationals wasted little time in picking up the $9 million option for 2015 on outfielder and the team's leadoff batter Denard Span. Span made the decision easy after arguably having his best ever season in 2014 as he batted .302 with 31 stolen bases and 94 runs scored. Since becoming a regular back in 2008 with the Minnesota Twins, Span had been a pretty boring fantasy baseball investment due to his utter lack of pop and for the fact he didn't exactly light up any one category. Still if Span can replicate his 2014 haul, we are looking at a three-category helper who fits in nicely as an outfielder 3. **PROJECTION: .282 4 HR 43 RBI 91 R 27 SB**

79. **Andre Ethier:** Unless he gets shipped out of town via trade, the fantasy baseball value of Los Angeles Dodgers outfielder Andre Ethier can't get any lower. A four-time 20-plus home run hitter in his career with the Dodgers, Ethier is now toward the bottom of the five-deep outfield hierarchy on the team. Ethier also has seen his home run rate go into the toilet **PROJECTION: .268 11 HR 55 RBI 51 R 2 SB**

80. **Austin Jackson:** The riddle that is Austin Jackson continues. There has been no rhyme or reason to Jackson's year-to-year numbers in his still-young career and that has made him one of the more frustrating players to own since he broke into the majors back in 2010 with the Detroit Tigers. Jackson looked like the next power/speed five-tool player early on but his utter lack of any sort of consistency and a sky-high K rate have combined to degrade him into backup outfielder status in fantasy baseball. The Tigers joined many of Jackson's owners in running out of patience with the guy, sending him to the Seattle Mariners at last season's trading deadline. Overall Jackson hit the 20-steal mark for the first time since 2011 which was nice but only 4 home runs and a .256 average leave a ton to be desired. Stop trying to figure this one out. **PROJECTION: .262 7 HR 45 RBI 67 R 16 SB**

81. **Logan Morrison:********SEE FIRST BASEMAN RANKINGS!****

82. **Chris Coghlan:*******SEE THIRD BASEMAN RANKINGS!****

83. **Nick Swisher:********SEE FIRST BASEMAN RANKINGS!*****

84. **Juan Lagares:** If defense was a fantasy baseball category, Juan Lagares would be a top tier talent. Unfortunately defense has no place in the fake game which means the still-developing Lagares leaves a lot to be desired when it comes to his offensive numbers. Lagares wasn't horrible last season as he mostly served as the Mets' leadoff hitter. He used his speed there to swipe 13 bases and bat a respectable .281. However Lagares has limited power, with only 4 home runs in his 416 at-bats and he also has not proven he can stay healthy due to his all-out style in centerfield. Watch his progress but wait on making a play.
PROJECTION: .278 6 HR 52 RBI 62 R 16 SB

85. **Carl Crawford:** It is remarkable the depths Carl Crawford has fallen when it comes to both his numbers and his fantasy baseball value. Since his last top-notch season in 2010 with the Tampa Bay Rays, Crawford has been one gigantic mess. The biggest issue of course are the massive amount of injuries Crawford has suffered since signing that ridiculous free agent deal with the Boston Red Sox prior to the 2011 season. The physical maladies have robbed Crawford of much of his speed which is a huge problem considering that was the most valuable part of his game. Now just a part-time player in a crowded Los Angeles Dodgers outfield, Crawford has virtually no appeal left to his name.
PROJECTION: .284 7 HR 45 RBI 62 R 21 SB

86. **Coco Crisp:** Annually one of the better value plays in fantasy baseball, it surely looked like Coco Crisp began going over the statistical cliff in 2014. The negative signs came from everywhere as Crisp hit only 9 home runs (a drop from 22 the previous year), stole only 19 bases (the fourth straight season of decline there), and batted only .244 which was his lowest mark ever with more than 300 at-bats. Now 35-years-old, Crisp may not even hold a starting job this season as he continues to fade. It was fun while it lasted.
PROJECTION: .259 10 HR 45 RBI 65 R 17 SB

87. **Colby Rasmus:** Now we all can understand why Tony LaRusso got so frustrated with outfielder Colby Rasmus when he was managing the St. Louis Cardinals. Blessed with terrific natural power, hitting home runs has not been a problem for Rasmus. Pretty much everything else has been an issue as Rasmus posts terrible K rates each and every year which has resulted in a pathetic .246 career average now 6 full seasons in the rearview mirror. Rasmus has not done much of anything in the stolen base category either which would have helped offset some of the damage when it comes to his batting average. Thus what we have here is a one-trick power pony who

is now fully past his ceiling years. Both a real-life and fantasy baseball bust.
PROJECTION: .243 21 HR 67 RBI 55 R 5 SB

88. **Will Venable:** One of the more surprising performances of the 2013 season was the 20/20 season (22 HR/22 SB) that San Diego Padres outfielder Will Venable put up. Known for his decent stolen base ability but not much else, Venable's 2014 was determined to prove his previous year's numbers were legit. Venable failed in that endeavor however as his .224 batting average was the worst of his career and he would up with only 8 home runs and 11 stolen bases. Once again strikeouts were kryptonite for Venable who now is only a .252 career hitter. With Venable showing that his 2013 was a fluke and with his continued residence in Petco Park, we find it tough to find anything to recommend.
PROJECTION: .251 9 HR 48 RBI 63 R 21 SB

89. **Michael Bourn:** Speed doesn't age all that well as Cleveland Indians outfielder Michael Bourn could attest to. Long one of the more overrated players in fantasy baseball, Bourn saw himself get drafted in the high middle rounds due to his ability to contribute in only two categories (runs and steals). Now 32 years of age, Bourn's legs are betraying him as he stole only 10 bases last season and dealt with constant hamstring injuries. The fact Bourn collected only 10 steals in 444 at-bats show you how badly his legs are shot. Since Bourn supplies pretty much nothing else, his days as a fantasy baseball asset are completely finished.
PROJECTION: .255 5 HR 45 RBI 71 R 20 SB

90. **Matt Joyce:** If the fantasy baseball season only spanned from April through June, Matt Joyce would be a top-end outfielder 3. The Tampa Bay Rays veteran outfielder bats 30 points higher and has hit 57 of his career 88 home runs the first three months of the season. Of course the fantasy baseball season goes for six months and by the time July rolls around, Joyce takes his place on the waiver wire. In addition to his pre-and-post All-Star splits, Joyce is also ghastly against lefties given his .189 career mark. Mix and match according to the pitcher early on and than cut bait when the inevitable struggles arrive.
PROJECTION: .246 16 HR 51 RBI 56 R 4 SB

91. **B.J. Upton:** After signing a large free agent contract with the Atlanta Braves, Justin Upton's older brother B.J. had what many consider the worst season of any hitter in the majors in 2013. The numbers were enough to

make an owner lose his lunch on multiple occasions as Upton batted a ridiculously bad .184, while also managing to hit only 9 home runs and steal all of 12 bases. With the Braves locked in with Upton due to his contract, they had no choice but to stick him in the lineup for 2014 as well. Upton's 2013 campaign was so horrific that there was nowhere to go but up last season and he responded somewhat by batting .208, while boosting his home runs and steals to 12 and 20 respectively. Still the fact of the matter is that Upton is radioactive to own due to his pathetic batting average and his sliding power/speed numbers. While Upton will turn only 31 in August, he looks like a guy who has no shot to ever sniff his past as a 20-plus home run/40-steal outfielder 2. Ignore completely.
PROJECTION: .230 12 HR 59 RBI 74 R 23 SB

THE REST

92. **Jarrod Dyson:** Jarrod Dyson is the perfect example of how stolen bases can be found in large quantities on the waiver wire each season. Despite serving only as a part-time player for the Royals during the last three seasons, Dyson has stolen more than 30 bases in each of those years. The Royals have stuck by their belief that Dyson is not worthy of being a part of the everyday lineup and as along as that remains, he pretty much is a one-trick stolen base pony.

93. **Sam Fuld:** A few steals and nothing else. Fuld is a .236 hitter who is entering into the journeyman realm.

94. **Travis Snider:** Travis Snider never panned out in Toronto where the team made him their first round pick (14th overall) in the 2006 draft. The natural power that Snider possessed was always buttressed by an awful approach at the plate that has resulted in a .246 career batting average and a ton of strikeouts. The Blue Jays cut their losses on Snider during the 2012 season, sending him to the Pittsburgh Pirates where he has been a part-time guy since. Unless Snider finds a starting spot in the Pirates outfield and stops striking out in 30 percent of his plate appearances, he has zero fantasy baseball value.

95. **Ichiro Suzuki:** The end is near for future first-ballot Hall Of Fame Japanese outfielder Ichiro Suzuki. The former batting champ is leaking numbers all over the place and pretty much now is just an empty .280 average guy. Could grab hold of a platoon situation for one more season but this ship has sailed.

96. **Eric Young:** Another in the abundant class of cheap speed for 2015 fantasy baseball. Young served as a part-time outfielder for the New York Mets last season but still managed to steal 30 bases despite only collecting 280 at-bats. Unfortunately that was the extent of Young's contributions as he batted only .229 and proved himself a poor fit in the leadoff slot due to a terrible .299 OBP. Young figures to fill the same role for the Mets in 2015 that he did a year ago which means waiver territory.

97. **Seth Smith:** Seth Smith will be a guy you feel tempted to pick up once or twice during a given season but he will undoubtedly disappoint you again with his overall mediocre ability. At one time an intriguing Colorado Rockies outfielder who had some power and speed, Smith has been mostly waiver fodder after the team let him go to the Oakland A's prior to the 2012 season. Now in home run-killing Petco Park with the San Diego Padres, Smith will once again take his place in the waiver wire hotel.

98. **Emilio Bonifacio:*****SEE SECOND BASEMAN RANKINGS!*****

99. **Daniel Nava:*****SEE FIRST BASEMAN RANKINGS!****

100. **Nori Aoki:** Despite only entering into his fourth major league season as we approach 2015, Nori Aoki is already 33 years old. Thus it should be no surprise that Aoki's best season was during his 2012 rookie campaign. After hitting 10 home runs and stealing 30 bases in his 2012 debut, Aoki slipped all the way to 1 and 17 respectively in those two categories last year, which is worrisome. While Aoki is still a fine leadoff hitter as evidenced by his .349 OBP, the numbers simply are not there for fantasy baseball usage outside of five outfielder formats.

101. **Corey Hart:** Stick a fork in him. Corey Hart's career is in serious jeopardy as rampant knee problems have sapped him of his power and sunk his stock into the gutter. It is likely Hart is going to have to make a roster this spring given how much time he has missed and how ugly his bat has looked when on the field. Ignore outright.

102. **Garrett Jones:******SEE FIRST BASEMAN RANKINGS!****

103. **Jordan Schafer:** Jordan Schafer never came close to reaching the potential that some saw in him as a guy who could possibly hit around 15 home runs while stealing a bunch of bases. Instead Schafer has become a journeyman who struggles to hit for average. A pure one category stolen

base specialist at best. You can always find steals on the wire throughout the season so investing a draft pick here would be a waste.

104. **Chris Young:** Was simply brutal with the New York Mets before catching some late life after being picked up by the Yankees. Still Young's days as a starter both in real-life and in fantasy baseball are through.

105. **Ender Inciarte:** A virtual unknown prior to the 2014 season, the Arizona Diamondbacks gave speedy outfielder Ender Inciarte a chance to show his skills for a team looking to get younger. Inciarte proved up to the task as he hit .278 with 4 home runs and 19 stolen bases in only 418 at-bats. Overall Inciarte is a classic example of how stolen bases appear on the waiver wire pretty much throughout each and every season, thus lessening the need to draft speed-centric players until late. Think younger Nori Aoki here.
PROJECTION: .276 7 HR 38 RBI 67 R 25 SB

106. **David Murphy:** Drove in a lot of runs early on for the Cleveland Indians but Murphy eventually went back to his career norms as a waiver guy you add only when he is hot and injuries take down one of your starters.

107. **Michael Saunders:** Can hit the odd home run and steal some bases but Saunders is an average-killer who can't help you for more than a small hot stretch.

108. **Nate Schierholtz:** Fell back to his career norms as a bench guy after his surprising 2013 power output. Mediocre bat all the way.

109. **Chris Heisey:** Takes on some appeal when pressed into a starting spot for the Cincinnati Reds when injuries take out one of their starting outfielders due to decent enough pop and speed. No reason to bother until that injury hits.

110. **Peter Bourjos:** Forget about Bourjos once and for all as we are three seasons and counting of disappointing play. Great speed but he can't get on first base to use it.

111. **Junior Lake:** Took advantage of the awful state of the Cubs to hit some home runs and steal some bases last season. Will be pushed aside by the expected infusion of talent and due to his awful contact rates however.

112.   **Anthony Gose:** Has the ability to collect steals but Gose only batted .226 last season and has little pop.

113.   Arismendy Alcantara:***SEE SHORTSTOP RANKINGS!*****

114.   **Grady Sizemore:** The comeback season didn't go so well as Grady Sizemore went through two organizations in 2014. Stop living in the past.

115.   **Zach Walters:** Hit an impressive 10 home runs in only 127 at-bats last season but that was accompanied by a putrid .181 average. Monitor early on but wait on drafting.

116.   Kyle Blanks:***SEE FIRST BASEMAN RANKINGS!****

117.   **Cameron Maybin:** Can't see Maybin being another post-hype sleeper made good given his awful K rate/batting average and propensity to get injured.

118.   **Andy Dirks:** Missed all of 2014 with a neck issue but Dirks can crack some cheap home runs if he gets healthy. Put him in the watch lists.

119.   **Nolan Reimold:** We will never know how good Nolan Reimold could be due to the fact he can't ever stay healthy for more than a few weeks at a time. A backup at best in real-life baseball.

120.   **Josh Reddick:** We called the fluke that was Josh Reddick's 2012 breakout as his ridiculous K rate was eventually going to sink his numbers. Reddick is an occasional spot guy to use only on light schedule days in the hopes he could hit the occasional home run.

121.   **Carlos Quentin:** Gets hurt when he sneezes. The power remains very good but Quentin's medical history reads like an episode of Dr. Oz.

122.   **John Jay:** Good defensive player but that is as far as the positives go when it comes to John Jay. Oh and defense is not a fantasy baseball category.

123.   **Drew Stubbs:** Going to Colorado saved Drew Stubbs' fledgling career as he hit 15 home runs and stole 20 bases in only 388 at-bats as he took part in a platoon in the team's outfield. The most shocking part of Stubbs' season was the .289 batting average, as he hadn't hit over .243 the three years prior. You should throw that .289 average out however as it screams

outlier and for the fact Stubbs struck out 136 times in those 388 at-bats which means getting back up there is almost impossible without a ton of luck. The platoon will likely be back in play for Stubbs this season which means he carries value only in five outfielder formats at best. Overall the value is just not there.

124. **Gregor Blanco:** Gregor Blanco has some nice speed which helped him to steal 16 bases last season and the five home runs were also a nice bonus. Still Blanco is a limited player overall who doesn't play everyday which makes him unusable outside of spot start.

125. **Craig Gentry:** Another very cheap source of steals you can get on the wire whenever you wish. Overall though Gentry can't hit much at all and is really only a bench guy on his own team which doesn't jive with regards to being a useful.

126. **David Peralta:** David Peralta joins Ender Inciarte as part of the potential future look of the Arizona Diamondbacks outfield. Like Inciarte, Peralta showed some intriguing ability in hitting 8 home runs and stealing 6 bases while batting .286 in only 329 at-bats. It was a somewhat small sample size so try not to overreact to the numbers but Peralta is worth a late round grab in order to see where this could go.

127. **Brandon Barnes:** After the sudden breakouts of Charlie Blackmon and Corey Dickerson, fellow young outfielder Brandon Barnes deserves a long look. There is some sneaky power/speed ability here but Barnes has thus far shown he can't hit for average.

128. **James Jones:** Speesters such as Seattle Mariners outfielder James Jones are a dime a dozen in today's small-ball game. Stealing 27 bases will get you on the fantasy baseball map but Jones has zero power (literally) and is nothing to write home about when it comes to his batting average either.

129. **Kevin Kiermaier:** Very intriguing debut last season as Kevin Kiermaier hit 10 home runs and stole 5 bases while hitting .263 for the Tampa Bay Rays. Looking forward to seeing some more but not ready yet to use a draft pick.

130. **David Lough:** Some minimal power/speed ability here due to not having a full allotment of at-bats. Could work into some value if moved into a starting spot due to injury.

131. **Jackie Bradley Jr.:** So far it has been much adieu about nothing with regards to young Boston Red Sox outfielder Jackie Bradley Jr. He has shuttled back and forth from the minors to the Red Sox and to this point has not shown much of anything. With more prime prospects getting close to promotion, Bradley is in danger of being left behind.

132. **Nate McLouth:** After posting a nice comeback season for the Baltimore Oriole in 2013, Nate McLouth went back into oblivion after signing on to be the Washington Nationals' fourth outfielder prior to 2014. While McLouth has shown he can still run, non-guaranteed playing time makes him just another guy to leave on the wire.

133. **Jose Tabata:** Has never firmly claimed a starting outfielder role with the Pittsburgh Pirates and now is being passed by the younger Gregory Polonco. Tabata has proven he knows how to steal some bases but the rest of the numbers are ugly.

STARTING PITCHING

We have gone well beyond the point of being tired of listening to ourselves regarding our firmly stated fantasy baseball sacrament of NEVER drafting starting pitching early. Since we started business almost 10 years ago, this one principle has been the bedrock rule of our draft strategies. While there is no doubt that owning a Clayton Kershaw or a Chris Sale is a dominant addition to any roster, the fact of the matter is that using a first round pick (or using a pick in the first four rounds overall) on a starting pitcher is a terrible decision on a number of fronts. Chief among them is the incredible depth that the starting pitching fraternity has developed in this post-steroids era. Virtually every single hitting statistic is way down, with some by a huge margin over the last five to seven years. Whether it is the elimination of steroids and greenies is a debate for another book but the conicidence is too tough to ignore. As a result, pitching rules fantasy baseball which means you can wait until at the earliest Round 5 (and now likely even Round 6) to get your first starter and still wind up with a top notch pitching staff. Don't believe us? How about these names? Corey Kluber, Tyson Ross, Scott Kazmir, Phil Hughes, Garrett Richards, Jake Odorizzi, Sonny Gray, Yordano Ventura, Drew Smyly, Tanner Roark, Colin McHugh, Dallas Keuchel, Jason Hammel, and Zack Wheeler. Every one of those guys was a late round pick or an undrafted waiver pickup who all pitched to ridiculously great ERA's/WHIP's and top notch K rates. And there will surely be more where that came from this season as more pitchers emerge from the minors throwing gas. And even if you wanted to own a pure ace, you could have waited until the fifth round last season to snag Jon Lester, Cole Hamels. Zack Greinke, and Julio Teheran. How would that have worked out?

Again resist the urge to grab a starting pitcher until at least Round 5 and your team will be so much better for it. We didn't even discuss the fact that starting pitching is the most injury-prone position in the game, which makes any early pick there a huge gamble. Finally the fact a starter only goes once every five days means that you get less bang for your early investment bucks. A hitter will be in there every single day and have the ability to help in all five scoring categories. A starting pitcher meanwhile can only help in four, with wins being somewhat beyond their control. Do the right thing and stay far away from this group until you have at the very least four hitters anchoring your roster.

1. **Clayton Kershaw:** There is Clayton Kershaw, followed by a giant gap, and than every other starter for 2015 fantasy baseball. While we are in the era of pitching dominance, the numbers Kershaw have accumulated in his still-young career are beyond staggering. Consider that over the last two seasons, Kershaw has posted Sandy Koufax-like ERA's of 1.83 and 1.77. In addition, Kershaw's HIGH in ERA since 2009 is only 2.91. Want some more gems? How about the fact Kershaw's career WHIP is 1.06. And that he has struck out more than 225 batters during each of the last four seasons. Still only 27, the only issue that can derail Kershaw is injury, which of course you can say about any major league player. Kershaw has only dealt with a hip ailment over the last two seasons however and has not fallen victim to any serious issue with his pitching arm which is key. Ultimately you have to decide whether you want to use a first round pick on a pitcher, even one as ridiculously dominant like Kershaw given how extremely deep this group remains. When looking at numbers alone, Kershaw is in the discussion as the best player in the game.
PROJECTION: 22-4 1.97 ERA 0.91 WHIP 234 K

2. **Max Scherzer:** A year after winning the Cy Young Award, Detroit Tigers ace power pitcher Max Scherzer rejected a sizable extension from the team and instead gambled that he could post another monster season while aiming to cash in prior to 2015. Well Scherzer's gamble paid off as he went 18-5 with an ERA of 3.15 and struck out a career-high 252 batters. Having moved past some early elbow trouble when he first arrived in the majors, Scherzer is now a workhorse strikeout maestro who should be the second pitcher off the board once Clayton Kershaw is selected. While Scherzer still walks a few too many batters, his hit rate is among the lowest in the majors and he is a great bet to lead the majors in strikeouts.

PROJECTION: 19-5 3.11 1.16 WHIP 248 K

3. **Felix Hernandez:** While Yu Darvish, Clayton Kershaw, and Max Scherzer may have gotten more of the recent headlines the last few seasons, Seattle Mariners ace Felix Hernandez remains as dominant and durable as ever. Despite a long string of top level pitching, Hernandez may have had his best season ever in 2014 when he posted a career-best 2.14 ERA and 0.92 WHIP while striking out 248 batters in 236 innings. The 248 strikeouts were also a career-high, which shows you how potent Hernandez' stuff is when you consider his fastball has lost a tick or two since he first arrived in the major leagues. Durability is key here as Hernandez has pitched 200 or more innings 7 straight seasons and counting. Despite making his debut back in 2005, Hernandez turns only 29 in April. The cost is a tad cheaper than some other aces ranked around Hernandez as well, which makes him a slightly better buy overall.
PROJECTION: 16-6 2.88 ERA 1.11 WHIP 225 K

4. **David Price:** After dealing with some health issues that impacted his 2013 campaign, David Price was back to his old dominating self in a 2014 season split between the Tampa Bay Rays and Detroit Tigers. Not letting trade rumors distract him, Price posted by far the best K rate of his career last season in punching out a major-league leading 271 batters in only 248 innings. In addition, Price won 15 games while logging a 3.26 ERA. In moving from Tampa Bay to Detroit, Price doesn't see much of a change when it comes to both locales being pitching-leaning ballparks. Now that Price's health is back in order, there is no reason he can't once again be one of the more dominant aces for 2015. Just cut back some of last season's strikeouts as that looks like an outlier number to us.
PROJECTION: 17-7 3.27 ERA 1.09 WHIP 245 K

5. **Madison Bumgarner:** Saying that San Francisco Giants ace lefty Madison Bumgarner made the 2014 playoffs his own would be the understatement of the century. Bumgarner added his name to postseason lore as he won 5 games overall and saved the World Series-clinching Game 7 to grab MVP honors. Bumgarner's 5-inning/2-hit/shutout in relief to finish off the World Series was one for the ages and his postseason dominance overshadowed another excellent regular season when he pitched to a 2.98 ERA and 1.09 WHIP while going past the 200-K mark for the first time with 219. Turning only 26 in August, Bumgarner has a long run of ace-like pitching ahead of him. The only concern we have is the insane amount of innings he tossed last season. Counting both the regular and postseason, Bumgarner threw 292.1 innings. That is a huge red flag and has to be factored into

Bumgarner's 2015 price tag. Thus far he shown extreme durability since breaking into the majors but the draft price will come in at an all-time high given how much pub Bumgarner received last season. Those who are habitual readers of ours know we have pumped up Bumgarner as much as any other publication but this time around we are leery of an investment given how much wear his arm just withstood.
PROJECTION: 19-6 2.91 ERA 1.10 WHIP 208 K

6. **Yu Darvish:** It was one big mess of a 2014 season for overpowering Texas Rangers ace Yu Darvish to say the least. First Darvish began the season on the DL with a neck issue and than he was shut down in August with elbow soreness that lingered into the offseason. In between Darvish continued to show unparalleled strikeout stuff (182 punchouts in only 144.1 innings) and posted a terrific 3.06 ERA. Darvish was also a bit more hittable last season however and he also surrendered some more walks which perhaps was an indication that he was not feeling right. Either way, Darvish is another decent risk among the top ace power pitchers this season, especially considering his elbow was still being checked on as of this writing. If all breaks right Darvish will likely lead baseball in strikeouts and post a low-3.00 ERA but for now proceed with some caution.\
PROJECTION: 15-8 3.15 ERA 1.17 WHIP 201 K

7. **Stephen Strasburg:** We have been a bit leery with regards to investing in Washington Nationals ace Stephen Strasburg the last two seasons due to his violent delivery that makes him a sizable injury risk. Now two years-plus removed from Tommy John elbow surgery, Strasburg threw a career-high 215 innings last season as the Nationals took off the training wheels with regards to monitoring his workload. The result was Strasburg's best season ever in 2014 as he posted a 3.14 ERA and 1.12 WHIP while winning 14 games. There are few peers when discussing the dominant repertoire that Strasburg possesses, as he struck out a career-high 242 batters in those 215 innings. The violent delivery remains but Strasburg is as good as it gets.
PROJECTION: 15-7 3.08 ERA 1.11 WHIP 246 K

8. **Chris Sale:** Sort of along the same lines as Stephen Strasburg, Chicago White Sox ace lefty Chris Sale engenders some fear due to a history of elbow trouble. On stuff alone, Sale is right there among the best in baseball as his hit rate is incredibly low and his ERA during his first three full seasons as a starter were 3.05, 3.07, and last year's ridiculous 2.17. You will also find Sale right near the top in strikeouts and strikeout rate as he fanned 208 batters in only 174 innings last season. Oh but that elbow. Sale has now spent time on the DL in each of the last three seasons with elbow

and shoulder trouble and again like Strasburg, a wonky delivery is likely to blame. You are amost guaranteed at least one DL stint a year with Sale which is a major drawback when drafting him but the allure of those sweet numbers is very tough to pass up.

PROJECTION: 14-9 2.72 ERA 1.02 WHIP 215 K

9. **Johnny Cueto:** Sometimes it all comes together for a starting pitcher in one gigantic package of monster numbers and wins. Such a scenario unfolded for Cincinnati Reds ace Johnny Cueto last season as he won 20 games while posting career-bests with his 2.25 ERA and total of 242 strikeouts. It was an eye-opening season for Cueto in every sense of the word. Now Cueto was perennially one of the better pitchers in the game prior to 2014, reeling off a string of three straight seasons from 2011 through 2013 where he posted ERA's under 3.00 and WHIP's of 1.17 or below. However Cueto had never shown the crazy K rate he posted last season, as his previous career-high was only the 170 he collected in 2012. We are not fully buying 2014's strikeout explosion as it blares "outlier" and Cueto has a history full of health woes to be concerned about when debating whether to make an investment. Overall this is a guy you must weight the draft price on when determining your course of action.

PROJECTION: 17-7 2.57 ERA 1.07 WHIP 190 K

10. **Adam Wainwright:** It was another Cy-Young caliber season for Adam Wainwright in 2014 as he finished the regular season with career-lows in ERA (2.38) and WHIP (1.03) in winning 20 games. What was interesting is that Wainwright seemed to pitch more to contact as his K rate dropped noticeably. While the 179 strikeouts Wainwright posted last season was still a very good number, that total was 40 fewer that the year prior. Than during the postseason, Wainwright began complaining of elbow discomfort but ultimately pitched through it. Any sort of elbow issue with Wainwright is very concerning considering he already has a Tommy John surgery in his recent past. While the reports on Wainwright early in the offseason were positive, we are still leery of using a high draft pick on a guy who already has some questionable health issues. With the Cardinals having been a postseason mainstay the last few years, those very high inning totals that Wainwright has thrown during that span could be tied in to the elbow discomfort.

PROJECTION: 17-6 2.67 ERA 1.08 WHIP 186 K

11. **Zack Greinke:** No doubt overshadowed by a certain Cy Young rotation mate, Zack Greinke was terrific in his own right in winning 17 games for the 2014 Los Angeles Dodgers. Those who know us well remember that

Greinke is a guy we have fawned over for years, taking advantage of a cheaper than it should be draft price considering the guy puts up ace-like numbers on a yearly basis. It was more of the same for Greinke last season as he finished with a 2.71 ERA and went past the 200-K (207) mark for the first time since 2011. Grienke gives up his fair share of home runs and tends to struggle a bit on the road but few have had better hit rates over the last five seasons. Once again take advantage of the discount and draft Greinke as your staff ace.

PROJECTION: 17-8 2.65 ERA 1.14 WHIP 201 K

12. **Corey Kluber:** Those who had the foresight to pick up young Cleveland Indians hurler Corey Kluber early on last season were rewarded with the best starting pitcher value in 2014 fantasy baseball. Kluber was beyond incredible in his breakout Cy Young-winning season, posting an ERA of 2.44 and a WHIP of 1.09 while winning 18 games. Most impressive were the insane 269 strikeouts Kluber collected in his 235.2 innings, a K rate that was right there at the top of the major leagues. So what did we all miss here? Kluber did give some hints at what was to come back in 2013 when he pitched to a 3.85 ERA and 1.26 WHIP in 147.1 innings. In addition, Kulber posted some very good K rates while coming up the Cleveland minor league ladder. However the overall statistical package was off-the-charts for Kluber and he instantly gets lumped into ace territory as a result. There is some leeriness here given how Kluber turned into a top pitcher almost overnight but his minor league numbers pointed to him developing into a very good power pitcher. We do expect Kluber's ERA and WHIP to rise a bit now that major league hitters have more of a book on him but overall we are firm buyers.

PROJECTION: 16-7 3.08 ERA 1.10 WHIP 235 K

13. **Matt Harvey:** The first half of the 2013 season was otherwise known as "The Matt Harvey Show" as the young New York Mets fireballing pitcher took the league by storm. Earning the right to start the All-Star Game, Harvey unleashed his 98-mph fastball and tremendous secondary stuff in turning into an ace starter almost overnight. Unfortunately Harvey joined a recent growing trend of other young pitchers to succumb to Tommy John elbow surgery after 26 starts. The results prior to the injury were spectacular as Harvey posted a 2.27 ERA and 0.93 WHIP while striking out 191 batters in only 178.1 innings. Two of the main reasons Harvey ascended so quickly outside of his explosive power stuff, was the fact he successfully worked through some of his minor league control issues. In addition, Harvey doesn't give up home runs. Now the question is whether Harvey will be the same pitcher when he returns for 2015. We are very

bullish on Harvey however as he recovered from the surgery without incident and in fact was ready to pitch last August. The Mets were smart to hold him off until 2015, as they eye a playoff push. That means Harvey had even more time to recover from the surgery which will only make him stronger. If Harvey did not go under the knife, he would have been a top five starter without a doubt. There are some who will be leery of investing here off the surgery but the success rate is very high. The discount Harvey will provide will make him quite possibly the cheapest ace-like fantasy baseball pitcher for the upcoming season.

PROJECTION: 16-9 2.81 ERA 1.11 WHIP 209 K

14. **Julio Teheran:** While he doesn't possess the strikeout totals of most of the pitchers listed above him, the Atlanta Braves' Julio Teheran's ratios certainly are as good as anyone's. It took Teheran a few promotions before he relaxed and allowed his talent to bubble to the surface but the results the last two seasons have been stellar with ERA's of 3.20 and 2.89 while winning 14 games in each. The 186 strikeouts Teheran accumulated in 2014 are about as good as he is going to do here but at only 24, there is still a window left for another small step up in production.

PROJECTION: 15-9 3.09 ERA 1.09 WHIP 188 K

15. **Jon Lester:** Jon Lester certainly timed his best season since 2010 as he entered into free agency. In a season split between the Boston Red Sox and Oakland A's, Lester pushed his K rate way back up in striking out 224 batters and finishing with a cumulative career-best ERA of 2.46. It became apparent that two World Series-winning postseason runs and very large inning totals at a young age sapped some pop from Lester's arm in both 2012 and 2013, with his strikeout level falling below 200 in both seasons, while his ERA went as high as 2012's 4.82. However Lester seemed reinvigorated last season from the start and he seemed to get stronger as the year went on. Keep in mind that the 1.10 WHIP Lester posted last season is far from his career mark of 1.28 which is our only quibble. With a massive payday on tap, Lester has reaffirmed his past status as a lower-end fantasy baseball ace starter.

PROJECTION: 17-9 3.26 ERA 1.22 WHIP 190 K

16. **Cole Hamels:** Another perennial favorite of ours along the same lines as Zack Greinke and Madison Bumgarner as affordable fantasy baseball aces, is longtime Philadelphia Phillies lefty Cole Hamels. Always moderately priced despite consistently excellent numbers, it was more of the same for Hamels in 2014 as he pitched to a career-low 2.46 ERA and struck out 198 batters in 204.2 innings. Hamels annoys some people with his tendency to

struggle a bit out of the gate, and for his career-long home run issues. Also forget the low win totals the last two seasons as Hamels has gotten some of the worst run-support of any starter in that span. The big positives are that Hamels is incredibly stingy with the hits allowed and he has logged three 200-plus K seasons in the last five years. Trade rumors continue to surround Hamels but at 31 he still has a number of ace-like years left no matter the locale.

PROJECTION: 14-10 3.02 ERA 1.15 WHIP 204 K

17. **Jordan Zimmerman:** The title of "Best Pitcher In Baseball Without 200-K Stuff" would undoubtedly belong to the Washington Nationals' Jordan Zimmerman. Having lost a bit of velocity from 2009 Tommy John surgery, Zimmerman relied more on his very potent secondary stuff that resulted in a current streak of four straight seasons with an ERA under 3.25. Despite the fact Zimmerman will never be a 200-strikeout guy, he did whiff a career-high 182 last season which adds more value to his already very profitable stock. If you want a guy who will help you tremendously with your pitching ratios without costing a bundle, Zimmerman should be at the top of that list.

PROJECTION: 19-8 3.15 ERA 1.08 WHIP 177 K

18. **Tyson Ross:** While not exactly on the level of what Corey Kluber did last season, developing San Diego Padres hard-throwing starter Tyson Ross supplied some extreme value of his own in 2014. Ross actually made our Deep Sleeper list that we posted on the website last March, as we liked his above-average fastball and decent secondary offerings. Again like with Kluber, Ross hinted at what was to come in 2013 when he made 13 starts and recorded a terrific 3.17 ERA and 1.15 WHIP while averaging nearly a K/IP. Ross bettered those numbers last season as he was a pure sensation all the way through in posting a 2.81 ERA and 1.21 WHIP while striking out 195 batters in 195.2 innings. The young righty can really crank up the fastball and he wound up giving up only 165 hits which helped offset some shoddy control that resulted in 72 walks. If Ross can eat into some of those walks, his results could be scary. Reach a round or two early.

PROJECTION: 14-11 2.77 ERA 1.19 WHIP 199 K

19. **Sonny Gray:** The future is bright when it comes to starting pitching and one guy who will surely help carry the mantle is 25-year-old Oakland A's righty Sonny Gray. The former 18th overall pick in the 2011 draft had stardom written all over when Gray made his 2013 debut. The result was a spectacular 2.67 ERA and 1.11 WHIP in the heat of a pennant race. Gray was just as terrific in his first full major league campaign in 2014 as he won

14 games while compiling a 3.08 ERA and 1.19 WHIP while striking out 183 batters. Blessed with a vast arsenal of pitches, Gray keep the hits to a minimum and posts solid K numbers. He walks a bit too many batters but otherwise there is little to get on Gray about as he takes his place among the elite.

PROJECTION: 15-7 3.05 ERA 1.17 WHIP 186 K

20. **Gio Gonzalez:** Having been the only player to be cleared of any wrongdoing in the whole Biogenesis mess, it still appeared as though Gio Gonzalez' head was full of distraction early on in the 2014 season as he struggled through a horrific month of May when he posted a 7.98 ERA and 1.84 WHIP. Still that was the only bad month on Gonzalez' ledger as he rebounded to finish with a season ERA of 3.57 and a WHIP of 1.20. In fact you can say that Gonzalez quietly had one of his better years as the 1.20 WHIP was a career-low and he upped his K rate a bit in striking out 162 batters in 158.2 innings. The overall story remains the same here as Gonzalez' stuff can be impossible to hit at times and he continues to rack up the strikeouts at a good clip. In addition, Gonzlaez' 3.57 ERA last season was the highest that number had been in five years, which means we can pretty guarantee a finish in the 3.00 range. The negatives are control issues that tend to flare up multiple times during the season that sometimes push the WHIP upwards. Overall though Gonzalez remains a perfect low-end SP 2.

PROJECTION: 14-7 3.29 ERA 1.23 WHIP 191 K

21. **Gerrit Cole:** We are not there yet. The top has yet to be blown off for Pittsburgh Pirates fireballing youngster Gerrit Cole who managed only 138 innings in his first full year in the majors due to injuries. In addition Cole appeared to be fighting his stuff the first half of the season as he followed a 3.18 ERA April with an ugly 4.38 May and 5.59 June right before he hit the DL with shoulder fatigue. The fact that Cole suffered through shoulder fatigue that early in the season is a bit worrisome and his extremely hard-throwing ways no doubt had an effect. Once Cole returned to the mound in late July however, the talent took over as put up a 3.44 ERA and 1.05 WHIP the second half of the season, while ramping up the strikeouts to the tune of 60 in 52.1 innings. On stuff alone, Cole is as potent as any other starting pitcher in baseball. Able to touch 100 with the fastball and possessing a knee-buckling curve, comparisons to a young Justin Verlander remain right on down to some control problems. While Cole overall was a disappointment last season in failing to take the next step and only logging 138 innings, it is only a matter of time before the leap to an All-Star pitcher is made. That leap could come right off the bat in 2015 as Cole has another

season of experience under his belt and the raw talent to dominate. The fact that Cole's draft price has come down due to not carrying as much sleeper hype as he did prior to last year makes him one of the best value plays overall among pitchers. Give him another shot.

PROJECTION: 14-9 3.16 ERA 1.19 WHIP 188 K

22. **Jacob DeGrom:** Matt Harvey, Zach Wheeler, Noah Syndegaard,......Jacob DeGrom??? When talking about the amazing collection of young, hard-throwing pitchers in the New York Mets system, almost nobody mentioned the shaggy-haired Jacob DeGrom as being worthy of inclusion in this group. Five months and a Rookie of the Year Award later, DeGrom is on the short list of the best young pitchers in all of baseball. With the Mets needing an emergency starter for a May 15th date with the New York Yankees of all teams, DeGrom got the call and ended up immediately opening eyes by giving up one earned run in 7 innings and striking out six. While DeGrom took a tough-luck loss, the rest of his season was beyond eye-opening as he finished with a 2.69 ERA and 1.14 WHIP while striking out 144 batters in only 140.1 innings. The strengths here are obvious as DeGrom has a four-pitch arsenal that is highlighted by a 96-mph fastball that generates a bunch of swings and misses. Part of the reason DeGrom was off the prospect radar previously was due to having undergone an early Tommy John surgery. Upon his return to the mound however, DeGrom's fastball actually gained a few mph, which showed in his 2014 debut. While some will think that DeGrom is a bit of a fluke who took advantage of a league who had virtual no tape on him, we side with the argument that the potency of his stuff was the main reason for the breakout. The ballpark is obviously a big plus and while DeGrom could be on a bit of an innings limit, the kid looks for real.

PROJECTION: 15-9 3.29 ERA 1.16 WHIP 177 K

23. **Jeff Samardzjia:** Despite striking out 212 batters by the close of the 2013 season, many fantasy baseball owners of Jeff Samardzjia admittedly felt let down by his overall performance which resulted in a shaky 4.34 ERA and 1.35 WHIP for the rebuilding Chicago Cubs. Despite the less than ideal ratios, we argued loudly in defense of Samardzjia prior to last season and stated our firm belief that he was sitting on a monster campaign. The reason we felt Samardzjia was such a great buy centered almost solely on his 2013 advanced stats. One of the biggest areas of blame for Samardzjia's 4.34 ERA that year was due to one of the more unlucky BABIP numbers among all starting pitchers. Thus we banked on the idea that Samardzjia's BABIP would move back to the mean in 2014 and when combined with his 200-K power stuff, the possibility of an ace season was high for the cost of a

middle round pick. Well Samardzjia made us look very smart as he had the career season we all anticipated, pitching to a career-low 2.99 ERA and striking out 202 batters in a year split between the Cubs and the Oakland A's. The major impetus to the career numbers was the fact Samardzjia finally put his past control issues behind him for good, walking only 43 batters in 219 innings. Samardzjia is expected to be the staff ace for the A's this season and even though moving from the NL to the AL is mostly a negative, he ended up in one of its most pitching dominant ballparks so no worries there. While Samardzjia's ERA could in fact inch up to the low-3.00 region, nothing else really concerns us with the former Notre Dame wide receiver.

PROJECTION: 15-9 3.26 ERA 1.16 WHIP 205 K

24. **Alex Cobb:** So far through his first three seasons as a major league pitcher, the biggest challenge for Tampa Bay Rays starter Alex Cobb has been staying healthy. Just a season removed from suffering a scary batted ball that landed flush in his face, Cobb didn't even make it out of last April before he hit the DL with a serious oblique strain. However when Cobb has been on the mound, his numbers have been terrific as his ERA the last two seasons came in at 2.78 and 2.87. With an ability to reach the mid-90's with his fastball and with good secondary stuff, Cobb generates more than a few strikeouts along the way. If Cobb could ever stay healthy enough to make 30 starts, a run at a Cy Young is not out of the question. A terrific value.

PROJECTION: 14-8 2.91 ERA 1.16 WHIP 165 K

25. **James Shields:** The Kansas City Royals laughed all the way to the World Series bank last season with regards to the much-talked about trade two years ago when they sent top outfield prospect Wil Myers to the Tampa Bay Rays for pitchers James Shields and Wade Davis. While the Royals were instantly destroyed over trading Myers in the deal, the subsequent two years showed that they easily got the better end of things. While Davis was racking up incredible numbers in setup, Shields was filling the ace role for the Royals in terrific fashion. After a 3.15 ERA debut in 2013, Shields was once again excellent last season as he posted a 3.21 mark with a 1.18 WHIP. When you talk about durable pitchers, Shields has a place right at the top of any list as he has now gone 8 straight seasons of 200-plus innings pitched. Long one of the most affordable ace-level fantasy baseball starters, Shields's surface numbers were all impressive. However there are some disturbing signs lying beneath the surface of those numbers. The biggest potential issue is that Shields' K rate has dropped for three straight seasons, as his raw strikeout totals have gone from 223 to 196 to 180. Oftentimes a trending downard of the K rate for an established pitcher can be blamed on

arm fatigue. This would make sense in Shields' case as all of those 200-plus inning seasons could be taking some juice out of his pitches. This is the exact same thing we have seen out of similarly career high-inning pitchers over the last few years such as in the cases of Dan Haren, C.C. Sabbathia, and most recently Justin Verlander. While there is no science to say exactly that this is what is happening with Shields, the trends speak loudly. The trouble that could further escalate here is that if Shields is in fact losing velocity, his already high home run rate will go up even more. That in turn will spike the ERA and WHIP northward. While we love the amazing durability that Shields has shown throughout his career, we are always leery of pitchers whose arms have a ton of wear on them. You don't have to avoid Shields altogether but instead just be aware of the growing alarms that are starting to sound.
PROJECTION: 14-10 3.38 ERA 1.19 WHIP 188 K

26. **Lance Lynn:** First half hero and second half zero was the firm scouting report on St. Louis Cardinals pitcher Lance Lynn during his first two seasons in the team's rotation. Calling Lynn the new age Dan Haren due to his second half fades, was pretty much spot on given the evidence at hand. Still there was always hope that Lynn would eventually be able to gather up enough pitching strength to make it through a whole season at the top of his game and if accomplished, would move him into high-end SP 2 status. Well Lynn was finally able to achieve the feat last season as he actually posted a BETTER ERA in the second half (3.14/2.22) that helped him produce a career year. Being able to pitch effectively for a whole season elevated Lynn to a new statistical plane as he cut a full run off his season ERA and lowered his WHIP a few percentage points as well. While Lynn did lose some strikeouts, that is quibbling since pitching more to contact likely helped keep him fresh. The fact Lynn finally proved his stamina makes investing in him a much more comfortable exercise and as a result we can now feel better about endorsing him as a solid SP 2.
PROJECTION: 15-8 3.17 ERA 1.25 WHIP 182 K

27. **Doug Fister:** We were big-time proponents of new Washington Nationals starter Doug Fister as the 2014 season dawnedand for good reason. After coming over to the Nats in an offseason trade from the Detroit Tigers, the already very good Fister was staring at a career year in moving from the AL to the NL. Unfortunately a strained lat forced Fister to the DL even before the season started and he didn't make his return until May. Despite having only five months to pitch in, Fister still had that career year we anticipated as he picked up a total of 16 wins, while recording his best ever ERA at 2.41. Even before his arrival with the Nationals, Fister was quietly one of

the best pitchers in the American League as he recorded three straight seasons from 2011-2013 where his ERA hovered between 3.33 and 3.67. While Fister's K rate is never anything to write home about, his control is impeccable and hit rate better than average. The fact Fister now gets to continue operating in a pitching paradise and gets to feast on much weaker NL lineups mean an SP 2 campaign is once again likely.
PROJECTION: 17-7 3.08 ERA 1.10 WHIP 155 K

28. **Michael Wacha:** Talk about going from one extreme to the other. That statistical ride was taken last season by prized St. Louis Cardinals pitching gem Michael Wacha. After dominating while coming up the Cards' farm system and showing ace-like ability, Wacha forced the team to call him up midway through 2013. Showing incredible poise for his age, Wacha became an immediate difference-maker in the rotation in pitching to a 2.78 ERA and 1.10 WHIP while striking out 65 batters in 64.2 innings. As a result Wacha was an extremely sought after pitcher for 2014 fantasy baseball and rightly so considering his terrific control and high-powered arsenal. Wacha showed early on in the season that the hype was not misplaced as he stormed out of the gates with ERA's of 2.48 and 2.43 in April/May respectively. Unfortunately that is where the good times ended as Wacha began experiencing pain in his pitching shoulder that sent him to the DL in mid-June after some rough outings. Wacha stayed on the DL until September where he returned to take a 5.40 ERA beating to finish the regular season. What is really disturbing now is the fact that Wacha's velocity was down upon his September return, which made him so much more hittable. In addition, a shoulder injury for a pitcher is even worse than an elbow aillment as they tend to reoccur and cause more negative impacts on performance. We are incredibly worried about Wacha's immediate future given his shoulder troubles and thus won't pay much more than mean value for the guy. The light is dimming a bit on a guy who was shining just a few months ago.
PROJECTION: 12-8 3.41 ERA 1.17 WHIP 159 K

29. **Jose Fernandez:** Anyone that calls themselves a baseball fan had to shake their head in disappointment when the news got around that the best young pitcher in baseball, Miami Marlins fireballer Jose Fernanez, became the latest Tommy John elbow victim. Prior to the injury, Fernandez was in the midst of a season-plus run that was quite possibly the most dominant pitching in all of baseball despite the fact the kid was only 22-years-old. We have gone on record more than a few times in stating that we can't remember the last time we saw a pitcher come up with as incredible an arsenal of stuff than what was shown by Fernandez. Fernandez' 2013

rookie debut was out of this world as he pitched to a ridiculous 2.19 ERA and 0.98 WHIP while striking out 187 batters in 172.2 innings. What made Fernandez so amazing was the fact he could throw his 98-mph fastball with movement, while also showcasing a curveball that was already as good as any pitcher in the game. The movement on Fernandez' pitches was a sight to behold and it surely looked like amazing things were happening at the start of 2014 as well. In his first eight starts, Fernandez pitched to a 2.44 ERA and 0.95 WHIP while ringing up an insane 70 strikeouts in his first 51.2 innings. The elbow pain started after Fernandez' eighth start however and the Tommy John recommedation was quickly made. So now we sit here with Fernandez expecting to be out at least until the All-Star break as the Marlins play it very safe with their young stud. Just like with Matt Harvey and any other young pitcher coming back from the surgery, a full season is usually needed before the stuff comes all the way back. Three months of Fernandez is still better than most other starters but you obviously can't pay too high price for a guy who will only be out there for half the year. Still it shouldn't take Fernandez long to reclaim his top five status when he does get back onto the hill.

PROJECTION: 7-2 3.07 ERA 1.07 WHIP 125 K

30. **Anibal Sanchez:** The encore to veteran Detroit Tigers righty Anibal Snachez's 2013 career season (2.57 ERA/1.15 WHIP/202 K) was surely a letdown no matter how you look at it. A serious pectoral injury shelved Sanchez for a good chunk of the summer and when he returned in September, was relegated to bullpen duty. Prior to the injury, Sanchez was still a potent strikeout guy who was stingy with the hits allowed. That combination makes Sanchez a very solid major league power pitcher but his career-long trouble with staying healthy is beyond pronounced. If you can draft Sanchez as your SP 4, you did very well. Anything more and the risk becomes a factor.

PROJECTION: 14-8 3.61 ERA 1.16 WHIP 185 K

31. **Hisashi Iwakuma:** While he doesn't get the credit that countrymen such as Masahiro Tanaka or Yu Darvish receive, Japanese arrival Hisashi Iwakuma has quietly been one of the better pitchers in baseball since he signed with the Seattle Mariners prior to the 2012 season. Iwakuma really put his name on the fantasy baseball map however in 2013 when he posted a terrific 2.66 ERA and 1.01 WHIP while striking out 185 hitters. While Iwaukuma is not overpowering, he brings a four-pitch arsenal that does plenty to fool major league batters. We did throw some cold water a bit on Iwakuma prior to last season however due to the fact some of his 2013 breakout was based on some very lucky BABIP and strand rate numbers but overall we remained

interested. The BABIP corrected 3.52 ERA was still very useful for our purposes, so no harm done. Despite the ERA correction, there is still a lot to like here as Iwakuma doesn't beat himself with walks and he keeps the hit rate low. Home runs can be an issue once in awhile but otherwise this is a trustworthy SP 3.

PROJECTION: 15-8 3.48 ERA 1.07 WHIP 163 K

32. **Phil Hughes:** Sometimes all it takes for a fly-ball pitcher like Phil Hughes is to find a park that keeps baseballs in the stadium. Hughes found that type of ballpark in Target Field after signing on as a free agent prior to 2014 after getting his head beaten in the previous year with the New York Yankees. Hughes was a terrible match for the home run paradise that is Yankee Stadium and he habitually produced home/road splits that showed his ERA a full run lower on the road. Thus it stood to reason that Hughes set himself up for a nice comeback season in 2014 given his new locale. Well Hughes lived up to that bit of optimism as he stormed out of the gates with a dominant All-Star first half and ultimately finished out with 16 wins while recording a 3.52 ERA. In addition, Hughes' always solid strikeout rate improved even more in his pitching-favoring ballpark as he rang up a career-high 186 K's. As expected Hughes gave up 8 fewer home runs compared to his last year with the Yankees and that helped his terrific stuff to blossom in more friendlier confines. Hughes should once again be one of the better SP 3's in fantasy baseball this season and making matters more enticing, his draft price has not come all the way back to his current numbers due to how many people were turned off by him after his last year in pinstripes. Trust in the numbers.

PROJECTION: 15-10 3.48 ERA 1.14 WHIP 188 K

33. **Homer Bailey:** In going along with his career trends, Homer Bailey did the opposite of what was expected out of him last season. After years of poor pitching as he tried to find his MLB footing, Bailey finally broke through in 2012 and 2013 as he posted mid-3.00 ERA's with increasing strikeout totals that topped out at 199. After burning more than a few owners early on in his career when he failed to make good on some sleepers seasons, Bailey seemed to finally earn the trust of the fantasy baseball community as 2014 dawned. April would prove to be a compete horror show for Bailey however as he was hit all around the ballpark to the tune of a 6.15 ERA and ghastly 1.78 WHIP. The biggest issue were the 7 home runs Bailey gave up amid rumors he was tipping his pitches. Once Bailey worked through that issue, he began to improve immediately as each subsequent month resulted in better and better ratios. Bailey was at his best in June and July as he ramped up the strikeouts and kept the ball in the park. However the fun

came to an end early as Bailey hit the DL in August due to a flexor mass injury in his pitching arm and he never returned. Surgery was not needed and Bailey was pronounced 100 percent healthy for the start of the 2015 season. Since Bailey has been all over the statistical map in his career, it is almost impossible to figure out where he will end up with his numbers. What we can bank on is the fact Bailey has now posted mid-to-high-3.00 ERA's over the last three seasons and generally is in the 1.23 WHIP neighborhood. Home runs remain a problem and a prime threat to any Bailey start, which is annoying but overall he projects himself to be a decent SP 3 with no more remaining upside.

PROJECTION: 14-10 3.70 ERA 1.22 WHIP 172 K

34. **Ian Kennedy:** A fly-ball pitcher with a pronounced home run problem is always a bad match for an offensive ballpark like Chase Field in Arizona. Just ask Ian Kennedy who fits the pitching profile mentioned above, which got him run out of Arizona after a season-plus of terrible pitching followed a shockingly good 21-win campaign in 2011. Kennedy was very fortunate to be traded to the San Diego Padres midway through 2013 and that set hin up for sleeper status heading into last season. No longer having to worry about home runs in spacious Petco Park, Kennedy turned around his career by posting a 3.63 ERA and 1.29 WHIP. Even more impressive was the career-high 207 strikeouts. As long as Kennedy doesn't get traded (his name has come up repeatedly in rumors all offseason), a replication of last season's numbers is likely.

PROJECTION: 14-12 3.59 ERA 1.28 WHIP 197 K

35. **Hyun-Jin Ryu:** It is tough to stand out on a Los Angeles Dodgers pitching staff that counts Clayton Kershaw and Zack Greinke among its memebers but Korean veteran Hyun-Jin Ryu certainly does his best to keep up. Now two seasons into his major league career, Ryu has recorded ERA's of 3.03 and 3.38, while posting above-average strikeout rates. Unfortunately Ryu has had trouble staying healthy during his short stay with the Dodgers and that takes some bite out of his potential fantasy baseball impact. This is the kind of cheap and very effective arm you can grab in the middle rounds that will more than pay its own draft price. And if Ryu can stay healthy enough to make 30 starts, the payoff could be enormous.

PROJECTION: 14-7 3.32 ERA 1.19 WHIP 161 K

36. **Masahiro Tanaka:** For the first three months of the 2014 major league season, it appeared as though the New York Yankees were completely justified in spending the gargantuan amount of money it took to secure the services of top Japanese hurler Masahiro Tanaka. While not showing the

explosive fastball that countryman Yu Darvish possessed, Tanaka's ridiculous six-pitch arsenal and impeccable control made him an almost impossible chore for major league hitters to deal with. Tanaka immediately came out of the gate firing on all cylinders as he opened April with a 2.27 ERA, to go along with striking out 46 batters in 35.2 innings. Things only got better from there as Tanaka put up a 1.88 May and 2.19 June. A couple of rough outings at the beginning of July however raised some eyebrows and it soon was revealed that Tanaka had suffered a partial tear in his pitching elbow as it appeared he would join Matt Harvey and Jose Fernandez as recent big-name victims to go under the Tommy John knife. In a big shocker (and with the blessing of the Yankees), Tanaka chose to rehab the elbow instead of having surgery. This decision was loaded with peril as any further setback would have pushed back Tanaka's expected return date. Still Tanaka fought through the rehab and returned to the field in September where he didn't engender much confidence after posting a 7.71 ERA. There is a ton of uncertainty here as Tanaka goes into the 2015 season with the tear still in his elbow. A good comparison could be made to the St. Louis Cardinals' Adam Wainwright who pitched for a few seasons with a tear in his own elbow before eventually going through the Tommy John procedure. Any setback suffered by Tanaka during the season is likely to lead down that road which makes him one of the biggest risks among any big-name starting pitcher this season. While no one can argue the explosive stuff Tanaka showed at the start of 2014 is as good as it gets, there is a solid chance that pitcher doesn't exist anymore based on the current state of his elbow.

PROJECTION: 11-5 3.33 ERA 1.14 WHIP 163 K

37. **Alex Wood:** The Atlanta Braves have always been one of the more accomplished teams in baseball when it comes to developing pitchers. However they really screwed up big time last season when it came to Alex Wood. Knowing that Wood possessed a very talented right arm, the Braves made the decision to break camp with the kid in the rotation. Wood pitched even better than even the Braves expected as he posted a 2.93 ERA/1.13 WHIP in April. However in a truly maddening decision, the organization decided to remove Wood out of the rotation and instead placed him in the bullpen once the calendar flipped to May. It made absolutely no sense and Wood quickly struggled in the role so badly that he was sent back to the minors in order to stretch himself out again in order to rejoin the rotation. Brought back up in July, Wood reeled off three months of ace-like pitching to the tune of a 2.20 ERA and 1.08 WHIP while striking out 88 batters in only 86 innings. The former 2012 2nd round pick is the real deal, capable of striking out a batter per inning while posting an ERA that could match the

3.13 or the 2.78 from his first two seasons. The only positive of the Braves putting Wood in the bullpen is that it prevented him from striking out 200 batters which would have sent his draft price soaring. Be aggressive here as Wood has star written all over him.
PROJECTION: 15-10 3.20 ERA 1.5 WHIP 190 K

38. **Zack Wheeler:** Upward and onward we go with young New York Mets starter Zack Wheeler. While Matt Harvey and now Jacob DeGrom get more hype, Wheeler is more than doing his part to make the Mets' staff the envy of baseball. Coming into the season Wheeler had to work through two issues that were holding him back from reaching his full potential. The first was an utter lack of control and the second was a fastball that came in way too straight, thus hurting his strikeout rate. After a rough start to the season, Wheeler took a decent step forward with his development in 2014. While Wheeler still walked 79 batters in 185.1 innings, he was more efficient with his pitches which allowed him to go deeper into games and thus give himself a chance to collect wins. In additon, Wheeler really ramped up the strikeouts as he punched out 187 batters in those 185.1 innings. While Wheeler's overall 3.54 ERA and 1.33 WHIP were nothing mind-boggling, he is clearly on a trajectory upwards which means 2015 should be even better. We don't think Wheeler is the next Matt Harvey as some initially suggested but SP 2 territory can be reached this season if all breaks right.
PROJECTION: 14-10 3.41 ERA 1.29 WHIP 194 K

39. **Cliff Lee:** Father Time could be calling for Cy Young-winning lefty Cliff Lee based on what we saw in a busted 2014 season. Besides the fact Lee continued to lose some ticks on his fastball, the veteran was only able to make 13 starts due to a flexor strain in his elbow that lingered almost the entire season. In fact the elbow was such a problem that Lee was only cleared to begin a throwing program at the start of November which is undoubtedly concerning since he will be turning 37 this August. Even before he went on the shelf for good last season, Lee's hit rate and home runs allowed pointed upwards, yet another sign that age could be a factor. In Lee's defense, the three seasons prior to 2014's mess saw him record 200-plus K's all three times and posted ERA's that hovered between 2.40 and 3.16. Still while Lee is as smart and crafty as they come, investing in guys with this much negativity attached to their names at this stage of the game is a poor decision on more than a few levels.
PROJECTION: 14-11 3.45 ERA 1.12 WHIP 180 K

40. **Matt Cain:** We warned you. Another featured name on our 2014 All-Bust Team was San Francisco Giants veteran Matt Cain, who warranted

inclusion due to declining ability brought on by massive inning totals from the very start of his young career. However it was injuries more than performance that validated our bust selection for Cain last season as he spent time on the DL with bone chips in his right elbow, followed by surgery on his ankle to remove a bone spur. In between Cain threw only 90.1 innings where he wasn't horrible but still far from the former ace he was as recently as 2012. Now that Cain figures to be healthy to start the 2015 season, we must revisit the red flags that make him such as risk in the first place. Right along the same lines as rotation mate Tim Lincecum, Cain has lost velocity and as a result has seen his hit rate shoot up noticeably. Always prone to the home run ball even in his All-Star years, the loss of velocity has only exacerbated the situation for Cain. The result has been two straight years where Cain's ERA has hit the 4.00 mark or above. While Cain still posts good but not great strikeout rates, the threat of any one of his starts being blown up due to the home run ball makes owning this stock a hair-raising experience.

PROJECTION: 14-7 3.84 ERA 1.17 WHIP 171 K

41. **Francisco Liriano:** Instead of being consistently bad (as was the case for most of his career), perennial tease Francisco Liriano has actually put together two solid back-to-back seasons during his 2013-14 stay with the Pittsburgh Pirates. While Liriano will always be a WHIP-killer due to his career-long issue with walks, the hit rate is always terrific and he also continues to punch out more than a batter per inning which is where you want your power arms to be. We hope Liriano realizes his best value lies in remaining in the National League, as he is a free agent as of press time. If he does wind up staying in the non-DH league, we would buy in again as long as Liriano comes priced as a SP 4.

PROJECTION: 14-9 3.51 ERA 1.28 WHIP 173 K

42. **Andrew Cashner:** The storylines remain the same when it comes to hard-throwing San Diego Padres starting pitcher Andrew Cashner. Since being moved into the team's rotation for the 2013 season, Cashner has shown off a power repertoire and improving control that resulted in 3.09 and 2.55 ERA's the last two years. Always possessing the ability to dial up the fastball to the 97-mph range, Cashner has actually become more of a "pitcher" since moving into the rotation, primarily through inducing more contact in order to take advantage of the vast dimensions of Petco Park. Unfortunately we get small sample sizes on Cashner's talent due to persistent injuries allowing him to pitch only 123.1 innings last season. Obviously the ballpark is a major plus in Cashner's corner and he has thrown enough innings now as a starter to buy into the recent results. The

problem is that getting more than 150 innings out of Cashner would be considered a bonus, which in turn makes him not the most optimal way to use a draft pick.
PROJECTION: 9-8 3.02 ERA 1.14 WHIP 159 K

43. **Marcus Stroman:** Another young power arm that should be at the head of the class when it comes to future aces is Toronto Blue Jays righthander Marcus Stroman. Reminding us of a young Roy Oswalt, Stroman came up as a rookie in 2014 and pitched great in putting up a 3.65 ERA and 1.17 WHIP while racking up 111 K's in 130.2 innings pitched. What makes the numbers even more impressive is the fact that Stroman's ERA would have been a bit lower if not for the Blue Jays' idiotic idea to initially have him pitch out of the bullpen which he clearly wasn't comfortable with. Stroman is the kind of young pitcher we love in that he already has terrific control, which goes great with his nice K potential. The kid has all it takes to be a staff ace very soon so feel free to reach a round or two early to ensure he ends up on your roster this season.
PROJECTION: 14-8 3.32 ERA 1.14 WHIP 171 K

44. **Scott Kazmir:** The comeback story of Scott Kazmir continued for a second season in 2014 as the free agent signee of the Oakland A's won a career-high 15 games with an ERA of 3.55. Despite there being questions about whether or not he could hold up for a whole season after not having tossed at least 160 innings since 2007, Kazmir fought through 190 frames which also marked a career-high. Kazmir has lost some zip on his fastball which means he is no longer not even a 180-K guy but he remains very tough to hit and has improved his walk rate from his earlier days. The threat of injury remains very high here as imagining Kazmir staying in one piece two seasons running is asking a ton but the draft price remains affordable enough that it won't hurt much to find out if he can do so.
PROJECTION: 14-8 3.78 ERA 1.21 WHIP 165 K

45. **Jered Weaver:** We have been very rough on Los Angeles Angels veteran starter Jered Weaver the last few years which was based mostly on his vastly declining strikeout rate and rising ratios. Weaver earned back some respect from this publication last season as he won 18 games and posted a decent 3.59 ERA and 1.21 WHIP. The key to Weaver's season was his change in approach, a fact he spoke openly about. Instead of trying to rely on his fading fastball to get out of trouble, Weaver leaned more on his still effective secondary pitches to reinvent his approach. Clearly it is working for Weaver who is back to being a solid SP 3. Just don't expect anything

more than the 169 strikeouts he supplied last season and you won't be disappointed.

PROJECTION: 17-7 3.51 ERA 1.22 WHIP 162 K

46. **Jake Peavy:** There is a bit of late intrigue to the up-and-down career of Jake Peavy as the 2015 fantasy baseball season nears and it all has to do with his semi-new locale. After years of inflated ERA's and WHIP numbers while pitching in the American League for the Chicago White Sox and Boston Red Sox, Peavy is now back in the National League where he was a dominant Cy Young pitcher for the San Diego Padres. The ironic thing is that Peavy is as close to his old San Diego days as a pitcher can get after he was traded by the Red Sox to the San Francisco Giants last summer. The change in numbers was instantaneous as Peavy went from a 4.72 ERA with the Red Sox all the way down to a 2.17 mark in a dominant finish with the Giants. Clearly Peavy is a good notch or two below his Padres heyday but pitching in the very weak NL West makes him the rare aging veteran sleeper. We would absolutely use a late middle round pick on Peavy due to his new location alone and his stuff overall is still good enough to possibly supply SP 3 numbers.

PROJECTION: 14-10 3.48 ERA 1.14 WHIP 173 K

47. **Mat Latos:** A very dependable SP 2 when on the mound, getting into uniform has proven to be the greatest obstacle over the last season-plus for Cincinnati Reds starter Mat Latos. After compiling only 102.1 innings in 2014 due to surgery to repair a torn meniscus and later for shoulder trouble. Latos' 3.25 ERA and 1.15 WHIP last season were pretty much on par for his career marks. Still Latos is already on many DO NOT DRAFT lists after it was revealed he underwent yet more surgery in early November. A stem cell procedure was needed in order to regrow some tissue and cartilage in Latos' elbow, which already makes him a decent risk for 2015. One of the more easier players to project given his consistency since arriving in the majors back in 2009, Latos' awful recent health is starting to overshadow his possible impact.

PROJECTION: 14-10 3.42 ERA 1.16 WHIP 178 K

48. **Chris Archer:** Despite a rough April, Tampa Bay Rays righty Chris Archer recorded his second straight season with a low-3.00 ERA and in the process cemented his status as one of the better young pitchers in baseball. On the heels of his 3.22 ERA breakout in 2013, Archer pretty much finished in the same neighborhood last season with a 3.33 mark. Archer is a big kid at 6-3 who generates a ton of torque in his delivery and in the process picks up 170-plus strikeouts. His 1.28 WHIP last season is a bit ugly due to a

high walk rate but Archer should be able to iron some of that out as he continues to mature. Wins will be an issue on a rebuilding Rays squad but Archer is a solid buy when you combine his cheap draft price and good ratios.

PROJECTION: 12-9 3.39 ERA 1.24 WHIP 175 K

49. **Ervin Santana:** It was overall a successful one-year cameo for Ervin Santana in an Atlanta Braves uniform in 2014 as the veteran won 14 games while posting a 3.95 ERA. Santana's career has been defined by inconsistency as he flipped good years and bad years on more than a few occasions. This is another case of a guy who needs to stay in the National League as Santana's 179 strikeouts last season were the second-highest total of his career. If Santana does sign on with a National League team again, feel free to draft as a very good SP 5.

PROJECTION: 13-9 4.06 ERA 1.28 WHIP

50. **Yordano Ventura:** The 100-mph fastballs that Yordano Ventura tossed last spring training proved too tough to ignore as the Kansas City Royals had little choice but to put the kid into the team's rotation right out of the gate. Ventura lived up to the hype as he finished the season with a splendid 3.20 ERA while winning 14 games at the age of 23. There were some hairy moments along the way however as Ventura came down with some elbow soreness midway through 2014 that brought fears he would become the latest young hard-throwing pitcher who needed Tommy John surgery. Luckily for Ventura, no tears were found in his elbow and he returned to finish out the year with no further problems outside of sometimes shoddy control that pushed up his WHIP to 1.30. The talent is clearly evident but at only 6-0, durability is going to be a prime concern for future Ventura owners. The draft price will determine which way to go here as Ventura's injury risk is too pronounced for him to be anything more than a low-end SP 3.

PROJECTION: 14-9 3.18 ERA 1.27 WHIP 171 K

51. **Garrett Richards:** No one went from the highest of highs to the lowest of lows last season than Los Angeles Angels SP Garret Richards. Always possessing a fastball that comes close to triple-digits, Richards habitually undermined himself with awful control and terrible pitch efficiency which is why he was nothing but a waiver guy coming into the 2014 season. However Richards broke through in a major way, drastically reducing his walks and in the process letting his explosive fastball do all the work. The result was an All-Star selection, a miniscule 2.61 ERA, and a strikeout per inning pace. Fate than intervened in a late August start against the Boston

Red Sox when Richards stumbled covering first base that resulted in a gruesome torn left patellar tendon in his knee which required surgery. The original prognosis was that Richards would need 6-to-9 months recovery time which would put a return sometime between April and June. Fully buy into the results that Richards put up last season, as his was the classic case of a young starter who successfully fought through control problems to reach his top potential. The reduced draft price actually makes Richards a solid buy even if he misses a month or two.

PROJECTION: 3.17 ERA 1.10 WHIP 154 K

52. **Matt Shoemaker:** It was nearly a Rookie of the Year performance in the American League for previously unknown Los Angeles Angels starter Matt Shoemaker, who began 2014 in the bullpen and finished it as one of the hottest pitchers in the game. Shoemaker nearly threw a no-hitter versus the Boston Red Sox and overall finished the season with a 3.04 ERA and 1.07 WHIP as he won a ridiculous 16 of his 20 starts. Combining a 95-mph fastball and terrific control, Shoemaker has a bright future ahead of him and will be a great buy for 2015. The fact Shoemaker only tossed 136 innings and pitched on the West Coast helps to keep him under the radar which will only help you at the draft table.

PROJECTION: 15-7 3.29 ERA 1.08 WHIP 171 K

53. **Jason Hammel:** A free agent as of press time, Jason Hammel certainly timed his career season right as he hit the open market. After flaming out with three organizations due to a combination of poor pitching and ill health, Hammel took full advantage of an opportunity on a rebuilding Chicago Cubs team. Hammel had always possessed good strikeout potential, which he finally exhibited in a huge performance with the Cubs in pitching to a 2.98 ERA and 1.02 WHIP while striking out 104 batters in 108.2 innings. The biggest positive perhaps was that Hammel stayed healthy and his 95-mph fastball did a lot of the good work also. The Oakland A's were sufficiently impressed that they pulled off a trade for Hammel in order to help with their playoff push. However Hammel turned to mush with the A's, posting an ugly 4.26 ERA in a complete about-face performance from where he was numbers-wise with the Cubs. There is clear evidence that Hammel is a guy who has to stay in the NL to be fantasy baseball-worthy due his struggles with the A's, not to mention shaky results with the Tampa Bay Rays and Baltimore Orioles. If he does sign on with an NL squad, bump Hammel up to an SP 4. If Hammel stays in the AL, drop him to an SP 5.

PROJECTION: 12-11 3.66 ERA 1.21 WHIP 165 K

54. **Chris Tillman:** It was another decent step forward for young Baltimore Orioles righty Chris Tillman in 2014, as he lowered his ERA to a career-best 3.34 which went nicely with a 1.23 WHIP. In fact other than a drop in strikeouts, Tillman was pretty much the same pitcher he was in 2013 but with a tad more BABIP luck. What has to be mentioned here is that once again Tillman was a much better pitcher in the second half than he was in the first (4.11 pre-All-Star/2.33 after). Also don't look for much more than around 170 strikeouts as Tillman settles into his prime years. We always hate investing in AL East pitchers but Tillman has more than proved his good SP 4 value.
PROJECTION: 15-9 3.41 ERA 1.22 WHIP 160 K

55. **Justin Verlander:** We screamed to the rafters prior to last season about the foolishness of investing in fading Detoit Tigers veteran pitcher Justin Verlander, which was fully warranted given the carnage we saw over the next six months. The former number 1 pitcher in fantasy baseball began a decline in the 2013 season that was fueled by very noticeable drops in his velocity. The domino effect began to take shape as the loss of velocity spiked Verlander's hit and home run rates. Clearly sensing the problem, Verlander than tried to pitch too fine which ruined his control. The result was a bottoming out for Verlander in 2014 as he was hit hard almost all season to the tune of a 4.54 ERA and 1.40 WHIP. The numbers told the story here as Verlander gave up a staggering 223 hits in only 206 innings, clearly fooling no one. Perhaps even more concerning was the drastic drop in Verlander's K rate as he whiffed only 159 batters, which was a drop of 77 from the season prior. Pretty much everything went wrong for Verlander as he took the C.C. Sabbathia path from stardom to garbage. While it might be tough to imagine Verlander being so awful two seasons in a row, that lost velocity is never coming back. Neither is his standing as a top fantasy baseball pitcher. Cut your losses.
PROJECTION: 15-10 3.95 ERA 1.32 WHIP 170 K

56. **Jake Odorizzi:** If you are looking to buy low on a guy who seems primed for a major step forward, check out young Tampa Bay Rays hard-throwing righty Jake Odorizzi. Coming over to the Rays with Wil Myers in the James Shields trade, Odorizzi's first full season in the majors in 2014 was better than the 4.13 ERA and 1.28 WHIP looked. For one, Odorizzi showcased a power arm that rang up 174 strikeouts in 168 innings. That type of strikeout production in the American League is always eye-opening, what with the more potent lineups. The hit rate was also very good as Odorizzi only has to work through some control and home run problems to

reach his full potential. We see him turning into as good as an SP 2 if all breaks right.

PROJECTION: 14-10 3.67 ERA 1.24 WHIP 186 K

57. **Jake Arrieta:** The Chicago Cubs stumbled into a potential pitching gem in Jake Arrieta when they acquired him from the Baltimore Orioles midway through the 2013 season. Arrieta was pounded into submission during his Orioles tenure, so even the Cubs had little idea of what was about to take place. After a nice 3.66 ERA/1.12 WHIP finish to 2013 in 5 starts, Arrieta proceeded to take a huge leap the next season. While Arrieta made only 25 starts due to injury, the results were staggering as he posted a tiny 2.53 ERA nad 0.99 WHIP while striking out 167 batters in only 156.2 innings. Like with his former rotation mate Jason Hammel, Arrieta clearly needed to move to the National League to become useful. Based on the numbers, Arrieta makes the grade as a very good SP 4 whose K/IP ratio was very impressive. As long as the Cubs don't move him, Arrieta will be a quietly effective pitching asset for you.

PROJECTION: 11-11 3.49 ERA 1.08 WHIP 181 K

58. **Colin McHugh:** It looks like the New York Mets (and to a lesser extent the Colorado Rockies) jumped the gun in giving up on the hard-throwing Colin McHugh before they adequately saw his potential through. There is no denying that McHugh pitched as poorly as one could possibly pitch when given a chance at the major league level but the Mets (having put up a 7.59 and 10.29 ERA from 2012-13) before the Rockies followd suit after a 9.95 ERA cameo. However both organizations ignored the very high K rates that McHugh routinely put up in the minors, which was a fact the Astros bought into when they signed him prior to the 2014 season. Summoned from the minors to make a start at the end of April, the fantasy baseball community ignored the non-news. One start and 12-strikeouts later, McHugh was on his way to a terrific breakout season that culminated in a 2.73 ERA and 1.02 WHIP while he racked up 157 strikeouts in only 154.2 innings. Clearly McHugh's knack for the strikeout has followed him to the majors and the rebuilding Astros were the perfect team to establish himself with few expectations attached to his name. There is a good chance the ratios will rise as major league hitters have more of a scouting report on McHugh but especially in innings-capped leagues he more than makes the grade as an SP 4.

PROJECTION: 12-10 3.33 ERA 1.11 WHIP 172 K

59. **Dan Duffy:** Daniel Duffy has been a guy we have watched closely over the last few years as one of our prime deep sleepers. The young lefty racked up

some incredible strikeout totals while coming up the Kansas City Royals minor league ladder but once promoted to the big leagues, Duffy's utter lack of control usually sent him right back to the farm. A very similar case to Garrett Richards, Duffy only had to iron out the control kinks before his top-end stuff took over. It certainly looked like that is what was taking place last season as Duffy had a breakout campaign that few people talked about in pitching to a 2.53 ERA in his 149.1 innings. Despite the smallish innings total, Duffy showed great signs that he was ready to make the leap to above-average starter. Consider that Duffy drastically lowered his walk rate, which showed up in his 1.11 WHIP. Duffy also dialed back some of the fastball juice in order to pitch more to contact and thus trust the above-average Royals defense to get him outs. This is a classic sign of maturity for a young pitcher like Duffy and makes him one to target late in your draft due to the solid upside.

PROJECTION: 3.35 ERA 1.16 WHIP 158 K

60. **C.J. Wilson:** Known for extreme durability and decent pitching throughout his career, only one part of that scouting report came through for C.J. Wilson in 2014. While Wilson supplied his customary high-innings total, he would go on to post a career-high ERA as a starter at 4.51. Wilson walked a ton of batters, which is nothing new but his stuff was more hittable than ever. We worry a bit that all those very high innings totals are starting to take a bite out of Wilson's stuff and his status as even a SP 3 is in doubt.

PROJECTION: 14-11 3.97 ERA 1.33 WHIP 174 K

61. **Mike Minor:** A persistent shoulder problem held the Atlanta Braves' Mike Minor to only 145.1 innings pitches last season. In those 145.1 innings, Minor took a firm step back in his development as he was hit hard for most of them to the tune of a 4.77 ERA and 1.44 WHIP. Once again the big problem were the home runs as Minor surrendered an ungodly 21 which went a long way toward spiking his ratios. Minor's ugly 2014 campaign almost completely erased his 2013 breakout when he pitched to a 3.21 ERA and looked like one of the best young starters in the game. The shoulder and home run problems are two giant negatives when looking at Minor's immediate outlook and in turn make him a potentially volatile to own. While we wouldn't avoid Minor outright given his youth (he is still a young 27), the home run rate is a threat to almost any one of his starts.

PROJECTION: 12-9 3.98 ERA 1.16 WHIP 161 K

62. **Dan Haren:** The aging veteran is still getting outs after a tidy 4.02 ERA/1.18 WHIP 2014 campaign with the Los Angeles Dodgers. Durability has always been a Haren strength so you know he will be there when

needed. However the K rate has fallen off the map and Haren is unlikely to match his 2014 ratios at his advancing age. Use only in non-innings capped leagues.

PROJECTION: 14-9 4.23 ERA 1.20 WHIP 145 K

63. **R.A. Dickey:** We all knew R.A Dickey was headed for some rough seas after the New York Mets sold high on the 2012 Cy Young Award winner by dealing him to the Toronto Blue Jays prior to the 2013 season. The knuckleball mistakes got hit so much harder in Rogers Center and the American League as a whole, which showed up in Dickey's 4.21 ERA and 1.34 WHIP during his first year with the team. However Dickey did a nice job adjusting to the much more harsher surroundings in 2014 as he lowered his ERA back down under the 4.00 mark (3.71) while drastically reducing the hits allowed which shot down his WHIP to a tidy 1.23. Despite turning an ancient 40 last October, Dickey has a few good years left due to being a knuckleball guy. Just like the last two seasons, only draft Dickey as a SP 5 at best and try to avoid him in innings-capped formats.

PROJECTION: 14-12 3.98 ERA 1.25 WHIP 173 K

64. **Shelby Miller:** Boy did we look bad early on last season when it came to pushing the wisdom of drafting St. Louis Cardinals young power starter Shelby Miller. After a terrific 2013 debut (3.06 ERA/1.21 WHIP/169 K), Miller seemed poised to take the next step in his development for 2014. After a good April showing when he pitched to a 3.15 ERA, Miller reeled off four straight months where that mark finished at 4.30 or higher. Miller showed almost none of the strikeout ability that made him so intriguing in the first place and his control was horrific. Fortunately Miller figured things out in September as he posted a dominant 1.48 ERA but by than the damage was done. While Miller was lucky to finish with a composite 3.74 ERA, his WHIP shot way up to 1.27. That ugly WHIP was also indicative of how hittable Miller was and also how poor his walk rate ended up being. Clearly Miller was fighting his stuff last season and it took him way too long to make adjustments. The Cardinals also spoke volumes about how they thought of Miller's ability when they dealt him to the Atlanta Braves early in the offseason. While the pedigree of being a former first round pick and a good 2013 campaign are reminders of how potent Miller can be, the scars from last season are going to be tough to erase. Decent enough bounce back upside but we are not drafting Miller as anything more than an SP 4.

PROJECTION: 14-8 3.63 ERA 1.24 WHIP 156 K

65. **Tanner Roark:** Proof positive that pitching is deeper than ever in today's game, the Washington Nationals' Tanner Roark did his part in upholding

that argument with his eye-opening full-season debut in 2014. After being pushed into the rotation at the start of the season after Doug Fister got injured, Roark dominated from the get-go and never really let up on his way to finishing with a 2.85 ERA to go along with 15 wins. Roark was well off the fantasy baseball radar going into last season as he was only a 25th round pick back in 2008 but his four-pitch repertoire clearly was a chore for major league hitters to deal with. Not possessing much in the way of strikeout ability (only 138 K's in his 198.2 innings), Roark used his excellent control to paint the corners and draw weak contact. Those in innings-capped leagues may not want to get involved here due to the low strikeout total but Roark looks like another Kyle Lohse-type that can be a sizable help as your SP 4 or 5.

PROJECTION: 15-9 3.22 ERA 1.12 WHIP 144 K

66. **Carlos Carrasco:** Long on potential but short on results through parts of four previous seasons, not much was expected out of fading Cleveland Indians pitching prospect Carlos Carrasco. While no one ever doubted Carrasco's potent fastball, he was continually pounded when on the mound, which was highlighted in his pathetic 2013 campaign (6.75 ERA/1.76 WHIP). However the Indians gave him one last chance and stayed even more patient when Carrasco opened up April with a 6.46 ERA. The Indians ultimately moved him to the bullpen at the start of May where Carrasco proceeded to go back to the basics with his repertoire. Clearly the move worked as Carrasco gained more confience with every scoreless outing from the pen. He was so good that the Indians moved him back to the rotation in August after Justin Masterson was dealt. Carrasco made 10 starts total through the end of the season and the results were staggering as he followd a 1.82 ERA August with a 1.62 September. In 74 innings the last two months of 2014, Carrasco rang up a terrific 83 strikeouts as he rediscovered his power game. There is no doubt that Carrasco was a difference-maker down the stretch but you always have to be careful buying in fully on such a small sample size. Carrasco pitched too badly for too long to completely ignore his past. The arm is electric but tread cautiously here.

PROJECTION: 11-7 3.72 ERA 1.27 WHIP 167 K

67. **Matt Garza:** Once again Matt Garza mixed injuries with solid numbers last season. Garza failed to throw even 170 innings for the third year in a row but he threw well when on the mound as evidenced by his 3.64 ERA. The same trends have come to define Garza's career, which means you are never buying a full season if you do choose to make an investment. The K rate also slipped a bit which is also something to be aware of. We like

Garza as a very solid SP 5 to round out your rotation, as he is not dependable enough with his health to be rated as anything higher.
PROJECTION: 9-8 3.65 ERA 1.19 WHIP 146 K

68. **John Lackey:** After it looked like John Lackey's career was headed for disaster due to a 6.41 ERA horror show in 2011, the veteran righty pulled himself back off the cliff after missing 2012 due to having undergone Tommy John surgery. With a new elbow ligament giving some life back to his sagging stuff, Lackey reeled off a 3.52 ERA 2013 campaign which was followed by a 3.82 mark last season in a year split between the Red Sox and St. Louis Cardinals. We like the fact Lackey will now be pitching a full season in the much-easier National League and in a solid pitcher's park. There is still a ton of mileage on this 36-year-old arm however and overall Lackey is now pretty much a 3.60 ERA/160 K guy which is a clear step down from his early Los Angeles Angels era.
PROJECTION: 14-11 3.58 ERA 1.27 WHIP 161 K

69. **Kyle Lohse:** Few realize just how good a pitcher Milwaukee Brewers starter Kyle Lohse has been over the last five years and the main reason for this is due to a low K rate that had many fantasy baseball players thumbing their noses at him. The big picture shows that Lohse is a terrific buy when you consider his ERA has been between 3.54 and 2.86 over the last four years, which goes nicely with his WHIP ranging between 1.17 and 1.09 during the same span. This is a guy who clearly knows how to get outs and whose top-notch control ensures he doesn't beat himself. Lohse is a soft-tosser all the way, with his career-high in K's being a very modest 143 and it is that reason he gets so disrespected in the first place. Even in innings-capped leagues, Lohse is a guy who will help more (wins, ERA, WHIP) than hurt (strikeouts). Look at the big picture.
PROJECTION: 15-11 3.46 ERA 1.16 WHIP 142 K

70. **Jose Quintana:** Many weren't paying attention but the Chicago White Sox' Jose Quintana has made himself into a very useful pitcher for 2015 fantasy baseball. Those who saw the potential in his right arm were rewarded with a better-than-expected 2014 campaign when Quintana logged a 3.34 ERA while striking out 178 batters on a bad White Sox team. Now three seasons into his career, Quintana has yet to post an ERA higher than 3.76 and his K rate has improved each year as well. The best part of all this is the fact Quintana will only turn 26 this January which means you could maybe squeeze in another small leap in numbers this season.
PROJECTION: 12-11 3.43 ERA 1.23 WHIP 179 K

71. **A.J. Burnett:** After threatening retirement prior to 2014 due to not getting the contract he wanted from the Pittsburgh Pirates, A.J, Burnett instead took a one-year deal with the Philadelphia Phillies. Moving from a prime pitching ballpark to one that clearly favors hitting did nothing good for Burnett as his ERA shot way up to 4.59 as walks and home runs reared their ugly heads again. Now 38, Burnett needs to find a home in a National League park that favors pitching or else more of what we saw in 2014 is likely.
PROJECTION: 9-12 4.32 ERA 1.34 WHIP 188 K

72. **Yovani Gallardo:** We have now entered into the "Next Phase" of Yovani Gallardo's fantasy baseball career. At one time a 200-K ace pitcher, Gallardo has bled out K's badly over the last two years to the tune of totals that didn't get out of the 140's. With Gallardo's losing more than a few ticks on his fastball, he successfully pitched more to contact in 2014 in logging a useful 3.51 ERA. However Gallardo's 1.29 WHIP is a reminder of his horrible career control and now his hit rate is spiking due to the lost fastball juice. Saying Gallardo is even SP 4 now can be considered a stretch.
PROJECTION: 12-14 3.66 ERA 1.30 WHIP 149 K

73. **Tim Lincecum:** A year ago we told you in this very space that we had no idea where to rank fading two-time Cy Young Award winner Tim Lincecum. This time around we have no such trouble as Lincecum is fresh off his third horrible season in a row and he ultimately shows no signs of even remotely being the star pitcher he once was. There is no need to rehash the obvious here with regards to Lincecum's arm being shot from all those crazy inning totals early on in his career. The evidence is right there in front of us as amid all those ugly numbers. Things are so bad now that we wouldn't even bother using Lincecum as an SP 5. Seriously.
PROJECTION: 11-14 4.48 ERA 1.33 WHIP 165 K

74. **Marco Estrada:** A decent sleeper candidate the last two seasons due to a very low walk rate and above-average K rate, Marco Estrada ultimately drove his owners crazy due to a sky-high home run tendency that ruined more than a few of his starts. That is why it is shocking the Toronto Blue Jays and their home run haven ballpark would trade Adam Lind for him early in the offseason. Estrada is going to get rocked at home given his home run habits and his K rate will dip going to the AL as well. Avoid completely.
PROJECTION: 12-11 3.98 ERA 1.19 WHIP 167 K

75. **C.C. Sabathia:** We were already fully off the C.C. Sabathia bandwagon even before the 2014 disaster that was the veteran lefty's season. It is now pretty well established that Sabathia's massive velocity loss over the last four years has completely destroyed his fastball potency and as a result made him incredibly hittable as evidenced by the 4.78 and 5.28 ERA's the last two years. Yes Sabathia managed to strike out 48 batters in his 46 innings last season but pretty much every other statistic was a complete abomination. No doubt all those 220-plus inning campaigns have sapped Sabathia of more than a little of his arm strength and than there is the matter of last year's invasive season-ending knee surgery further clouding this ugly picture. Not a chance we could ever recommend Sabathia under any circumstances.
PROJECTION: 11-8 4.48 ERA 1.29 WHIP 155 K

76. **Matt Moore:** Young Tampa Bay Rays lefty Matt Moore lasted all of 10 innings in 2014 before a torn elbow ligament led to season-ending Tommy John surgery. The Rays are hoping Moore can make it back sometime in May and as of this writing he has not suffered any known setbacks. When looking back on all this, Moore was a disaster waiting to happen as his 2013 was marred by elbow trouble was a harbinger of what was to come later. When healthy, Moore is a very good strikeout pitcher who keeps the hits to a minimum. Unfortunately Moore has very poor control that spikes his walk rate and doesn't allow him to pitch deep into games, costing him wins. The cost will be bargain-basement but Moore was not the greatest investment even before the surgery.
PROJECTION: 8-4 3.77 ERA 1.32 WHIP

77. **Tajuan Walker:** Technically still a rookie, we expected at this point to be talking about Tajuan Walker as one of the best young pitchers in major league baseball. However a spring training shoulder issue became a season-long problem to the point that Walker pitched all of 38 innings in 2014. There is no use in going through those innings due to the small sample size and instead we will delve back to the general scouting report on Walker being a prime power pitching prospect who has front-of-the-rotation ability. Walker fights his pitches from time-to-time which leads to walks but the strikeout ability is immense. Obviously the ballpark is as good as it gets for a pitcher and the much lower hype volume surrounding the kid make investing here even more of a good idea. Try again.
PROJECTION: 12-12 3.76 ERA 1.25 WHIP 173 K

78. **Tim Hudson:** The ageless Tim Hudson continues to bat back Father Time as he was generally successful in his first season with the San Francsico Giants in 2014. Once again using his sinkerball with great success, Hudson posted a 3.57 ERA and 1.23 WHIP while tossing 189.1 innings. The 9 wins were low for sure but Hudson got some terrible run support most of the season. Hudson was very smart in choosing to sign his free agent contract prior to last season with a National League team in a pitching-favoring park, which no doubt helped extend his already Hall of Fame career. One of the best pitchers of his generation that no one talks about, Hudson should be able to sneak through another year of useful ratios.
PROJECTION: 14-8 3.58 ERA 1.24 WHIP 127 K

79. **Michael Pineda:** Those who were new to fantasy baseball in 2014 likely had little clue as to who New York Yankees starting pitcher Michael Pineda was. After all, the last time Pineda pitched in a major league game was back in 2011 when he was an All-Star rookie with the Seattle Mariners. Persistent shoulder trouble kept Pineda out of action for both the 2012 and 2013 seasons before he finally made his return last April. With virtually no expectations given how long he was out, the Yankees had to be very pleased by what they saw as Pineda gave up only 56 hits in his 76.1 innings, while also logging a splendid 1.89 ERA and 0.83 WHIP. The low innings total was due to yet more injuries, which kept Pineda out for April all the way to August. Of course there was also that ridiculous pine tar suspension but Pineda still pitched great when he came back from that stupid incident. Pineda is still a power pitcher as his fastball was once again reaching the upper-90's last season but his body has to go along with the program for him to help us out. The price remains very cheap for Pineda given how much time he has missed the last three seasons but on stuff alone he is well worth a late round look.
PROJECTION: 9-5 3.17 ERA 1./05 WHIP 144 K

80. **Dallas Keuchel:** Joining Colin McHugh on the Houston Astros starting rotation breakout tour was lefty Dallas Keuchel in 2014. After getting blown up the previous two seasons to the tune of ERA's over 5.00 in both years, the light bulb seemed to go on for Keuchel as he never had an ERA over 3.58 in any one month. What really helped Keuchel turn the page on his ugly 2012 and 2013 campaigns was getting his gopher ball habits under control. After giving up 20 home runs in only 153.2 innings in 2013, Keuchel cut that number drastically to 11 in 200 innnings flat last season. While Keuchel doesn't have nearly the K rate that McHugh has, he limits walks and keeps the hits down which are obviously prime recipes for success.

PROJECTION: 12-8 3.48 ERA 1.19 WHIP 149 K

81. **Henderson Alvarez:** Another soft-tossing special here as the Miami Marlins' Henderson Alvarez proved himself as one of the better pitching values of last season in winning 12 games with a 2.65 ERA. Alvarez deserves the soft-toss label due to a very low K rate (only 111 whiffs in only 187 innings) but he clearly uses the team's spacious ballpark to his advantage. Like most soft-tossers, Alvarez gives up a lot of hits (198) but compensates with a tiny walk total (33). There is always more risk of a blowout in any given start without the K potential but Alvarez was too good for too long last season to think he was a complete fluke. Push the ERA above 3.0 and draft as an SP 5 guy.
PROJECTION: 14-11 3.52 ERA 1.23 WHIP 128 K

82. **Alfredo Simon:** There were more than a few jokes made along the way last season in the case of the Cincinnati Reds' Alfredo Simon, who was actually charged with attempted murder a few years ago (the charges were eventually dropped) before he found his way back to the major leagues. Mostly a terrible reliver in his career, Simon transitioned into the starting rotation for the Reds prior to the start of 2014 and more awful results were expected. Simon got the last laugh of course as he was one of the bigger surprises the first half of the season as he earned an All-Star nod by compiling 2.70 ERA and winning 12 games. Simon tired a bit during the second half (4.52 ERA) which was no surprise since he was moving into uncharted innings territory but overall the righty was a terrific value play. Anyone who finishes a season with a 3.44 ERA as Simon did in 2014 clearly knows how to get outs and chalking that completely up to a fluke would be silly. Simon has a good fastball that he complemets with nice offspeed stuff that generate outs. His K rate was much higher as a reliever though and ultimately we think Simon will get hit around more this season now that major league batters are getting a good read on him again. Last season was likely as good as it gets and Simon will only go down from this point on.
PROJECTION: 14-10 3.96 ERA 1.23 WHIP 137 K

83. **Mike Fiers:** You wonder why the Milwaukee Brewers didn't find a rotation spot sooner for Mike Fiers last season given the fact that the veteran righty was one of the best pitchers in baseball the last two months of 2014. Beginning the year in the minors, Fiers had a brief call-up in June where he pitched in four games out of the bullpen. When a need arose in the rotation early in August, Fiers was summoned as second time to fill that void with little expectations. Fiers was absolutely incredible however as he pitched to

a 1.80 ERA August with a 4-1 record. That was followed by a 2.43 ERA September (where he added 2 more victories). Despite a fastball that tops out at around 88-mph, Fiers generated a ton of swings and misses as he racked up 76 K's in 71.2 innings. We have seen this out of Fiers before when looking back at his 2012 performance (3.74 ERA/1.26/135 K in 127.2 IP) but a subsequent pounding the next year got him sent back to the minor leagues. Fiers will turn 30 in July so he is still young but he has to prove that he can hold up over a full season with regards to continuing fooling major league hitters. We will gladly take a shot in the late middle rounds on the K potential alone.

PROJECTION: 11-6 3.57 ERA 1.14 WHIP 163 K

84. **Bartolo Colon:** Despite turning 41 during the 2014 season, the New York Mets were applauded for giving a two-year contract to free agent pitcher Bartolo Colon last winter. Wanting a veteran presence in the team's very young rotation, GM Sandy Alderson felt that Colon's rubber arm and ability to continue getting outs with his top notch control and still solid stuff would be great teaching tools. Colon certainly did his part to earn the money as he won 15 games on a losing team while posting a 4.09 ERA and 1.23 WHIP. The Mets dangled Colon in trade talks last July but nothing came of it and at least for now the team is preparing to have him in the 2015 rotation. Colon is a good fit at Citi Field as his home run rate is quite high due to lost velocity. Always around the plate with his stuff, Colon doesn't walk anyone, which helps keep his WHIP low and ERA decent despite his age. The 151 strikeouts Colon collected last season are pretty much his maximum output at this stage but he sneaks in as a dependable SP 5 even in innings-capped leagues.

PROJECTION: 16-11 4.02 ERA 1.24 WHIP 144 K

85. **Derek Holland:** You pretty much have to completely toss out the 2014 "season" for Texas Rangers lefty Derek Holland who logged all of 37 innings while missing the majority of the year due to needing knee surgery after falling over his dog last January. That serious case of bad luck interrupted what was looking like a rise to possible stardom for Holland who took a major leap to prominence in 2013 when he put up a 3.42 ERA and struck out 189 batters while calling Texas' launching pad ballpark home. The talent is well above-average here and Holland looked very sharp upon his late-season return in 2014 which quieted some fears. There are some negatives though such as the fact that being a lefty starter is always a rough ride in Texas due to the home run tendencies of the place and Holland's control can be hit-or-miss. However this could be the quietest

190 strikeouts in the league this season so be sure Holland has a place on your sleeper list.

PROJECTION: 12-13 3.53 ERA 1.28 WHIP 174 K

86. **Jon Niese:** The lone lefty in the New York Mets rotation, veteran Jon Niese continues to post solid ratios (career 3.87 ERA) but the rest of the profile is medicore. Entering his sixth season as a member of the team, Niese' career-high in strikeouts is a modest 155 and that came back in 2012 as annual DL stints for shoulder trouble continue to hurt his counting numbers. In addition, Niese puts a solid amount of runners on base as evidenced by his career 1.35 WHIP. A good enough SP 5 in all formats, Niese is really better suited for non-innings capped leagues.

PROJECTION: 10-10 3.51 ERA 1.26 WHIP 149 K

87. **Chris Young:** The shocking AL Comeback Player of the Year, Chris Young stayed healthy enough last season to post a 3.65 ERA and 1.23 WHIP in winning 12 games for the Seattle Mariners. This after Young failed to pitch at all in 2013 due to yet more injuries. There may not have been a bigger health mess than Young over the last six years but when on the mound the hulking 6-10 righty gets outs with a fastball that comes in faster than it looks due to his long release point. Obviously Young can't be trusted to stay on the mound for even 100 innings so don't exert yourself drafting him even in the late rounds.

PROJECTION: 7-4 3.75 ERA 1.25 WHIP 95 K

88. **Jason Vargas:** No matter the location, the story remained the same for Jason Vargas. A decent pitcher who has posted ERA's under 4.00 in three of the last five years, Vargas was a home start gem and a road start bum. That is until his first season with the Kansas City Royals in 2014 when he flipped the script on that trend. No matter how the numbers break down, Vargas remains a guy who will supply a mid-3.00 to low-4.00 ERA with a mediocre strikeout rate. You an do better.

PROJECTION: 12-11 3.82 ERA 1.28 WHIP 135 K

89. **Bud Norris:** Bud Norris is that classic high-strikeout pitcher you always feel the pull to pick up but than one look at his usually awful ratios keep you from making that mistake. There is no doubt that Norris and his awful control have burned more than a few owners over the years who were seduced by his high K potential but the veteran righty actually comes off his best season in 2014. Norris recorded wins in 15 games on a divison-winning Baltimore Orioles team to go along with an ERA of 3.65. Norris' control remained ugly but he reduced his hit rate, which was all the more

impressive since he made the move from the National to the American League. In fact some of Norris' improvement could be the result of pitching more to contact as his K rate dropped noticeably but his ERA went down for the ride as well. Maturation could be in play here but regardless Norris is too risky to depend on as anything more than a SP 5.

PROJECTION: 14-10 3.90 ERA 1.25 WHIP 162 K

90. **Hiroki Kuroda:** Still no word yet on whether or not Hiroki Kuroda will pitch in the majors this season, return to Japan, or just simply retire. The 40-year-old veteran still showed he has the goods to be a successful pitcher in 2014, as he put up a 3.71 ERA and 1.14 WHIP in his third season for the New York Yankees. Few realize just how good a career Kuroda has had, as he has yet to post an ERA north of 3.76 in his 7 major league seasons, nor has he registered a WHIP higher than 1.22. After Kuroda struggled badly the last two months of 2013, there were questions whether he had the stamina to make it through a full season at his age. Kuroda swatted away those thoughts a year ago as he had his best monthly ERA last September at 2.81. We would like to see Kuroda sign for one more season in the easier National League but no matter where he ends up, count on more useful ratios and a mediocre K rate.

PROJECTION: 14-10 3.75 ERA 1.16 WHIP 149 K

91. **Wily Peralta:** When looking at the advanced numbers, it was amazing that Wily Peralta was able to win 17 games last season. Anyone who gives up 23 home runs, walks 61 batters, and gives up a hit per inning needs some sizable batted ball luck to register a 3.53 ERA. Peralta's 1.30 WHIP is more indicative of what type of pitcher he really is and with a K rate that is just average, this one has bust written all over it.

PROJECTION: 11-12 3.93 ERA 1.32 WHIP 156 K

92. **Drew Hutchinson:** It was a mixed bag of numbers for Drew Hutchinson in his first full season for the Toronto Blue Jays in 2014. A 4.48 ERA was not too hot but the 184 punchouts in 184.2 innings certainly were nice. Obviously Hutchinson's power arsenal would play much better in the National League but he has room to get better in 2015. If Hutchinson can be more economical with his pitches and keep the baseball in the park a bit better, a move toward going under 4.00 with the ERA is likely. Worth the cost to find out given the strikeout impact.

PROJECTION: 12-14 4.10 ERA 1.24 WHIP 188 K

93. **Edinson Volquez:** The Pittsburgh Pirates organization once again reaffirmed itself as the Lourdes for struggling pitchers. It started with A.J.

Burnett, ran through Francisco Liriano, and continued on with Edinson Volquez last season as the former walk-plagued washout put up a career year that no one could have predicted. Volquez posted his best hit rate ever in 2014 which helped lead to a career-low 3.04 ERA and 1.23 WHIP. Those numbers are a mile from where Volquez usually resided in previously and speaks to how they clearly are doing something right in Pittsburgh. Of course we can never feel too comfortable in completely buying into Volquez' 2014 statistical haul given how horrible he was for pretty much his entire career. Volquez did dial back the strikeouts last season which is always a sign of a pitcher trusting his stuff more but we need to see more of what he showed in 2014 in order to buy in totally.

PROJECTION: 11-8 4.05 ERA 1.26 WHIP 155 K

94. **Drew Smyly:** The Detroit Tigers have such a surplus of starting pitching that a guy who has the look of a solid SP 4 is currently on the outside looking in when it comes to the 2015 rotation. Long man duty looks like the calling for Drew Smyly at least at the start of the season for a second year in a row given the crowded nature of the Detroit rotation. That is a bit of a shame considering how good he pitched down the stretch in 2014. With the Tigers making a playoff push, Smyly was virtually unhittable in August (1.50 ERA) and September (2.31). Smyly's stay in the rotation last season coincided with the health-challenged absence of Anibal Sanchez and the same situation could unfold in 2015 given how brittle the latter is. Smyly was a second round pick of the Tigers in 2010 so the pedigree is there for the guy who struck out 44 batters in his last 48.2 innings. Not the worst idea to use one of your last picks on this upside play.

PROJECTION: 10-7 3.88 ERA 1.27 WHIP 159 K

95. **Brandon McCarthy:** It has been a bit of a roller coaster ride for veteran righthander Brandon McCarthy over the last few seasons. McCarthy broke through in 2011 and 2012 when he registered 3.32 and 3.24 ERA's with the Oakland A's, showcasing a deep pitching repertoire that kept hitters routinely off balance. After signing with the Arizona Diamondbacks prior to 2013, McCarthy proceeded to have a truly horrific season all the way around as he posted a 4.53 ERA and suffered a scary HBP to the skull that could have killed him. More struggles ensued once McCarthy made it back to the D-Backs for 2014 amid reports that the coaching staff wouldn't allow him to use his offspeed stuff. A trade was soon consummated with the pitching-desperate New York Yankees that was the impetus to a big rally for McCarthy's season. Being the rare pitcher who posted much better results in going from the NL to the AL, McCarthy pitched like a staff ace for the Yankees as he won 7 of his 14 starts to go along with a 2.89 ERA

and 1.15 WHIP. In addition, McCarthy boosted his K rate to its highest mark in years. A free agent at press time, McCarthy is back in play as a solid SP 4. He is a little light in the strikeouts but McCarthy's ratios work.
PROJECTION: 14-10 3.57 ERA 1.17 WHIP 121 K

96. **Mark Buehrle:** The rubber arm of Mark Buehrle continues to chug along in showing no signs of age as he comes off his best season since 2005. Despite being 35-years-old, pitching in the roughest divison in baseball in the AL East, and once again showing nothing in the way of strikeouts, Buehrle registered a 3.39 ERA while winning 13 games. One of the more amazing stats among pitchers of this generation is the fact Buehrle has thrown 200 or more innings for 14 straight seasons. The story of his career remains the same as Buehrle is pretty much nothing more than a late round grab in non-innings capped league.
PROJECTION: 12-9 3.84 ERA 1.33 WHIP 122 K

97. **Justin Masterson:** Maybe now everyone will listen to us regarding our strong contention that Justin Masterson is one of the more overrated pitchers in fantasy baseball. The hype meter went into overdrive when Masterson put together a career-year in 2013 by posting a 3.45 ERA, while ringing up 195 strikeouts for the Cleveland Indians. We never for a second bought into the numbers, as we wrote in last year's guide, due to the fact it screamed "outlier" since Masterson had never approached those statistics before. Masterson also got very lucky with his strand rate and BABIP, which figured to blow up on him in 2014. Blow up it did, as Masterson was arguably one of the worst pitchers in all of baseball last season as he was hit around in both leagues (the Indians dealt him to the St. Louis Cardinals at the trade deadline). The result was a pathetic 5.88 ERA and a K rate that plummeted back to his career norms. A free agent as of this writing, we wouldn't touch Masterson no matter where he went.
PROJECTION: 12-12 4.23 ERA 1.27 WHIP 155 K

98. **Travis Wood:** Anyone could have told you that the 2014 season put up by Travis Wood (3.11 ERA/1.15 WHIP) was not to be repeated. Wood was incredibly fortunate with both his BABIP and strand rate that year which left his ERA not indicative at all when it came to how good a pitcher the guy really was. Thus the fallout in 2014 when Wood's luck corrected itself which was beyond ugly. Getting hit hard from the get-go, Wood was a complete liabiliy to own for most of last season as he finished with a 5.03 ERA and 1.53 WHIP. In fact Wood's hitting was more impressive than his pitching.
PROJECTION: 9-14 4.35 ERA 1.26 WHIP 145 K

THE REST

99. **Jesse Hahn:** Deep sleeper alert. We surely want to see more of young San Diego Padres righthander Jesse Hahn who could be the latest Petco Park pitching gem. Despite garnering only 14 starts last season, Hahn was very impressive in posting 7 wins with a 3.07 ERA and striking out 70 batters in 73.1 innings. The fastball can touch 95 and Hahn's repertoire goes deep. Like other young power pitchers, control is an issue, as are home runs. Obviously the home run problem is negated by the vast dimensions of Petco Park and we love arms which can miss bats like Hahn's can. Keep him in mind late.

100. **Josh Collmenter:** Now four years into his MLB career, Arizona's Josh Collmenter has yet to post a season ERA higher than 3.69. Able to mix speeds effectively to compensate for an ordinary fastball, Collmenter continually draws weak contact and keeps walks to a minimum which is key without the strikeout ability. Avoid in innings-capped formats.

101. **Carlos Martinez:** It is always a good idea to be aware of any young St. Louis Cardinals pitcher due to the team's great record of developing prospects. Martinez is very interesting in a Carlos Carrasco kind of way, what with his top end fastball and developing secondary stuff. Needs a rotation spot to be worth anything however so monitor his standing as spring training gets underway.

102. **Dillon Gee:** Dillon Gee failed to build on the huge second half of 2013 that put him on the fantasy baseball map last season. The smallish righthander remainded a top-notch control guy who could paint the corners but Gee was a bit more hittable as his ERA spiked to 4.00 with a WHIP of 1.25. Gee won't ever hurt you as he can strike out 150 guys with solid ratios but poor health makes him unreliable.

103. **Drew Pomeranz:** It was a small 69 inning sample size but Drew Pomeranz could be another Oakland A's pitching asset this season if he claims a rotation spot. Pomeranrz has a live arm that is capable of good strikeout totals and the ballpark works. Monitor early to see if he grabs a rotation spot and draft accordingly.

104. **Charlie Morton:** Charlie Morton has posted 3.26 and 3.72 ERA's the last two seasons which is probably better than you thought. The guy is a crafty veteran who possesses top control that compensates for the lack of

K's. Another guy you can grab off waivers or draft late in non-innings capped leagues.

105. James Paxton: James Paxton pitched well when on the hill last season but health was huge challenge for the Seattle Mariners righty as he amassed only 74 innings due to a long DL stint for a strained back muscle. He will get another chance to stick in the rotation for 2014 where his solid K rate, tremendous ballpark, and decent stuff could supply a quiet sleeper campaign.

106. Yusmeiro Petit: Once again the San Francisco Giants waffled Yusmeiro Petit from the bullpen to the starting rotation as needed in 2014. Through it all Petit continued to show explosive power stuff that can be unhittable at times. Petit has done more than enough to be given a chance to start from the beginning of 2015 and if he does claim a spot, this could be among the cheapest 175 strikeouts you can get. Watch closely in the spring and get ready to pounce if he does in fact land a rotation slot.

107. Mike Leake: Another guy who should only be used in non-inning capped leagues. Mike Leake has impressed with 3.37 and 3.70 ERA's the last two seasons but the 164 strikeouts he collected in 2014 were about the best you can expect there, which is nothing but a mediocre number. Think Kyle Lohse with much less of a track record.

108. Ubaldo Jimenez: It took only one season for the Baltimore Orioles to admit to themselves they blew it by signing Ubaldo Jimenez as a free agent prior to the 2014 season. After a nice comeback with the Cleveland Indians the year prior when he posted a 3.30 ERA, Jimenez was hit hard all last year to the tune of a 4.81 mark. The 1.52 WHIP Jimenez also put up shows how awful his control is and how his hit rate is also nothing to brag about. One guy you should have no business looking at under any circumstance.

109. Danny Salazar: We ate a ton of crow on Danny Salazar last season but we weren't alone. The high-powered fastball of Salazar was still immense but he was a complete mess with his lack of control and leaving balls all over the plate. 35 walks and 13 home runs given up in 110 innings is horrific and is the main reason for the unsightly 1.38 WHIP. Salazar still hinted at his potential in striking out 120 batters but lots of work needs to be done here before we can trust the kid again. Watch early though to see if a breakthrough takes place and than jump back on the bandwagon.

110. **Tony Cingrani:** Sort of along the same path as Danny Salazar, Cincinnati's Tony Cingrani bombed last season when many expected a full breakout. Cingrani showed none of the potential he exhibited in 2013 when he registered a 2.92 ERA and 1.10 WHIP while striking out 120 batters in only 104.2 innings. While Cingrani still struck out a batter per inning last season, his walk and home run rates were a mess and he gave up a hit per inning, which doesn't work for keeping tidy ratios. He is not guaranteed a spot in the team's rotation this season but is still interesting if given a chance.

111. **Dan Straily:** Dan Straily always carried some intrigue due to his strikeout ability but he has been rocked when given a long look by the Oakland A's. Wait for Straily to prove himself over a longer stint before you dive back in.

112. **Ivan Nova:** Tommy John surgery will keep Ivan Nova out until at least the summer which means he can safely be ignored. Nova was getting rocked before going under the knife last season anyway as he once again was all over the plate with his inconsistent stuff. Nova has simply not developed into a pitcher that can be trusted and now he is coming back from major surgery. No thank you.

113. **Hector Santiago:** Hector Santiago's conversion from reliver to starter has gone well enough as he pitched to a 3.75 ERA last season while striking out 108 batters in 127.1 innings. Alas Santiago's 1.36 WHIP is a major problem which can be blamed on terrible control that followed him fron the bullpen. Also Santiago still has not been able to pitch deep into games yet which severely limits his wins potential. Spot start only.

114. **Miguel Gonzalez:** Miguel Gonzalez has been a solid starter in his three-year major league career, never having posted an ERA higher than 3.78. In fact Gonzalez has finished with an ERA under 3.30 twice in his three seasons and that is especially impressive when you consider he pitches in the rough AL East with the Baltimore Orioles. This is a soft-tosser all the way who will forever collect mediocre K rates. Good as a SP 5 in non-innings capped setups only.

115. **Wei-Yin Chen:** Wei-Yin Chen has quietly been an effective pitcher in his three-season tenure with the Baltimore Orioles but he has given up more hits than innings pitched the last two years which shows you how shaky he can be. In addition, Chen will struggle to even approach 150 K's which means he is very limited in what he can do for your roster.

116. **Clay Buchholz:** Clay Buchholz was hit as hard as any pitcher in baseball last season and remains a horrible fit in the American League due to the fact he doesn't possess above-average strikeout stuff. Another disaster waiting to happen.

117. **Jorge De La Rosa:** Yeah he is still hanging around. At one time all us took a chance on the hard-throwing Jorge De La Rosa but ultimately ended up disappointed due to his Coors Field ballpark, injuries, and epic control issues. Now 34, De La Rosa is not young anymore and he is losing strikeouts as he ages, which was the prime reason we picked him up in the first place. Leave this one alone once and for all.

118. **Jesse Chavez:** Was terrific early on out of the rotation but eventually moving into uncharted innings territory made Jesse Chavez much more hittable. Chavez was soon moved to the bullpen where he finished the rest of the season. Will likely stay in the bullpen to begin 2015 and thus have little to no fantasy baseball value.

119. Roenis Elias: Young lefty did some nice things as a rookie for the Seattle Mariners in 2014, pitching to a 3.85 ERA while striking out 143 batters in 163.2 innings. Actually pitched better on the road than at home which says something. A kid to monitor early on.

120. **Bronson Arroyo:** Tommy John surgery spares no one and that includes one of baseball's most durable pitchers over the last decade. We are referring of course to Bronson Arroyo whose first season with the Arizona Diamondbacks was cut short due to the ligament transplant operation. It is very rare for older pitchers to have the surgery but no matter. Arroyo won't be back until late summer and he wasn't much of help outside of spot starts even before he went under the knife. It was a decent career but Arroyo's days of relevancy seem finished.

121. **Jarred Cosart:** Average righty who is still very young at 25. Bombed out of the Houston Astros organization before finding a new home with the always welcoming Miami Marlins. The control is awful here and with just an all right K rate, there is nothing here to get excited about.

122. **Nathan Eovaldi:** Eovaldi can routinely touch the upper 90's with his fastball but the K rate has never matched the impressive speed. After a nice 2.58 ERA April, Eovaldi turned back to the mediocre starter he always has been. Over the last five months of 2014, Eovaldi posted an ERA of 4.31 or

higher in four of them. In other words you don't need to waste much time with this.

123. **Tsyoshi Wada:** The Chicago Cubs wisely re-signed Japanese import Tsyoshi Wada early in the offseason after a very intriguing rookie debut in 2014 that saw him pitch to a 3.25 ERA in 14 starts. A rotation spot is there for the taking and Wada has some potent strikeout stuff that is of interest. A good last round lottery grab that could pay off nicely.

124. **Jaime Garcia:** It is very rare when you get the chance to see Jaime Garcia pitch for the St. Louis Cardinals as he is always dealing with one injury or another. He threw very well in his 43.2 innings last season and Garcia has registered ERA's under 4.00 every year from 2010 through 2013, which counts for something. Leave a spot open for Garcia as a last round pick.

125. **Odrisamer Despaigne:** The Cuban Revolution is well underway right now when it comes to big-time talents arriving on a yearly basis from our neighbors to the south. Odrisamer Despaigne falls right in line with this group as the Havana native had a nice debut in 2014 for the San Diego Padres in ringing up a 3.36 ERA and 1.21 WHIP. Despaigne paints the corners well and can ramp up the fastball when needed. He is obviously helped immensely by Petco Park, which alone makes Despaigne someone to watch closely. Take a late round stab and see if he can build on his solid results from last season.

126. **A.J. Griffin:** Like with rotation-mate Jarrod Parker, don't look for A.J. Griffin to return to the Oakland A's until the summer at the earliest. A guy you always stream at home but bench on the road, Griffin should be ignored completely.

127. **Brandon Beachy:** Brandon Beachy can't catch a break as he failed to make it out of spring training last season before having to undergo Tommy John surgery for thre second time in his career. Once one of the most promising power pitchers in the game, Beachy is now just another name who won't even appear in a major league game again until late in the summer.

128. **Jarrod Parker:** Jarrod Parker was one half of the dual Tommy John surgery attack on the Oakland A's starting rotation last spring training (A.J. Griffin was the other). As a result of the surgery, Parker is not expected back until June at the earliest. A decent pitcher, who posts usable ratios

combined with a just all right strikeout rate, Parker could help the second half of the season if he has no setbacks with the elbow. Revisit later.

129. **Scott Feldman:** Aging veteran always gives a solid account of himself but overall Scott Feldman carries little fantasy baseball value. Always seemingly pitching on bad teams and possessing a poor K rate, Feldman can pretty much be ignored in drafts.

130. **Kevin Gausman:** After bombing out in his 2013 debut, hard-throwing Baltimore Orioles pitching prospect Kevin Gausman took some baby steps last season as he continued with his development. Gausman registered an impressive 3.57 ERA and won 7 games in 20 starts but there are still some issues here such as a high walk rate contributing to a 1.30 WHIP. The potential is there but Gausman still has some more work to do before he becomes usable.

131. **T.J. House:** T.J. House had some good starts down the stretch of the season in his 2014 debut but a 1.32 WHIP and only 80 K's in 102 innings are not overly impressive. The former 16th round pick of the Cleveland Indians is only needed for spot start duty.

132. **Jeff Locke:** Jeff Locke has had some nice stretches of very good pitching over the last two seasons but he also has shown he can go weeks with getting his head pounded in. A career 1.36 WHIP is all the evidence you need to know about how hittable Locke can be and he doesn't possess the strikeout ability to make himself worth more than a guy you use when he is hot.

133. **Chase Anderson:** Picking up 105 K's in 114.1 innings was interesting but Chase Anderson was a placeholder in the Arizona Diamondbacks rotation and not part of the future solution. No thank you.

134. **Tom Koehler:** A 3.81 ERA put Tom Koehler on the fantasy baseball map last season but a 1.30 WHIP and mediocre K rate should get him off. While Koehler had some dominant outings last season, the guy looks like a classic stremable play when needed.

135. **Gavin Floyd:** The Atlanta Braves stupidly put Alex Wood in the bullpen in order to open up a rotation spot for veteran Gavin Floyd but in actuality the latter pitched well in his 54.1 innings as shown in his 2.65 ERA. Still Floyd is a been there/done that boring pitcher who has some tiny value in non-innings capped leagues.

136. **Ryan Vogelsong:** Another aging pitcher who needs to stay in the NL to at least salvage some value. Vogelsong was a nice story a few years ago when he made it back to the major leagues but he should not be on any roster this season.

137. **Shane Greene:** Took advantage of an injury-plagued New York Yankees rotation to appear out of the blue to post 81 strikeouts in 78.1 innings for the team which opened some eyes. Green had an ERA over 4.00 at Triple-A before his promotion however and eventually the league caught up to him toward the end of his major league innings. Feel free to monitor but don't draft until we see Greene reach another level.

138. **Joe Kelly:** Boston Red Sox soft-tosser Joe Kelly may not even have a rotation spot this season so there really is no reason to make a play on the guy. Kelly has helped in the past in short spurts but that was in the easier NL with the St. Louis Cardinals. The AL won't be kind.

139. **Martin Perez:** Yet another Tommy John surgery victim, Martin Perez is not due back until late summer. Perez was really on the way to a breakthrough campaign last season until the elbow gave out but that story is no longer intruiging. Pass.

140. **Aaron Harang:** Apparently Aaron Harang was not ready to be chased out of the league as he had a mini-comeback season with the Atlanta Braves in 2014 in posting a 3.57 ERA and winning 12 games. A 1.40 WHIP showed how many runners Harang still puts on base which means he remains dangerous to own. Likely going right back to oblivion.

141. **Jeremy Guthrie:** More of the same out of Jeremy Guthrie as he generally posts an ERA around 4.00 and a WHIP above 1.25 while posting a mediocre K rate. A better real-life pitcher than a fantasy baseball one.

142. **Tyler Skaggs:** Revisit this in 2016 as Tykler Skaggs won't be ready to pitch until very late in the season due to Tommy John surgery.

143. **J.A. Happ:** If you are drafting J.A. Happ, you should be doing something else.

144. **Jeremy Hellickson:** Once a highly regarded prospect in the Tampa Bay Rays organization, the team finally threw in the towel on Jeremy Hellickson by dealing him to the Arizona Diamondbacks early in the offseason. While

getting out of the AL East and the American League as a whole should make Hellickson more interesting, his gopher ball tendencies are a horrible match with Chase Field. Tread carefully.

145. **Josh Johnson:** Tommy John surgery stuck a fork in the intriging San Diego Padres signing of former All-Star power pitcher Josh Johnson in 2014. It has been a terrible struggle for Johnson to stay healthy over the last four years and his stuff has diminished during that period as a result of all the maladies he has suffered through. Look for a return sometime in the summer but overall Johnson is becoming pure waiver trash.

RELIEF PITCHERS

We are pretty sure we don't have to go into great detail here as far as suggesting you not even look at this extremely volatile group until the middle-to-late-middle rounds of your draft. Consider that not even a month into the 2014 season, over 10 closers who began the year holding onto the ninth inning gig were already out of a job. And things only got crazier from there. When the dust cleared, only 15 closers stayed in the role for their original team all season long. With injuries, demotions, and trades constantly turning over this group, there is absolutely no need to pick a closer any earlier than the middle rounds. We would even suggest waiting until the late middle rounds as you can pick up saves all season long if you can manage the waiver wire.

New York Yankees (David Robertson-Dellin Betances): As of this writing, David Robertson is a free agent who was presented a $15 million qualifying one-year offer by the New York Yankees to return. That is an extremely high number for a reliever so Robertson might bite at that level of salary. On numbers alone, Robertson was one of the best closers in the game last season as he converted 39 saves with a 3.08 ERA and an extreme 96 strikeouts in only 64.1 innings. Long one of the most potent strikeout relievers in the game, Robertson transitioned the Yankees seamlessly away from the Mariano Rivera period. If Robertson does depart in free agency, the Yanks have a ready-made solution in fireballer Dellin Betances. A failed starter prospect, Betances went wild in his 2014 rookie season in posting a tiny 1.40 ERA and striking out an insane 130 batters in 90 innings. The Yankees worked Betances hard but he never showed any signs of fatigue or wear. It is very rare when a reliever can pass the 100-K mark, which only adds to Betances' potential value. If saves come along for the ride, Betances could challenge for the top tier with Craig Kimbrel and Greg Holland.

Boston Red Sox (Koji Uehara): The Boston Red Sox re-committed to Koji Uehara as the team's closer early in the offseason, signing the Japanese sensation to a two-year deal worth $18 million. Uehara was more hittable last season as his ERA rose to 2.52 from the previous year's 1.09 but he still punched out 80 batters in only 64.1 innings. Turning 40 in April, there is always concern about injury and more falloff at that advanced age. A possible red flag was the ugly finish to last season for Uehara as he posted 5.56 and 6.23 ERA's in August and September respectively. With closer volatility at an all-time high, we would let Uehara pass if given the choice.

Baltimore Orioles (Zach Britton): We told you the Tommy Hunter choice as the Baltimore Orioles closer to begin 2014 was destined to fail. Fail it did as Hunter barely made it out of the gate before his soft-tossing ways proved a poor match for the ninth inning. Enter former failed starting pitching prospect Zach Britton, whose high-mileage fastball but lack of good secondary stuff made him an interesting replacement. Britton became the latest closer success story to go down this path as he put up a 1.65 ERA and 0.90 WHIP while converting 37 saves. Britton's K rate was a bit lower than most closers as he struck out 62 batters in 76.1 innings but the overall results were terrific. There is a threat of a one-year wonder as Britton has less margin for error than the fireballing class but the fact he didn't wilt in a playoff push shows you at least mentally the kid checks out.

Toronto Blue Jays (Brett Cecil-Casey Janssen): As of press time, 2014 closer Casey Janssen remains a free agent but the Toronto Blue Jays are well-stocked with hard throwing relievers that could step into the ninth inning if he ultimately departs. While Janssen has always pitched well when healthy, persistent shoulder trouble makes him unreliable. In addition, Janssen had his worst season statistically in 2014 with his 3.94 ERA and 1.18 WHIP. After pitching to an ERA of 2.56 or less from 2011 through 2013, Janssen was hit pretty hard at times last season, accounting for the rise in ERA. Another red flag was the fact Janssen struck out only 28 batters in 45.2 innings as his K rate fell off the map. When you consider Janssen was previously a K/IP guy, the drop-off there possibly is an indication that his shoulder issues are sapping his arm strength. As a result, looking at possible replacements is the key here and Brett Cecil should head that class as we move toward the 2015. Over the last two seasons out of the pen (again after being a failed starter), Cecil posted ERA's of 2.82 and 2.70 while striking out 146 batters in only 114 innings. Aaron Sanchez is can also be looked at as a darkhorse candidate given his explosive stuff as well so keep close tabs on this situation in March.

Tampa Bay Rays (Jake McGee): The Tampa Bay Rays found their closer for the present and maybe for the future as hard-throwing Jake McGee proved a good fit during the 2014 season. McGee had generally been a solid setup man for the Rays since breaking into the major leagues back in 2011 but saves proved elusive until last season when he finished 19 games while posting a tiny 1.89 ERA. The strikeout rate checked out as well, with McGee striking out 90 batters in only 71.1 innings. While McGee does not have much of a track record pitching in high-pressure situations, the low-key Tampa Bay environment should give him a good chance to be a solid and cheap source of saves.

Detroit Tigers (Joe Nathan): After having arguably his best of many great seasons in 2013, the Detroit Tigers gave a two-year free agent contract to a nearly 40-year-old Joe Nathan prior to 2014 in thinking the former Stony Brook product would solve their perpetual issues in the ninth inning. Well Nathan only made the Tigers' adventures closing out games more pronounced last season as he went through long stretches of terrible pitching that resulted in an unsightly 4.81 ERA and 1.53 WHIP. The Tigers would have removed Nathan from the closer role given his struggles but they had no one else capable of doing the job until trading for Joakim Soria late. Soria is back in setup for now as manager Brad Ausmus plans to go into the 2015 season with Nathan at closer again but this is a situation that could change quickly. Given how poorly Nathan pitched in 2014 and also given his age, the much more capable Soria is a good bet to lead the Tigers in saves. Soria himself pitched very well last season coming back from Tommy John surgery and thus is the much better choice to close games.

Cleveland Indians (Cody Allen): Cleveland Indians manager Terry Francona is one of the best in the game at what he does but the one area he mysteriously got wrong early on last season was the team's closer situation. Defying all conventional wisdom on the issue, Francona decided to go with the awful John Axford in the ninth inning to start the season, which of course ended up with disastrous results. After auditioning the rest of his bullpen for a few weeks, Francona correctly decided that strikeout artist Cody Allen was the best man for the job. Allen rewarded Francona's selection by dominating with a 2.07 ERA and striking out 91 batters in 69.2 innings pitched. As long as Allen keeps on doing what he is doing, a long future lies ahead of him as an above-average closer.

Kansas City Royals (Greg Holland): While many will say that Craig Kimbrel is the best closer in baseball, the numbers suggest that Kansas City Royals stopper Greg Holland is at least his equal. After getting his control issues squared away prior to the 2013 season, Holland has reeled off tremendous ERA's of 1.21 and 1.44 the last two years. With a K rate as good as anyone in baseball and flat in his prime, Holland is as safe a bet as anyone to be the top closer in the game this season.

Minnesota Twins (Glen Perkins): After a rough April, Minnesota Twins closer Glen Perkins reminded all of us that he is quietly one of the best stoppers in fantasy baseball. The southpaw has lacked in the flash department due to the fact the Twins have been so bad the last few years but on the numbers alone, Perkins ranks with the best of them. Last year's 3.65 ERA was more than a full run higher than where that number came in for Perkins from 2011 through 2013 but the K rate is still imposing. Turning a still young 32 this March, Perkins remains one the better closer buys when you consider track record and the cheaper price he costs compared to some other names around him in the rankings.

Chicago White Sox (Jake Petricka): The Chicago White Sox bullpen was nothing but an ulcer-inducing mess in 2014. After presumptive closer Nate Jones couldn't make it through April before missing the virtually the entire season with injury, the White Sox foolishly turned to multiple failed closer Matt Lindstrom to hold the fort. Lindstrom bombed as expected which than began a run through pretty much the entire White Sox bullpen before youngster Jake Petricka stabilized things a bit by recording 14 saves with an ERA of 2.96. That should give Petricka a leg up on being the closer to begin 2015 but he has bust written all over him. For one, Petricka's 1.37 WHIP last season shows you how he relied on good BABIP fortune to post his 2.96 ERA. When that number normalizes this season, Petricka will be in major trouble. In addition, Petricka has very little margin for error as well since he only struck out 55 batters in 73 innings. The fact Petricka doesn't miss bats is a major problem in the ninth inning, where having a potent K rate is a major part of the gig. Avoid at all costs.

Texas Rangers (Neftali Feliz): Joakim Soria reestablished himself as a closer the first half of the 2014 season after the Texas Rangers took a chance on him in coming back from Tommy John surgery. However Soria was dealt to the Detroit Tigers at the trade deadline and that brought former All-Star closer Neftali Feliz back into the ninth inning picture. Having battled arm/shoulder injuries of his own going back to 2012, Feliz actually pitched well as he posted an ERA of 1.99 and 0.98 WHIP while recording 13 saves. However Feliz' velocity was down more than a little from his 2011 heyday as he struck out only 21 batters in his 31.2 innings. The decrease in velocity from his pre-injury seasons heightens the bust potential going forward with Feliz. Another injury could be right around the corner as Feliz will try to navigate a full season for the first time in years and the drop in his K rate is always a major red flag to keep an eye on. Watch out.

Los Angeles Angels (Huston Street): After a career year that was highlighted by the fact he stayed healthy for a whole season for the first time, the Los Angeles Angels didn't hesitate in picking up his $7 million option for 2015. The Angels acquired Street at last season's trade deadline from the San Diego Padres with the idea he would solve their ongoing issues in the ninth inning. Solve them Street did as he was unhittable for large stretches of the season to the tune of a 1.37 ERA and a total of 41 saves. The Angels historically have supplied some of the highest save opportunities in the league for years and so Street is as good a bet as anyone to lead baseball in that statistic. The bigger issue is whether Street can stay healthy for two years running, which is a big uncertainty given his long medical history. Be that as it may, Street has burned so many owners over the years that his draft price is never extraordinarily high.

Seattle Mariners (Fernando Rodney): It was a typical year for Seattle Mariners closer Fernando Rodney in 2014. He picked up a high allotment of saves (48) on a team that historically plays close games, he posted a solid ERA (2.85), struck out a high rate of batters (76 in 66.1 innings) and issues with walks blew up his WHIP (1.34). Rodney is always seemingly walking a tightrope in his appearances, due to the walks and a hit rate that is higher than some of the other top closers, which can be heartburn inducing. However Rodney is aging like a fine wine as he turns 38 in March. Always very durable, Rodney should be right on target in replicating last season's numbers in 2015.

Houston Astros (Chad Qualls): It had been a long and trying road back to a closer role for Houston Astros stopper Chad Qualls. After serving as a quality ninth inning man for the Arizona Diamondbacks from 2008 through 2009, Qualls began a five-year odyssey that took him to 7 different MLB organizations as he struggled to pitch even adequately. After seemingly being down to his last shot to stick in the major leagues, Qualls re-discovered his stuff in 2013 with the Miami Marlins as he pitched to a 2.61 ERA. That got him back to the Houston Astros for 2014 (Qualls made his major league debut there in 2004 and pitched four years for the team) where he reclaimed a closer role with solid success. Overall Qualls finished 19 games while posting a solid ERA (3.33) for a second season in a row. Closing games for the Astros is a rough deal given the fact the team supplies few opportunities and historically have jettisoned their stopper at the trade deadline on a yearly basis. The same deal could very well happen to Qualls this season as well. We wouldn't bother here unless Qualls is hanging around late in your draft.

Oakland A's (Sean Doolittle): It didn't get as much attention as it should have but Oakland A's lefty Sean Doolittle had a tremendous breakout season in 2014 as the team's new closer. After being given the closer role after both Jim Johnson and Luke Gregerson failed in spectacular fashion, Doolittle unleashed his hellacious stuff (89 strikeouts in only 62.2 innings) and impeccable control (8 walks allowed and a WHIP of 0.73). There really was nothing Doolittle didn't do well last season and he is in line to be a top ten closer for 2015. A perfect low-cost closer anchor for your team.

Atlanta Braves (Craig Kimbrel): Atlanta Braves closer Craig Kimbrel goes into the 2015 season once again considered the top ninth inning man in all of fantasy baseball. Kimbrel has now posted ERA's of 1.01, 1.21, and 1.61 the last three seasons, with a K rate that is out of this world. Kimbrel gave us a brief shoulder scare early on last season but he came through it just fine. Will be the first closer drafted and deservedly so.

New York Mets (Jenrry Mejia-Jeurys Familia): On the surface it would appear as though Jenrry Mejia is the clear choice to once again serve as the New York Mets closer for the 2015 season. After all Mejia had a breakout season a year ago in moving to the back of the Mets' bullpen once it became clear he could not pitch consistently enough in the rotation. While Mejia always seemed to be dealing with some sort of nagging injury, he would go on to finish 28 games while pitching to a 3.65 ERA. The ERA is a bit misleading as Mejia had a 5.06 mark before he moved to the bullpen. Despite all the positives, there is a real chance that top setup man Jeurys Familia could overtake Mejia for the right to pitch in the ninth inning for 2015. Familia has durability that Mejia doesn't have and also posted a breakout year last season in pitching to a tiny 2.21 ERA. This is another situation which must be watched closely this spring in order to see if a changing of the guard takes place.

Philadelphia Phillies (Jonathan Papelbon): It seemed as though Philadelphia Phillies closer Jonathan Papelbon was a human form of radiation when it came to 2014 drafts, so high a degree did the fantasy baseball community try to avoid him. With his fastball down more than a few ticks and coming off a 2013 season when he was more hittable than ever, there was certainly some evidence that Papelbon was ready to implode as he turned another year older. However we went the other way in talking up the value play that Papelbon presented and correctly pointed out that the veteran's stuff was still good enough for him to succeed at a high level. Well Papelbon went right along with the script as he posted one of his better seasons in 2014 by pitching to a 2.04 ERA and 0.90 WHIP while recording 39 saves. The only semi-negative was a K rate that continues to decline but otherwise Papelbon was as good as any closer last season. While the Phillies would love to find a taker for Papelbon due to his contract, his skill set obviously shows he can remain a top ten closer and maybe better.

Washington Nationals (Drew Storen-Tyler Clippard): The very solid Rafael Soriano era at the back of the Washington Nationals bullpen is over, as the veteran closer lost the job to former top prospect Drew Storen during the second half of the 2014 season. With Soriano a free agent that the team has no interest in bringing back, Storen will likely open up 2015 in the hot seat. Storen comes off a dominant 2014 season when he pitched to a miniscule 1.12 ERA and 0.98 WHIP while collecting 11 saves post-All-Star break. However Storen melted down to the highest order in the postseason, helping the Nats to a first round exit versus the San Francisco Giants, which calls into question his mental ability to carry the gig all season. The very capable Tyler Clippard is still around as a solid alternative if Storen struggles early. Tread carefully with this.

Miami Marlins (Steve Cishek): One of the very best closers in baseball over the last two years has performed in relative anonymity with the Miami Marlins. We of course are referring to Steve Cishek who has posted ERA's of 2.69, 2.33, and 3.17 over the last three seasons when saving games. Showing a quirky delivery that induces a ton of strikeouts (84 K's in 65.1 innings in 2014), Cishek has survived the last few trade deadlines when rumors indicated the Marlins would send him packing in their ongoing rebuilding plans. The Marlins are now on the cusp of contending again and will rely on Cishek to stabilize things in the ninth inning once again. Based on the numbers, he is up to the task and has proven to be one of the more reliable stoppers in baseball.

Chicago Cubs (Hector Rondon): After having arguably the worst ninth inning situation in baseball in 2013 and early last season, the Chicago Cubs finally seemed to hit on a potential closer when they put the hard-throwing Hector Rondon into the hot seat. Showing good control and strikeout stuff, Rondon finished 29 games for the Cubs last season with a terrific 2.42 ERA and 1.06 WHIP while punching out 63 batters in 63.1 innings. While the Cubs are far from contention, Rondon is a guy they can build around when it comes to their bullpen. Rondon is anything but a sure thing given that he has not even closed games for a full season but the early results are promising.

Milwaukee Brewers (Francisco Rodriguez-Will Smith): As of this writing, Francisco Rodriguez is a free agent which leaves the back end of the Milwaukee Brewers bullpen a bit unsettled. However Rodriguez had strongly indicated his desire to return to the Brewers and he surely owes them a discount after the team gave him one last chance to pitch in high-pressure situations last season when it appeared his career was almost finished. Rediscovering some of his lost fastball speed, Rodriguez boosted back up his K rate and the results were superb as he posted a 3.04 ERA and 0.99 WHIP. Even more impressive was the fact Rodriguez posted his best walk rate ever. As great as Rodriguez was last season, there is still major risk here as he is now 33-years-old. In addition, memories of how poorly Rodriguez pitched in 2012 and 2013 remain fresh and a threat to reoccur.

Now if Rodriguez does move on as a free agent, top strikeout setup man Will James would be a decent fallback option. James struck out 86 batters in only 65.2 innings last season, with an ERA of 3.70. There are control issues here though so James could be a high-wire act.

St. Louis Cardinals (Trevor Rosenthal): The full-season debut of fireballing top St. Louis Cardinals pitching prospect Trevor Rosenthal as the team's closer didn't go as smoothly as most thought it would. Drawing spring training comparisons to Craig Kimbrel or Greg Holland, Rosenthal failed to bring the flash consistently as he went through a few prolonged struggles that had many questioning his ability to hold onto the closing gig. Overall Rosenthal finished up with a 3.20 ERA which is a bit high for a hard-throwing closer. The 1.41 WHIP was even worse and a disturbing number that was a result of a terrible 42 walks in 70.1 innings. Rosenthal still brought the heat as he racked up 87 strikeouts but he has to do better. Jason Motte is back again and another year removed from Tommy John surgery which means the leash won't be as long as it was last season for Rosenthal. We still like the potential here but some of the shine has worn off for sure.

Cincinnati Reds (Aroldis Chapman): It was a very scary start to the 2014 season for Cincinnati Reds All Star closer Aroldis Chapman as he didn't even make it out of spring training due to getting nailed in the face by a comebacker. Chapman suffered facial fractures in the incident and didn't make his debut until May 11th. Still once he was back on the mound, Chapman was his old 100-plus-mph self as he rang up an unfathomable 106 strikeouts in only 54 innings. That marked the third straight season Chapman has crossed the 100-K mark, which is like 250 for a starter. Those in innings capped leagues know how valuable Chapman is under that setup. The 2.00 ERA and 0.83 WHIP Chapman put up last season was par for the course for him and he remains right there with Craig Kimbrel and Greg Holland in the top tier.

Pittsburgh Pirates (Mark Melancon): The short but effective tenure of Jason Grilli as the Pittsburgh Pirates closer came to end in 2014, opening the door for All Star setup man Mark Melancon to finally make a ninth inning gig all his own. Melancon showed that there was no need to hold an audition for 2015 as he pitched to a 1.90 ERA and 0.87 WHIP while punching out 71 batters in 71 innings. At only 29, Melancon is now in his early prime years, which sets him up as to be the Pirates closer for years.

Arizona Diamondbacks (Addison Reed): Maybe the Chicago White Sox knew what they were doing when they surprisingly traded away young closer Addison Reed to the Arizona Diamondbacks prior to the 2014 season. While no one ever could argue about the potency of Reed's stuff, there are issues with the home run ball and a lack of control that make his ninth inning appearances tough to stomach. Reed's 4.25 ERA last season was indicative of his troubles and he sits here as one of the more risky closer investments for 2015. Not for us.

San Francisco Giants (Santiago Casilla): It was shocking to see how poorly Sergio Romo pitched out of the ninth inning for the World Series-winning San Francisco Giants early last season after a 2011-2013 run where he was one of the most dominant relievers in the game. Romo's situation was another reminder of how volatile the closer fraternity is each and every season and it is why we continue to preach resisting the urge to draft here until the middle rounds. Be that as it may, the Giants came through Romo's struggles just fine as manager Bruce Bochy turned to ace setup man Santiago Casilla to put out ninth inning fires. Put out fires Casilla did as he posted a 1.70 ERA and 0.86 WHIP while closing out 19 games. Remember that Casilla had issues closing games in 2012 which opened the door for Romo to take over, so he is anything but a given.

Los Angeles Dodgers (Kenley Jansen): It started to look like Los Angeles Dodgers closer Kenley Jansen would be the latest stopper to go from awesome to awful from one season to the next early in 2014 when he opened up the year by posting ERA's over 4.00 in two of the first three months. However Jansen harnessed his stuff better in the second half and dominated from that point on as he finished with an ERA of 2.76 while striking out 101 batters. This is Jansen's show all the way and it will take a very long run of struggles before he has his closing job threatened.

San Diego Padres (Joaquin Benoit-Dale Thayer-Kevin Quackenbush): With Huston Street having been sent to the Los Angeles Angels at the 2014 trade deadline, the back end of the San Diego Padres bullpen went up for grabs.

Joaquin Benoit took over when Street was dealt and that made perfect sense given his high-strikeout ways and run of dominant pitching since 2010. A free agent at press time, Benoit would be the easy call to close games again for San Diego if he re-signs. If for some reason Benoit doesn't return, a battle between Dale Thayer and Kevin Quackenbush would take place for the right to pitch in the ninth inning.

Colorado Rockies (LaTroy Hawkins): It was very surprising to see Colorado Rockies closer LaTroy Hawkins make it through the entire season finishing games for the team given his age and the threat of him being dealt at the July 31 trade deadline. Hawkins wrote his own narrative however as he pitched to a 3.31 ERA and 1.20 WHIP while recording 23 saves at the age of 41. Another year older, Hawkins remains a major risk to fall off the map with his numbers and he once again could be a threat to be traded on a rebuilding Rockies team.

Be sure to check out our Monday "Closing Time" feature at www.thefantasysportsboss.com where we delve into all the latest news and happenings coming out of the world of the ninth inning.

THE LAST WORD

As a final reminder, we strongly advise all of you to stick with us on our website at www.thefantasysportsboss.com where we have all the corners covered in staying on top of the 2015 fantasy baseball season. From posting daily injury and general news briefs, to sharing our weekly analysis features, our staff goes the extra mile to break down every nuance of the game. In addition, look for our updated second draft guide "Post-Free Agency Edition" sometime in late January where we update the rankings and some captions, while also delving into all the trades/signings from the Hot Stove season. It is always a fun yet rocky ride but we will be with you all the way through. Let's do this.

17286366R00097

Made in the USA
San Bernardino, CA
07 December 2014